shadows of things to come

A PROPHETIC LOOK AT GOD'S UNFOLDING PLAN

RICK JOYNER

A
JANET
THOMA
BOOK

THOMAS NELSON PUBLISHERS
Nashville

Published in Nashville, Tennessee, by Thomas Nelson, Inc.

Unless otherwise noted, Scripture quotations are from THE NEW AMERICAN STANDARD BIBLE®, Copyright © The Lockman Foundation 1960, 1962, 1963, 1968, 1971, 1972, 1973, 1975, 1977. Used by permission.

Scripture quotations noted AMPLIFIED are from THE AMPLIFIED NEW TESTAMENT. Copyright © 1958 by the Lockman Foundation (used by permission).

Scripture quotations noted KJV are from THE KING JAMES VERSION.

Scripture quotations noted NKJV are from THE NEW KING JAMES VERSION. Copyright © 1979, 1980, 1982, Thomas Nelson, Inc., Publishers.

Library of Congress Cataloging-in-Publication Data

Joyner, Rick, 1949–
    Shadows of things to come : a prophetic look at God's unfolding plan / Rick Joyner.
    p. cm.
    Includes bibliographical references.
    ISBN 0-7852-6784-0 (hardcover)
    1. Church history. I. Title.

BR150 .J69 2001
270—dc21
                                 00-068232
                                    CIP

Printed in the United States of America
1 2 3 4 5 6 7 8 9 10 QWD 06 05 04 03 02 01

Contents

Acknowledgments

I WISH TO ACKNOWLEDGE RAY HUGHES FOR HIS article "The Forgotten Legacy of Sam Jones," Keith Davis for his article "The Apostolic Ministry of John G. Lake," Stephen Mansfield for his article "The Hidden Calling," and Gail Harris for her article "An Odyssey of Reconciliation." All these articles were adapted from the *Morning Star Journal* for this book.

In writing on church history, I used insights from many different church historians, borrowing heavily from *History of the Christian Church,* two separate multivolume works by Philip Schaft and Henry C. Sheldon. For continuity and flow I have used Sheldon's excellent work as an outline. Another source I used was *The History of Christianity* (consulting editors John H.Y. Briggs, Dr. Robert Linder, and David F. Wright). I have also used many of all these authors' insights, though they are rephrased to make the language more contemporary and to contribute my own views. Most of the commentary in this history is my own, and may or may not find agreement with any others unless I specifically quote them.

Though I have studied history for many years, I am not a historian or an academic. This book is not intended to be an academic or objective view of history, but a cursory examination of history for the sake of insight into our own times. Keep in mind that this is necessarily a superficial study of this great subject. One of my motives for writing it is to instill in readers a desire to search these matters out more deeply and therefore to have a fuller understanding to share with the Body of Christ. For more in-depth study, I highly recommend Philip Schaft's and Henry C. Sheldon's works, as well as *Christian History* magazine and other great resources.

Foreword
The Greatest Treasure

THIS BOOK IS ABOUT THE QUEST FOR THE greatest treasure the world has ever known. This treasure has nothing to do with silver and gold but with something infinitely more valuable—the truth. Truth is the quest of the noblest souls who have ever walked the earth. The fact that you have picked up a book like this indicates that you are almost certainly one of these seekers of truth. True seekers always find what they are looking for. They also always come up with the same ultimate answer—*all of the treasures of wisdom and knowledge are found in Christ.* Jesus is the Truth. We cannot know the truth about this world, or the world to come, except by looking through His eyes. That is what we are seeking—to see the world with His eyes.

In this book we will seek the Lord's perspective on the past, present, and future. It is not possible to understand the present adequately without at least a general knowledge and understanding of the past. A sound knowledge and understanding of the past and present are required to look prophetically into the future and understand it. The reverse is also true: we cannot truly understand the present, or the past, without having at least a general understanding of the future as revealed through biblical prophecy. That is why the Lord has always given some knowledge of the future to those who walked with Him. Because of this, even Enoch, who walked with God, also prophesied, as we see in Jude 14. "A cord of three strands" is not easily broken, according to Ecclesiastes 4:12. The cord of three strands that we are seeking to weave in this book includes an accurate perspective of the past, present, and future.

THE WELL THAT NEVER RUNS DRY

Every genuine seeker of truth will ultimately come to the understanding that the Bible is the "mother lode" of the treasure we seek. Its value is far beyond our ability to measure. It is an infinite vein of something far more valuable than any earthly treasure—the truth. It is also the map that will lead us to a correct understanding of all the truth that can be found on this earth. There are also treasures of truth in history. The very word *history* contains the two words *His story*. True history is the revelation of God's dealings with man and, through that, the revelation of His nature. But only with the Bible as our guide will we be able to interpret and understand the facts of history accurately.

The Bible itself is comprised mostly of either history books or prophetic books, which are history written in advance. One of the most valuable commodities in the world is knowledge of the future. The more confidence we have in that knowledge, and the more specific it is, the more valuable it becomes. As we approach the end of this age, we know by the Scriptures that this knowledge of the future will increase, just as we are promised in Acts 2:17–18:

> "And it shall be in the last days," God says,
> "That I will pour forth of My Spirit upon all mankind;
> And your sons and your daughters shall prophesy,
> And your young men shall see visions,
> And your old men shall dream dreams;

Even upon My bondslaves, both men and women,
I will in those days pour forth of My Spirit
And they shall prophesy."

One result of the Lord pouring out His Spirit is that His people begin to have prophetic experiences and to prophesy. The above text indicates that at the end this prophecy is greatly increased. However, this knowledge of the future is not given to us for our entertainment. We will need this knowledge to make it through the times and accomplish our purpose.

Today some of the church rejects the idea that the Lord still speaks prophetically, in spite of such obvious promises in the text above. Though the majority of Christians now seem to believe and expect Him to speak to His people in this way, even those who have received such knowledge have seldom used it properly. Our goal is not to just have this great treasure (prophecy), but to use it in the right manner, for the Lord's purposes and for His glory, not our own.

If our purpose for gaining this knowledge is right, and our preparation for applying it is sound, we can expect more and more prophecy as we get closer to the end of this age. Our main preparation will be our devotion to a godly character and our commitment to live for the Lord, not just ourselves (2 Cor. 5:15). That is why I have sown many biblical references to a godly character and properly handling the Word of truth throughout this work. Our goal is not just to know about God, His ways, and what He is doing, but to be changed into His image as we behold His glory (2 Cor. 3:18).

1

The Quest of Kings

The Truth of the Past That Prepares Us for the Future

It is the glory of God to conceal a matter, but the glory of kings is to search out a matter. (Prov. 25:2 NKJV)

What makes something a treasure is the fact that it is rare or hard to get. By its very definition, treasure is not cheap. Neither is the knowledge of the truth, nor is prophetic knowledge. The devil has sought to release many counterfeits in order to cheapen what is real. Even so, the Lord has hidden the great treasure of prophetic knowledge in the Scriptures so that only those who are led by His Spirit are able to acquire real truth. His Spirit is the personification of His nature. The Spirit leads those to this truth by a path that promotes character, spiritual maturity, and wisdom, which is the ability to apply knowledge correctly. Let us never lose sight of the fact that we need godly character even more than knowledge.

When the Lord brought the children of Israel out of Egypt, they carried the great treasure of Egypt with them. However, the Lord did not immediately take them to the closest shopping mall so they could spend it. He took them to the wilderness, a place where this treasure probably became a burden. Then they were willing to exchange it for something infinitely more valuable than anything they could have ever purchased—a tabernacle for God so that He could dwell among them. That is what we must seek above all things—His presence with us.

The understanding of God's ways is a priceless treasure that is not easily found, even though the world overflows with books and tapes claiming to tell how to find it. Certainly some of them do, but they are much more rare than we probably think, and even harder to find through all the clamor of the pretenders.

Treasure hunters are also very rare. Our modern culture has fed a powerful addiction to convenience, which makes each succeeding generation even more impatient than the previous one. Everyone is in an increasing hurry, but very few people can tell you where they are going. In this environment, Mel Fisher stands out as one of the most extraordinary men of our time.

Mel Fisher is a quiet, unpretentious, former chicken farmer from the Midwest who seems almost quintessentially ordinary. His easygoing, grandfatherly nature belies the fact that he is known around the world as "the king of the treasure hunters." He is a modern Indiana Jones, and his story is no less remarkable than that of Steven Spielberg's character. Those who are seeking the heavenly treasure can learn a lot from this remarkable man.

Mel spent a large part of his life seeking the great treasure that was lost on a single Spanish galleon, the *Atocha*, which sank in a storm more than 350 years ago. There was evidence that the treasure on that one vessel was worth hundreds of millions of dollars. Many believed that the sinking of the *Atocha* was just a legend, but Mel happened upon a trail that he believed to be authentic.

Even so, the ocean is very big, and the galleon could have gone down anywhere over hundreds of square miles off the southern coast of Florida. With his little boats and a crew that he could only afford to pay fifty dollars a week, he spent years following the trail through disappointments, setbacks, and heartrending disasters. He did it with so little encouragement that his resolve, patience, and endurance must be considered one of the extraordinary stories of the twentieth century.

Mel invested all that he owned on his one quest. He did not have a Plan B if he failed; his commitment to his quest was total. He and his little band would sometimes go for years scouring the bottom of the ocean finding little more than a nail, a few musket balls, or a single Spanish coin. After each such discovery, the ocean seemed to take it personally, and would smite them back with a blow that seemed far more devastating than they could ever afford. But as Mel's wife stated, "If we had quit, we would have been defeated for the rest of our lives." So they never considered quitting as an option. They plodded on.

One of Mel's greatest trials came after one of the team's most encouraging finds. They recovered a silver bar that matched the bill of lading from the *Atocha*. Their excitement was obviously great, but it seemed that the entire world rose up to challenge their find. Articles were written accusing them of fraud, scheming to use their find as a ploy to attract naive investors. Then the IRS stepped in to confiscate what Mel's crew had found, and ruled that if any treasure were found it would all belong to the government.

It looked as if Mel would receive nothing for his years of toil. Having already spent millions of dollars, mostly borrowed, just scouring the sea, now he would have to spend six million more fighting the government in court. It was a terrible and demoralizing blow, but still he pressed on, even though he did not know whether he would be able to keep the treasure if he found it.

Then one day Mel's oldest son, Dirk, found some ancient Spanish cannons. They checked the serial numbers and verified that they were from the *Atocha*. The team was ecstatic. Two nights later the sea struck back with its cruelest retaliation yet. While the crew was sleeping, their boat developed a leak, capsizing without warning. Dirk, his young wife, and another crew member died.

The team was devastated, but still they refused to quit. Then the cannons they had found proved to be another cruel hoax from the sea. The galleon had broken into many pieces and was scattered over a very wide area. The cannons proved not to be anywhere close to the precious cargo. Their "great find" would actually cost the venture years of fruitless searching in the wrong place. Still they did not give up.

Finally an encouraging victory did come. After years of bitter fighting in the courts, Mel won his case. He had to go all the way to the U.S. Supreme Court, which gave a five-to-four decision in his favor. The ruling established Mel's ownership of the treasure that he found, and protected it during the salvage process. Even so, he still did not have anything to claim. He knew that if they did not find some treasure soon, all of the courage and resolve in the world, and even a Supreme Court decision, would not help them. They simply would not have any more support.

On a hunch, Mel decided to look for the *Atocha*'s sister ship, which had gone down in the same storm. In just a few months his team found it, and enough treasure to keep them going. Mel then returned to his primary quest, the *Atocha*. For several more years his team continued, day after day, in seemingly fruitless searching. After spending nearly twelve million dollars, Mel barely had enough money to meet his payroll for two more weeks. Everyone knew that the end was certainly near. Then, to the astonishment of people all over the world, with Mel now more than sixty years old, voices crackled over the radio from his little salvage boat—they had found the *Atocha*! With it they found veritable mountains of silver and gold bars, large caches of silver coins, precious jewels, silver and gold plates, and so many uncut emeralds that they alone would ultimately be valued at more than four hundred million dollars. What may have been the longest treasure hunt in history resulted in one of the greatest discoveries in history.

A Greater Treasure

Mel Fisher is now a hero to thousands. Few men have ever held their course and persevered against such opposition to attain their goal. If he could give so much for the treasure on the *Atocha*, how much more valuable is the eternal treasure of knowing God's ways? How much more devotion, resolve, and endurance should we have in searching God's Word to understand the unfolding of His plan? The Bible, which often lies on shelves gathering dust, contains greater treasure than any ever to be found in a Spanish galleon.

In many ways true students of history often feel a lot like Mel Fisher during his years of sifting through empty sand. Yet, the treasures of wisdom and knowledge I found studying history simply cannot be valued in human currency. They reveal the glory of God, and the marvelous ways He has chosen to reveal His dealings with fallen men. What greater treasure could be found on earth?

Even so, many still refuse to study the past. Let me tell you why I believe they are wrong.

WHY STUDY CHURCH HISTORY?

The failure to understand church history has resulted in some of the most devastating and unnecessary mistakes made by the modern church. This is a weakness that affects our theology and eschatology (view of the last days), as well as the way that we relate—or fail to relate—to the modern world. This lack of understanding has also been used to sidetrack almost every denomination into pursuing fruitless and expensive projects that divert many believers from their true purpose.

As the proverb states, "Those who do not know history are doomed to repeat it." This has certainly proven true for the church. Each generation falls into the same traps and loses the same battles by making the same wrong decisions. At the same time, we have repeatedly missed some of the greatest opportunities for advancing the gospel. How can we end this tragic cycle? The answer may seem too simple: by studying church history.

Many think of history as dates and dead people. Unfortunately, uninspired teachers often reduce it to that. However, those who are inspired will not only glean wisdom and understanding from the past, but they will also be given a remarkable compass for navigating through the present while they prepare for the future.

A SOURCE OF BOLDNESS

The great statesmen in history seem universally to have known that the knowledge of history would greatly enhance their ability to deal with the present. Winston Churchill, for instance, led the conflict against the greatest evil of his time using the lessons he had gleaned from his extensive study of history. He often quoted, and followed the lead of, great leaders of the past when he was confronted with some of the most challenging problems of the most terrible war yet fought upon the earth. In this way he inspired his people with the knowledge that similar threats had been overcome before and could be overcome again. He also did not have to "reinvent the wheel" every time he was confronted with problems that others before him had faced. As he asserted, this enabled him to give even more attention to the problems that were unique.

It is no coincidence that almost every strategic battle in history was won with the same tactics. And almost every great spiritual advance was released in basically the same way. What are these tactics? How can we implement them for our own times? These questions will be answered in this book.

Even so, the most that any one book can do is give us generalizations. These can point the way to more specific applications, but we must each find our own special course as we follow the Lord for our own life. Knowing history and prophecy can help, but only if we are sensitive to the leading of the Lord in the present. Our goal must always be to apply the knowledge that we are learning in our own present walk.

This book is a general study of church history, the present state of the church, and the prophecies of the future, combined. In each chapter we will view a period of church history, relate it to our present conditions, and then use it to see where we are headed. We will also view some events that prophecy asserts will come. We will seek to establish all of these on the solid foundation of Scripture. The Bible prophesies our present and future with accuracy and wisdom so that we can not only endure the times but even prevail through them. That is our goal. We want not just to know what is coming but to use this knowledge to glorify the name of the One who has established all things, and upholds them by His Word.

The spiritual treasures that can be mined from knowing the experiences of our spiritual ancestors can make the difference between whether we are relevant or irrelevant in our own time. What was it that took so many ordinary people and enabled them to do such extraordinary deeds? What helped them recover from terrible mistakes and keep marching forward until the victory was won? What made seemingly weak, insignificant people arise to confront the great darkness of their times, and push it back? And finally, how can we apply the lessons to our own calling?

STAYING ON THE TRAIL

One of the foremost journals for conservative evangelical leaders found in its own study that less than 1 percent of their articles contained even one reference to Scripture! This is a sure way for us to drift from the path of life. Charles Spurgeon once stated that he could find ten men who would die for the Bible for every one who would read it! It seems that this is still true. For all the talk about the need to use Scripture as the foundation for all doctrine, those who talk about it the most often do it the least. Is that not why Paul wrote to Timothy to "pay close attention to yourself and to your teaching" (1 Tim. 4:16)? Maybe we, more than anyone else, need to hear our own messages.

I will use a lot of Scripture in this book and often quote the text for your convenience. Please do not skip over these passages. If we really love the truth, we will care enough to search out and verify what is written in God's Word. You may even want to compare these verses with other references or Bible versions; those who will be trusted with the greatest truths will esteem truth enough to search for it. If you have a question about anything, do not accept it until you have searched it out. Ask the Lord to confirm it to you. You will be amazed at how you will see a particular Scripture in a way that you have never seen it before. Or perhaps a book or tape will be given to you that has the answer. In this way you will know that the Lord is teaching you.

I believe that this book includes some of the most important and valuable material I have ever written. It is also the first book I remember writing that I hoped not many people would read. I did not acquire what you are about to read cheaply. My prayer is that it will only fall into the hands of those with the wisdom to use it properly. Like all truth, some knowledge in this work is powerful enough to do great good (to bring healing and unity) or to do great damage (to create even more division) to the Body of Christ. My prayer is for the former, but I know that sometimes there must be division before true unity comes. We cannot be trusted with the greatest treasures until we want the truth simply because we love truth, regardless of what it does to us.

We See Through a Glass Darkly

I am neither a trained theologian nor a historian. My credentials for writing this book are that I love God, I love the church, and I love the truth. Even so, I recognize that there are weaknesses that come from my not being a trained theologian or historian. On the other hand, there are also some advantages that come with a lack of professional training, which allow me to see things that trained professionals may not see, and to avoid a few of the traps that have often hindered our knowledge of the past. Let us look at a few of those traps before we go on.

TRUTH CAN BE DANGEROUS

For those who will search for treasures in church history, I want to share what I have learned that can spare you from falling into three needless traps, or wasting a lot of time and effort following fruitless trails that I have already stumbled through. It is important that I do this now, before we begin the quest.

Trap One

A great deception is to judge a person's or institution's entire history from a small slice of its existence. For example, I once had an acquaintance who wanted to meet a friend of mine. On the day of his visit, my friend was having an unusually bad day. He was uncharacteristically abrupt and impatient, and my acquaintance went away disappointed, stating that my friend was hardly the man of God he had expected to meet. This was a very unfair assessment. He was judging my friend's whole character, and even his life, on the basis of an encounter that lasted just a few minutes.

Likewise, some of the greatest preachers in history were deemed very poor preachers by reporters who heard just one of their sermons. Even the best preachers have bad sermons occasionally. Probably just as many poor preachers were judged great by some who just happened to visit their worship services when they were having an uncharacteristically good day.

We cannot judge denominations, institutions, or movements accurately if we do not look at their entire history. The Roman Catholic Church today bears little resemblance to the same church during Luther's time. The same is true of the Lutheran Church. The Catholic Church in South America tends to be very different from the Catholic Church in North America, as do the other denominations in both places. Honest Catholics will acknowledge that there have been popes who make some of today's most ruthless dictators seem benevolent. The same could be said for some leaders of the Reformation. When we look at these dark times in history, we are not trying to imply anything about the present state of these denominations. Many made great and necessary corrections after previous excesses. Some have not, but if I am trying to imply anything about their present state, I will make that clear.

Trap Two

History is often distorted because historians tend to record only significant events, which are always, by the nature of reporting, extremes. For example, when we think of the Age of Napoleon, we usually think of the great battles. However, all of the battles together took up less than 1 percent of the time during that period, and only a small fraction of the people in Europe actually participated in them. A true picture of that period would have to be almost entirely devoted to normal families working their farms or shops, passing through life without ever even seeing a battle, much less fighting in one. But a "normal" life of that time is not interesting enough to record in history.

In the same way, the evening news is a gross distortion of real life. Far less than 1 percent of the population is involved in the events that make the news—the murders, accidents, and political issues. It is improbable that the news will ever take the time to cover the happy family on a picnic or friends gathering for a game of bridge. These events may not be interesting enough to make the evening news, but they are a much more accurate description of real life.

The same is also true of the church. The only churches or ministries featured in Christian publications tend to be those that are doing something extraordinary. Similarly, Christian television tends to carry only the extraordinary. It is true that these exemplary churches or ministries may be helping set a course for the church, but they are not an accurate reflection of the present life of the church. The real, substantial work of the kingdom is accomplished by the day-by-day faithfulness of average pastors and laypeople. I will include a few stories in this book about "average" Christians who are doing great things for the kingdom. However, we must keep in mind that we do not have to do anything extraordinary to help the advancement of the kingdom; we just need to be obedient and faithful. We may not do anything to make the news, but over a lifetime, our faithfulness can add up to substantial accomplishments, and even have a greater impact than much of that covered by the news or recorded in history. We must view the average Christian or the average church to define Christianity accurately in our time, but almost no reporter or historian would be interested in that story. So, at best, what we are seeing as we look at history is only a fraction of the reality of the times.

Trap Three

I once heard a remarkable story on a radio news commentary. It was about a man who was wandering the streets of Dallas, Texas, broke and homeless. When he asked a passerby for some change for a cup of coffee, the man was so moved with compassion, he gave the tramp all the money he had. This one act of generosity turned the hapless drifter's life around, and now he is a successful businessman. Ironically, the compassionate benefactor was Lee Harvey Oswald, and the event took place the day before he shot President Kennedy. There is good in the worst of men, and evil in the best of them, but history rarely records both.

Napoleon's ambitions resulted in the deaths of millions of young men, as well as the destruction of so much property and land that it would be impossible to tally. Even so, he had a concern for the common man, and his innovations in law and government have made life better for literally millions of men and women since.

Adolf Hitler's cruel leadership probably resulted in more death and destruction than that of any other single individual in history. His name will forever be one of the ugliest scars on human history. However, even Churchill acknowledged that if Hitler had died in 1938, he would have been considered one of the greatest leaders of all time.

When Hitler came to power, Germany was suffering under some of the worst economic and political conditions a nation has suffered during modern times. Unemployment was between 50 and 75 percent. The government was bankrupt, and the German mark actually fell to an exchange rate of four *trillion* to a dollar before it was declared totally worthless. Mobs ruled the streets, perversion was rampant, and the entire nation tottered on the brink of either anarchy or becoming a Soviet state.

In just four years Hitler not only balanced the budget, but he also paid off the national debt while building the most powerful economy in the world. He brought employment to near 100 percent. He restored Germany's national dignity and built the most powerful army in the world. He did all of this while the whole world was staggering through the Great Depression. He also drove pornography and other forms of perversion from German soil. There has never been such a swift and complete transformation of a nation in the history of the world.

The apostle John explained that there are many antichrists (see 1 John 4:3), and there have been many throughout history. As a Swedish journalist, Torbjourn Freij, once told me as we sat in a Berlin café pondering Hitler's life, history seems to be an ever-rising and tightening spiral. As we get closer to the top, each antichrist is more like the ultimate Antichrist who will be revealed at the end. In this way Hitler is more like the Antichrist than Napoleon, and so forth. If we are wise, we will understand these antichrists and learn to discern them much earlier in their careers. Most of the church in Germany was so fooled by Hitler that they helped establish his power base, with some church leaders actually calling him "a messiah."

Could this be what Paul meant when he warned that the man of sin would take his seat in the temple of God, which is the church, displaying himself as being God? There have been numerous antichrists in history who have used the church this way. Are we doomed to keep repeating history because we fail to understand it? Some of these antichrists may have begun with genuine good intentions but were corrupted by their power. Others had unpromising beginnings but somehow accomplished great and noble feats that elevated the lot of mankind, while sowing great deception into the church.

As you read the coming chapters, keep these traps in mind. History deals in generalizations, and generalizations are never completely accurate. However, they do give us a paradigm for understanding the present and the future.

My hope is that after reading this book you will want to explore the writings of others who are more equipped to address these issues. Because we all see in part, and therefore no one person can see the whole picture, we need to put the parts together to form the complete picture. Even though much of the following material is a composite of studies made by many others, there are still pieces left that must be found to form the complete picture. Because I am weak in theological and historical training, friends who have these backgrounds have helped me immensely. I think that they have, likewise, been helped by me. We all need each other, and we particularly need those who are the least like us.

Maybe in your searching you will find some understanding that no one has found before. This is not to imply that anything will ever be added to Scripture, but maybe you will be the one who sees how certain biblical prophecies have been fulfilled or will be. The only qualification that you need for this is to be a seeker of truth. The truth you find may get some needed shaping by other pieces that other people provide, but that is all a part of the plan. The fastest way to fall to delusion and deception is to begin thinking that we do not need the rest of the Body of Christ.

We must also keep in mind that, with history, we are looking through a glass almost as darkly as when we view the future. If you have ever played "Gossip," the game where one person whispers a story to the person next to him or her and so forth around the room until it returns to the first person, you have been amazed by how much the original story has changed. History has similarly been passed through many hands and changed by each one, sometimes a great deal. However, the Holy Spirit can lead us to the truth, and we must depend on Him to do it. We must "examine everything carefully; hold fast to that which is good" (1 Thess. 5:21).

MY AGENDA

To be an accurate historian, one almost has to be without bias or agenda. I cannot claim to be without bias, and I definitely do have an agenda. I do pray for the Spirit of Truth to guide my studies and the presentation of what I find, and that my agenda will be the Lord's. Even so, you have a right to know my agenda, which I will try to explain briefly.

My goal is to examine the very foundations of modern Christianity. I do this not to attack or condemn, and I do not want to be preoccupied with mistakes. I desire to differentiate between what God has built and what man has created, with the hope that we will be able to abandon fruitless endeavors, correct the harmful ones, and concentrate on what will advance the cause of Christ. We can do this best by seeing the city that God is building.

I also intend to honor those who paid such a price to walk in truth and deliver to us what we will need for continuing the advance. Only one of the Ten Commandments had a promise attached to it: "Honor your father and your mother, that your days may be prolonged in the land which the LORD your God gives you" (Ex. 20:12). This is reaffirmed in Ephesians 6:2–3. Our own spiritual longevity will be determined by the humility with which we honor those who went before us, who made our way straighter and who spiritually gave birth to us. The pride of new spiritual generations—thinking that they are better than those who preceded them—is a stumbling block that has tripped up every generation to date.

Therefore, when we examine the mistakes of previous generations, it is not to dishonor but to learn from them. For our sake, the Bible does not hide the mistakes of even its greatest heroes. If we are wise, we will maintain the humility to acknowledge that without their examples we would be prone to make the same mistakes. Some of the greatest heroes in church history also made some of the greatest mistakes, seemingly opening the windows of heaven and then turning around and opening a gate of hell. We want to view these so that we can clean those windows—and maybe even repair some of them—and also close the gates of hell, the openings the enemy has used to gain entry and do his deadly work. The church has the authority to close them (Matt. 16:18).

Our main goal is to find out how to win, not how to lose. We must resolve to fight until truth, righteousness, and justice prevail. This can only be accomplished one way. As the apostle Paul stated in Colossians 1:28–29: "We proclaim Him, admonishing every man and teaching every man with all wisdom, that we may present every man complete in Christ. For this purpose also I labor, striving according to His power, which mightily works within me."

The biblical prophets all had a profound knowledge and understanding of history. They used illustrations from that history to illuminate their visions of the future. Likewise, the depth and quality of our prophetic perspective will be determined to a great degree by our knowledge and understanding of history. It seems that the height to which the

Lord will take us to view the future is determined by how deep our roots are in His Word and by the span of our worldview that we gain by interpreting history and current events by the Scriptures.

As Psalm 119:105 states, "Thy word is a lamp unto my feet, and a light unto my path" (KJV). The Scriptures clearly show the path of life through human history, and on into the future. Therefore it cannot be overemphasized that we must continually let the Scriptures shine on the knowledge we are finding. If we deviate from this, we will deviate from the path of life.

As I stated earlier, something is a treasure because it is either rare or hard to get. We will be finding treasures of wisdom and knowledge that will be well worth the effort of our study. At times it will be like an adventure that keeps us on the edge of our seats, and at times it can seem boring and tedious because we must dig so deeply in one place before we get to the gold. However, inevitably the greatest treasures are the ones that are the hardest to find. Could God have designed knowledge in this way—to separate immature and mature believers?

LOST TREASURE

Many of the ideas you are about to read I have not heard others speak or write about in the thirty years I have been a Christian. However, they were all taught, preached, and believed by generations of believers before us. They seem to have been treasures that gave insight into the prophecies of Scripture, yet they have obviously not been understood and passed on for several generations. I only found them because some old books seemed miraculously to find their way into my hands. I felt that these treasures were so great that I have since spent much more time reading old books than new ones.

As you read, please understand that I am not writing for scholars or theologians, but for *treasure hunters*. When I was finding many of the truths you are about to read, I was not thinking about writing this book, or any book; I was just seeking to know the truth. I therefore neglected to record where I got some of the information and am limited in the references I can give.

Except for the Scriptures, history is where I have spent most of my life seeking the treasures of wisdom and knowledge. It was only after years of studying history that I began to have prophetic experiences in which much of the general knowledge I had gained from both the Scriptures and history was illuminated and tied together. These experiences took many random pieces and formed them into distinguishable patterns and pictures. I could not have understood the future without some knowledge of the past, but neither could I have understood the past without some knowledge of the future. This book is my most comprehensive attempt to unify what I have come to understand of the past, the present, and the future together.

2

In the Beginning ...
The Map That Guides Us

THROUGHOUT THE AGES, MEN HAVE SEARCHED for truth. Some have sought diligently for this great treasure, like Mel Fisher, until they found it. Others have twisted through blind alleys and dark corridors to arrive at falsehood. One man who could be called "the blind of the blind" was Pontius Pilate. Pilate, an influential representative of one of the most powerful empires the world has ever known, asked the question, "What is truth?" The fact that he asked this question while looking at Truth Himself made it the most ironic utterance ever recorded. It is not clear whether Pilate asked this question scornfully or with sincerity, but the power of the empire he represented was used to flog, beat, and then crucify the Truth. It is, therefore, one of the ultimate demonstrations of human blindness. Earthly power and influence never have been a basis for finding the Truth.

Neither has human intelligence nor goodness been able to come to the knowledge of the truth. The seemingly righteous and wise religious leaders of Jesus' time manipulated the Roman Empire into crucifying Him. These religious leaders were the custodians of the prophecies that spoke of His coming—and even spoke of their own rejection and persecution of Him—but still they could not see. Religion, too, can be a great hindrance to finding the Truth. In fact, from the time when the Truth Himself walked the earth until now, human religion has been the most persistent and deadly enemy of the Truth.

Saul of Tarsus is a good biblical example of what religion will do to a man. Though he considered himself to be a protector of the truth, he was a persecutor of those who loved the Truth. Saul would come to know Jesus and would one day become arguably the chief of the apostles, but his religion did not lead him to this great change. He had to be struck blind before he could see. The same is true of everyone who seeks to establish his or her own righteousness through religion. Instead, these people need to be reduced to helplessness like Saul, who had to rely on someone else to guide him for a time. Simply speaking, pride is the thickest veil to keep us from discerning truth. That is why Jesus said,

> "For judgment I came into this world, that those who do not see may see; and that those who see may become blind." Those of the Pharisees who were with Him heard these things, and said to Him, "We are not blind too, are we?" Jesus said to them, "If you were blind, you would have no sin; but since you say, 'We see,' your sin remains." (John 9:39–41)

The fastest way to know the Truth is to start from the position that *we know that we do not know* and that we need help from above. As James 4:6 declares, "God is opposed to the proud, but gives grace to the humble." A basic character trait found in every real seeker of truth is genuine humility, which makes one much more prone to listen than to speak. True humility opens one to learn from sources that others overlook, and what is born of God is most often found in the most humble circumstances. Wise men will still go to even the most lowly places to find Him.

The Bible is our compass and our map, and it is the most accurate one ever made. Of course, no map is useful unless we know where we are on it. Church history was prophesied in advance in astonishing detail, yet few modern writers have given much attention to this historical perspective. This glaring omission has been costly, causing much of the church to drift instead of having the confidence to confront our times boldly. When we see our present location in the unfolding of God's plan, as well as our own purpose in it, we can also see where we are going with much more clarity. This must be a primary goal of our search for truth.

Our Present Location in God's Plan

The first step to understanding our purpose, and how to fulfill it, is to gain knowledge of God's plan. Many Christians have a basic knowledge of the plan of salvation but very little understanding of the Lord's ultimate plan to establish His kingdom on earth. Conflicting and confusing doctrines have filled the void. As we see in Matthew 24:14, the gospel of the kingdom, not the gospel of salvation, must be preached throughout the world before the end comes. Every believer should have a sound understanding of this gospel if he or she is to be used significantly in this great purpose.

This is not to belittle the gospel of salvation. This message is so great, so unfathomable in its glory and majesty, as well as the depth to which it reveals the nature of God, that it is easy to understand why many cannot see beyond it. We will probably spend eternity marveling at its wonders. That we can be born again with everything in our life being made new is a gift beyond measure. However, when we are born, we are just beginning life. To be born again is the beginning of the matter, not the end. Our calling is to be ambassadors of the heavenly kingdom.

The Bible follows a consistent path that leads to a certain conclusion: the establishment of God's kingdom on this earth. Once we understand the unfolding plan of God in the Scriptures, we are much more able to interpret the great forces and events of human history, all of which are intended either to prevent or to prepare for the revealing of God's ultimate purpose. As the path becomes clear to us, we can more easily discern the great forces behind human events so that we will not be easily pushed off the path.

Many of the greatest failures have come when those entrusted with the truth—the sword of the Spirit for their times—failed to use it. Understanding history is not the answer to all of our problems, but it will greatly help us overcome many of them, and give us the boldness to seize the day.

So, let us begin at the beginning so that we can more fully understand our place in the unfolding plan of God.

IN THE BEGINNING

The first verse in the Bible is also the most important: "In the beginning God created the heavens and the earth" (Gen. 1:1). The understanding of this one verse is the foundation of all truth. Before we can comprehend the end of the age, or our present purposes, we must first understand the beginning.

In the beginning God . . . These are possibly the four most important words ever written. These four words alone are worthy of a lifetime of study, and will be the basis for an eternity of worship. We exist because of God; therefore, we owe Him everything.

It is not surprising that at the end of the age, the most pressing philosophical controversies still revolve around our origin. Understanding our own beginning is the beginning of understanding. When we accept this one fact, that God created us, we no longer have an excuse; we are compelled to serve Him. This one truth sets the course of our lives, and the way men have dealt with this truth in the past has set the course of history.

When we answer this one question correctly, the answer to all other questions is possible. If we answer it incorrectly, the door opens to almost every form of darkness and deception.

THE ULTIMATE DELUSION

In contrast to the simple truth that God created us, men have formulated many theories about our origin, which they assert with great confidence. Even the most brilliant and widely accepted of these theories are easily debunked with a child's logic, which is a revelation in itself. The devils must be laughing at the foolishness of what our scientists and educators have compelled men to believe, but, as the Lord said, we must become like a little child to enter the kingdom.

Without seeing God as the Creator, we are left to believe that our creation just happened by accident. As a professor once said, the odds are better for a tornado to hit a junkyard and leave behind a perfectly built Boeing 747 jetliner than for all of the order and symmetry of this universe to have happened by accident. As another educator once said, the odds are better that an ape could throw a handful of chalk at a blackboard and have it form the theory of relativity than for our existence to be the result of chance.

Consider the following facts: if you took the distance of the earth from the sun and reduced it to a scale of one hundred miles, and if, over that one-hundred-mile distance, the earth deviated the equivalent of just *one-eighth of an inch*, we would either fry or freeze. Even if the earth's orbit just happened to fall into the tiny slice of space where life could be sustained, we must also consider how the earth tilts and spins in such a way that the seasons are perfectly controlled. This tilt and rotation must be precise to keep one side of the planet from freezing over, which would quickly cause the earth to wobble out of its tiny slice of space where life can be sustained. We are still far from being able to develop a computer that can even figure the odds of all this happening by chance. In fact, one study acknowledged that it had not even been able to compute the odds that the gases found in our atmosphere would come together as they did to support life on the planet.

These are just a few of the multitudes of combinations of events that had to take place for life to exist on earth. The belief that any of this just happened by chance should be grounds for insanity, but for some reason men easily swallow this foolishness. Science has accomplished much for mankind, but the acceptance of such theories as evolution reduces science to a mental level that tempts us to think that maybe *some* men may have evolved from the apes, and they did not evolve very far!

When we understand that we had our beginning in God, that He made us for *His* purposes, then we are compelled to return to Him. The truth of our beginning is also the beginning of all truth. If He made us, we are His. His purpose and His plan must guide us. The depth to which we understand this one truth can determine the spiritual strength of our entire life, just as the strength of a foundation will determine the magnitude of what can be built upon it.

The Second Beginning

So what does all of this have to do with the church history? When we address the beginning of the church, we are observing a second beginning, the beginning of a new creation with consequences no less profound than the first creation. The church does not represent a new beginning for just a few chosen people, but a new beginning for the entire creation. That is why Paul asserted that "the creation waits eagerly for the revealing of the sons of God" (Rom. 8:19).

The first-century church really had only one thing going for them—God. The Lord was with them. The Lord had His first leaders in a place where they were completely dependent on Him; if the Lord did not show up, they were helpless. That is precisely the foundation that we must return to: *In the beginning . . . God.* There is no other explanation for what happened. No one would just naturally follow fishermen, tax gatherers, and peasants, who had proven their unfaithfulness by deserting their Lord when He needed them the most. Unless the Lord was with them, the first church leaders had no hope of accomplishing their purpose of building the church.

The beginning of both creations can be summed up in one word—*Jesus.* He is called "the Beginning of the creation of God" (Rev. 3:14), not because He Himself is created but because the entire plan of creation began with Him. In fact, the Scriptures make it clear that Jesus is the Creator, as we see in the following texts:

In the beginning was the Word, and the Word was with God, and the Word was God. The same was in the beginning with God. All things were made by him; and without him was not any thing made that was made. (John 1:1–3 KJV)

For by him were all things created, that are in heaven, and that are in earth, visible and invisible, whether they be thrones, or dominions, or principalities, or powers: all things were created by him, and for him: And he is before all things, and by him all things consist. (Col. 1:16–17 KJV)

In everything God created He was looking for His Son, and He is looking for His Son in us. The goal of our life is to be found in Him; it is also the ultimate goal of the whole creation, the new and the old, the heavens and the earth.

The church was originally conceived in the heart of the Father as a fitting bride for His Son, just as Eve was the perfect helpmate for the first Adam. The church did start out in such a way that this was an unquestionable reality. From that point on, the history of the church could be summed up as, "after the beginning . . . man."

If we are to understand church history, we must see it in the context of the whole plan of God. When we see His entire plan, we can understand why He would let the first creation fall into such depravity, and then let the new creation follow the same course. Yes, the new creation also fell, following a remarkably similar path as the original creation. In His great wisdom God gave man, the crowning glory of His creation, the freedom of choice. He knew that there could be no true relationship unless there was the freedom not to relate. In addition, there could be no true obedience without the freedom to disobey. He did not put the Tree of the Knowledge of Good and Evil in the Garden in order to cause man to fall, but so that man could prove his devotion and obedience.

Even so, the Lord knew from the beginning that man would choose wrongly, eat of the Tree of Knowledge, and rebel against Him. And He knew that when man fell, death and deception would mar the beauty of His glorious creation. He made us anyway, knowing that the darkness would one day make His light even more glorious to those who would behold it. He loved His first creation, but planned from the beginning to bring forth a new creation that would transcend the glory of the first one. He also determined that the glory of the second would result in the redemption of the first.

That is one reason Jesus is referred to as "the last Adam." His help-mate, the church, also partook of the forbidden fruit of the Tree of Knowledge, falling into a terrible depravity. However, unlike the first Adam, Jesus did not follow His bride. That is why He is the "last Adam," not just the second one. He kept His place; He obeyed and never ate of the fruit of sin. That is why He can now redeem both the new and the original creation. He will restore His bride, and she will one day again be "without spot or wrinkle." Then, together, we will bring restoration to the rest of creation.

We cannot try to build the church of God upon charismatic preach-ers, regardless of how true their preaching is or how great their gifts. The true church will only be built upon the one Foundation, Jesus Christ Himself.

We should always ask the question, Why are people coming to our churches? Is it because they agree with our doctrine? Is it because of our dynamic ministry? Is it because of our facilities? Our music? Or is it because the Lord Jesus Himself is in our midst, and we are all being joined to Him?

The apostolic burden was not to bring the church into a certain form but to see Jesus formed within His people. There is a difference. One is Christ-centered; the other is man-centered. The more church-centric the church became, the quicker she fell into the prophesied apostasy.

In the New Testament narrative of the beginning of the church, we see that those who were converted were added to the church. Today some of our greatest evangelists estimate that only about 5 percent of those who "make decisions for Christ" are added to the church. We should be thankful for even these, but can we really call this fulfilling the Great Commission? What has caused this slide to just one out of every twenty? Can those who are not really joined to the church even be called "converts" if we are going to comply with the biblical definition of the word? Those are questions that twenty-first-century Christians must answer.

THE TEACHINGS OF JESUS OR PAUL?

After the first century, the institutional church, which evolved over the next twelve hundred years, claimed to be based upon the seat, or authority, given to Peter. His ministry and message were the main focus of that time, and the church reflected it. Like Peter's own life, spectacular victories followed shocking errors. The Reformation really began with a rediscovery of the epistles of Paul, and since then the church's main emphasis has been on Paul's theology. In a sense, the Reformation seemed to be Paul arising to rebuke Peter, as he did in Antioch.

Paul was unquestionably one of the great builders of the New Testament church; his theology and revelation set a true course for Christianity. Even so, Paul is not the foundation of the church; Jesus is. Since the Reformation we have tended to use Paul to interpret Jesus, rather than the other way around.

This is not to imply that Paul's epistles do not deserve to be Scripture, or that they are not pure words from God. However, we will misinterpret them, and misapply them, if they are not rightly built upon the foundation of the teachings of Jesus. Likewise, the teachings of Jesus will be misinterpreted, and misapplied, if we try to view them through the teachings of anyone else, rather than as the foundation for all other understanding.

Paul's teachings made many great and insightful references to the kingdom of God, but they mostly dealt with the practical issues of the church and some basic doctrinal issues. The church is a part of the kingdom of God, but it is just a part. Conversely, the Lord's teachings were devoted to the kingdom and only made a couple of references to the church. Unless the church is viewed from this perspective, we will become church-centric rather than Christ-centric and we will not have a kingdom perspective.

When the church becomes self-centered, she loses her ability to see the glory of the Lord and to be changed by that glory. She will also have a distorted view of the kingdom, and therefore a distorted view of her relationship to the world.

THE TWO WILL BECOME ONE

The new creation, the church, was so much in the heart of God from the beginning that we can see church history prophesied with astonishing clarity in Genesis 1–2, in the account of the seven days of creation.

HISTORY IN THE SEVEN DAYS OF CREATION

Second Peter 3:8 states: "Do not let this one fact escape your notice, beloved, that with the Lord one day is as a thousand years, and a thousand years as one day." We must understand that prophetically, sometimes a day represents a thousand years. This is why the millennial reign of Christ is sometimes referred to as "the *day* of the Lord." We also can determine the length of time that man has been on the earth by adding up the genealogies in Scripture. We must give or take a hundred years, because a period in the book of Judges is a little ambiguous, but generally we know that it has been about six thousand years since Adam was created. Therefore, we are coming to the end of the sixth prophetic, one-thousand-year day.

This is also the beginning of the seventh one-thousand-year day, or the prophetic Sabbath. The Lord Jesus is called "the Lord of the Sabbath," and therefore the history in creation prophesies that the seventh prophetic one-thousand-year day will be His millennium. During that time Jesus establishes His reign over the earth.

This was obviously a prevailing view of many early church fathers, such as Barnabas. The epistle of Barnabas was included in the canon of

Scripture by many early church leaders, such as the Ante-Nicene Fathers, Clement of Alexandria, Justin Martyr, Origen, and others. It is even included in the Didache or "Teaching of the Twelve," which was written in A.D. 100; the evidence that it is the authentic writing of Barnabas who served with Paul is quite solid. However, this epistle is not in the modern canon of Scripture and should not be esteemed as Scripture. Still, early church writers quoted it so often that Barnabas's epistle can be a good source for understanding and confirming early church doctrines. Here is what Barnabas had to say about the one-thousand-year day:

> And elsewhere he saith; If thy children shall keep my sabbaths, then will I put my mercy upon them. And even in the beginning of the creation he makes mention of the Sabbath. And God made in six days the works of his hands; and he finished them on the seventh day, and he rested the seventh day, and sanctified it. Consider, my children, what that signifies, he finished them in six days. *The meaning of it is this; that in six thousand years the Lord God will bring all things to an end. For with him one day is a thousand years; and himself testifieth, saying, "Behold this day shall be as a thousand years." Therefore, children, in six days, that is, in six thousand years, shall all things be accomplished.* (13:2–5)

This thought did not seem to be comprehensible to those who formed the modern canon of Scripture, but now it makes perfect sense. We can also see how the seven days of creation made an amazing outline of the history of man, which would unfold over the next six thousand years.

On day one, God separated the light from the darkness. During the first one-thousand-year period of man's history, we have the fall of man and the beginning of the conflict between light and darkness.

On day two, the waters were separated. During the second one-thousand-year day, the Flood occurred and the waters that had been over the earth in a mist came down in the first rain.

On day three, God gathered the waters into seas. Waters often represent peoples (for instance, "the waters which you saw where the harlot sits, are peoples" [Rev. 17:15]). In the third one-thousand-year period of man's history, man built the Tower of Babel and formed people into nations.

On day four, God separated the day and night and created the sun, moon, and stars. During the fourth one-thousand-year day, the Lord Jesus was born (the sun), Satan was fully revealed as the one who rules the night (the moon), and the apostles led the church (the star). In Scripture the apostles are often spoken of as stars. This was the true separation of light and darkness on earth.

On day five, God created the "great sea monsters." During this one-thousand-year period, the powerful and monstrous religions of the world were formed that were to rule the "seas" or peoples, such as Islam, Hinduism, and some of the powerful and dominating institutions of Christianity that would devour so many.

On day six, the creatures multiplied. During this one-thousand-year period, we see every religion and philosophy in the world multiplying into many offshoots. At the end of this day we also have man created in the Lord's image. When we come to the end of this period, the world is going to see a church that is re-created in His image, without spot or wrinkle, walking in the "measure of the stature which belongs to the fulness of Christ" (Eph. 4:13).

On day seven, God rested. The next one-thousand-year period of man's history will see the return of the Lord and the setting up of His kingdom. Then "the Lord of the Sabbath" will reign over the earth as promised.

This is just a general outline of what is contained prophetically in the days of creation. Could this have just been coincidence? No. The Lord knew the end from the beginning, and a prophetic repetition flows throughout the Scriptures, which should release in us a powerful confidence in the One we serve and in whose plan we seek to walk. His Word is clear that He knew not just these major events that would take place but that He also knew you and me from the beginning and is able to accomplish His purpose in our lives as well.

It is now time for the church to once more be born again. We must return to our beginning. Many have been hearing this call for years but have interpreted it as meaning that we need to return to the *ways* of the first-century church. There is some merit to this idea, but our goal is much greater than that. We need to return to the One who did the works. The Lord is going to insist on building His own house. When it is done right, He is going to return to live in it.

As we see in Revelation 3:20, the Lord is on the outside of most of our churches trying to get in. He is a gentleman and will not force Himself upon His bride. Building on the foundation of Jesus is much more than just teaching about Him. It is also more than just inviting Him in, though that would be a good start for most of us. Ultimately, we are going to have to let Him do the building.

During the Middle Ages, Francis of Assisi, one of the great leaders of the church, was walking with a friend who was pointing out the glories of their city cathedral. Observing the great treasures of the church, the friend remarked that the church could no longer say, "Silver and gold have I none." To which Francis replied, "And neither can we say, 'In the name of Jesus rise up and walk.' " Many great things have been done in the name of the Lord, but how many of them have actually been done by the Lord?

The Lord has blessed many great works and movements, and He has even occasionally visited a few with His manifest presence. However, it does not seem that there has been a church since the first century about which it could be said that the Lord truly dwells with her. Isn't this our quest—to find the city that God is building, the place where He wants to dwell?

3

The Men Who Led Us
Our Apostolic Foundation

IN THE EARLY CHURCH IT WAS OBVIOUS THAT THE Lord might manifest Himself and do extraordinary works through any believer at any time, but He did have leaders. These leaders did not have authority just because they were appointed, but because the Lord was with them in their leadership. Peter boldly stepped beyond the present limits to preach the gospel on the day of Pentecost, and then to the Gentiles at the home of Cornelius. Because Peter followed the Lord, he repeatedly led the church in the new directions that the Lord wanted to go in. The apostles were used to perform great miracles, even raising the dead. Leadership was not just a position; it was an action verb! Such was the nature of the apostolic ministry that laid the foundation in the first century, and we can expect the apostolic authority at the end to be like it.

Will there be true apostles again? Yes. The Scriptures are clear about this, and we will examine them. Are there apostles in the church today? Maybe. Many Christians call themselves apostles, and what are now being called apostolic movements encompass the fastest-growing segment of the Body of Christ. These movements are already having such a sweeping impact that they are even being called the Second Reformation of the church. However, do those who are now called apostles measure up to the biblical stature of that ministry? Are the movements they are generating truly carrying the church to another level of maturity or effectiveness in carrying out the Great Commission? These are questions that should be examined, but how do we do this?

First, we must examine the biblical requirements for apostolic ministry, and the mandates for this ministry that are clearly laid out in Scripture. This is not to imply that our goal is to seek to be another first-century church. We are no longer in the first century, and our calling is to build not another first-century church but rather the twenty-first-century church. Even so, the biblical stature for this ministry, and for the church, is established in Scripture as the plumb line for judging what is authentic from what is not. Some of the things promoted by the new apostolic movements, and some of their fruit, seem to be truly apostolic. Some of the things promoted, and the fruit of some, seem to fall far short of true apostolic ministry.

The sheer magnitude of these movements now requires their examination by all responsible church leaders. My goal for examining them is to "hold fast to that which is good" (1 Thess. 5:21) and not waste time on what is not. If true apostolic ministry is being restored to the church, we will miss out on one of the great spiritual opportunities of all time if we do not recognize it. If we call those who do not measure up to the biblical stature of apostles by that name, we are allowing a tragic devaluation of our spiritual currency. This will only hinder the recognition of the authentic when it comes. This issue may be one of the most important for the church to face in these times.

What Is an Apostle?

The following are some of the more prominent characteristics of an apostle that we can derive from the New Testament:

1. Apostles are spiritual fathers.

In the first century it was important for the church to recognize the leaders who were ordained by the Lord. It was also the nature of the apostolic leaders to recognize and support what the Lord ordained through any believer. For example, when they heard that Samaria was receiving the word of the Lord through Philip, apostles were sent to help lay a solid foundation in the believers there. When they heard that the Gentiles in Antioch had received the word, they sent Barnabas to help encourage and establish them. In this the leaders did not just lead but followed the Holy Spirit and supported His ministry through whomever He chose to use. They were building a body, not just a platform for their own ministry. This was so fundamental to the apostolic ministry that one's apostleship could in fact be judged by the men and women who were released into ministry through that individual.

Paul warned the Corinthians, "Though you might have ten thousand instructors in Christ, yet you do not have many fathers; for in Christ Jesus I have begotten you through the gospel. Therefore I urge you, imitate me" (1 Cor. 4:15–16 NKJV). The same is true in the church today. There are many outstanding teachers and preachers, but not many fathers. Many are called spiritual fathers because of their age; but just as most men become fathers when they are young, being a spiritual father has little to do with age. A spiritual father reproduces his ministry in others. Very few of the recognized ministries presently do this.

Even so, just the ability to reproduce one's ministry in others does not make one an apostle. All of the equipping ministries are supposed to do this. Being apostolic is more than just reproducing one's ministry in others, it is also seeing Christ formed in the whole church.

2. Apostles establish churches.

Establishing churches was an obvious result of apostolic ministry in the first century. However, there is a big difference between establishing churches and building franchises. The Lord is the only One who can build His church. From the beginning He has chosen to do this through apostles, whom He uses as "wise master builders." However, not all churches were established through the apostles. In fact, one of the most notable churches in the first century, the church at Antioch, was not founded by apostles, yet it was used to give birth to some of the most remarkable apostles of all time, Paul and Barnabas.

The God who makes every snowflake different obviously still likes to be creative. Every prophet and apostle in Scripture was unique; likewise, we can err by overdefining what an apostle is. The basic issue is that the Lord will be both the designer and builder of His own house. If we are going to be a part of a truly apostolic church, we must ask ourselves, "Are we building a church the Lord wants to dwell in, or are we building mostly to attract people?" If our true motivation is to attract people, we will not build a ministry that will bring the manifest presence of the Lord. If we build something the Lord truly inhabits, we may or may not attract many people to it, but that is not our concern. Even though the Lord desires for all men to be saved (1 Tim. 2:4), people today are conditioned to be drawn by many things that the Holy Spirit will not endorse with His presence. There are places where the conditions are such that His presence will not draw many people, and there are places where He will draw far more than a human organization can contain. We are not here to be big or small, but to abide in Him so that He can abide in us. The apostolic vision was God living in people—not bricks. When one grasps the true faith, he does not go to church, but he *becomes* the church. We must also consider that just building churches does not make one an apostle. Evangelists, pastors, teachers, and prophets may all be used to establish churches, as well as those who are not recognized as being in one of the equipping ministries.

3. Apostles are committed to the diversity of ministry needed by the church.

Again, the first-century church at Antioch was not birthed by apostles but by ordinary believers who started sharing the gospel with the Gentiles. Still, this church gave birth to new apostolic ministries. It is likely that if the apostolic team from Jerusalem had birthed this church, the new type of missionary apostle released through Paul and Barnabas might not have come forth from here. It takes a new wineskin to hold God's new wine. However, the Lord is also going to serve "refined, aged wine" at His banquet that He is preparing for all people (Isa. 25:6). We should have a taste for both!

The great churches that emerged during the first century received ministry from the apostles sent out from both Antioch and Jerusalem, the new and the older, more established church. Likewise, today the churches that will arise to become truly significant will probably receive apostolic ministry from a number of different movements.

It is obvious from the New Testament that the first-century apostles encouraged the churches to receive ministry from other apostles. Paul gave letters of recommendation to many, and acknowledged how one would plant and the other water the seeds that God would use to bring forth fruit. Peter also encouraged those to whom he wrote to receive Paul's ministry. We should beware of any ministry that is reclusive or exclusive in its relationship to other movements in the Body of Christ, as this is sure evidence of motives, agendas, or strongholds present that will divert the ministry far from what would be truly apostolic.

Just as the high priest in the Old Covenant was from the tribe of Levi, but carried the stones that represented all of the tribes of Israel on his breastplate, so our High Priest carries all of His people on His heart. So will everyone who is truly joined to Him. If our primary goal is to build our own church or movement, we will never be truly apostolic. Our goal must be to see God's kingdom built, not to build our own kingdoms. This necessitates a constant devotion to seeing the whole church built up. This will require interchange between the ministries and movements. Isolationist tendencies are therefore a sure sign of a serious diversion from true apostolic Christianity.

4. Apostles impart God's government.

We cannot have a revelation of Jesus without understanding that He is the King of kings. Jesus is the ultimate representative of God's authority, and if we are becoming like Him, we will both walk in and help to establish His authority on the earth.

However, the Lord made it clear that His authority was not like that of the Gentiles or present human authority. His authority was based on love and service. The most devastating mistakes in church history have been the results of church leaders imposing a government in the form of human authority rather than kingdom authority.

The government of God is not a system or organization but an anointing. When men derive their authority from a position in a system, they can maintain influence long after the anointing has departed from them. Though it seems that some of the most important truths of God's government have yet to be discovered by the modern church, the apostolic church will not be built just by tearing down what now exists. Earthly governments are also ordained by God for the purpose of keeping order until His kingdom comes. Let us also not confuse the fact that although His authority is based on love and service, it still involves discipline and judgment.

5. Apostles have seen the Lord.

When Paul was defending his own ministry, he asked the Corinthians, "Am I not an apostle? Am I not free? Have I not seen Jesus Christ our Lord?" (1 Cor. 9:1 NKJV). Paul obviously saw this as a requirement for apostolic authority. Jesus is the pattern of the house that the apostle is commissioned to build. Moses had to go up on the mountain to see the pattern for the tabernacle, the first dwelling place of God on the earth, before he could build it. Now contemporary apostles must see the glory of who He now is, and have this branded on their hearts and minds.

When we are captured by the glory of who He is, we will not be so prone to be distracted by plans and programs that may seem good but are still the inventions of men. Devotion to patterns and formulas is a basic symptom of witchcraft, which is the counterfeit of true spiritual authority. If we are to be delivered from the tendency to use human devices for trying to accomplish the purposes of God, we must see Him on His throne in such a way that it is much more than a doctrine to us. True apostolic ministers must have literally seen the resurrected Christ.

John G. Lake, an Episcopal minister in Zion, Illinois, during the early part of the twentieth century, demonstrated the nature of apostolic ministry through his continual search to know and see Jesus. At the turn of the twentieth century, John Lake had undergone a powerful salvation experience and a powerful sanctification experience. He then received an impartation of the gift of healing. At each juncture, those around Lake tried to convince him that he had received the baptism of the Holy Spirit, yet his heart burned for more of God than ever before.

Searching for something that would satisfy the longing of his heart, he began to fast, pray, and wait upon the Lord for nine months. At the end of this period, Lake had an awesome experience with the Lord. Finally his heart was content that he had received the baptism of the Holy Spirit, which would produce the nature and character of Christ within him.

During the winter of 1913, Lake presented a teaching to the Church of England entitled "Triune Salvation," which revealed a key secret to his power and intimacy with God. In this study Lake emphasized the important significance of our complete redemption on all three levels of human life—spirit, soul (mind), and body. Lake taught that the average Christian tended to stop at the redemption of the spirit. However, Lake believed that it was equally important for the believer to allow the Holy Spirit to sanctify the soul and the body in order for the individual to become the habitation of God.

The sanctification of the soul literally involves the impartation of the mind of Christ. John Wesley defined *sanctification* as "possessing the mind of Christ." This level of consecration is essential for our thoughts to be perfectly in tune with the Lord's thoughts and our ways consistent with His ways. Because all ministries will basically impart what they are, not just what they teach, a true ministry is much more zealous for Christlikeness than for good organizational or administrative abilities.

Possibly the ultimate articulation of the true apostolic burden is found in Galatians 4:19: "My children, with whom I am again in labor until Christ is formed in you." Paul was not just seeking to bring the church into a certain form, but rather to see Christ formed within the believers. That is still a basic difference between true apostolic ministry and the abundant substitutes that we have today.

Lake's "Triune Salvation" may or may not have been a perfect articulation of this, but he was right that true salvation involves the separation of the Christian from all that would defile, like alcohol, drugs, and sexual promiscuity. As he put it, "There arises in the heart the desire and prayer for the Spirit of God to eject, crucify, and destroy every tendency of the opposition of the Holy Spirit."

Lake also taught that the true apostle is a separated person: separated forever to God in all the departments of life—body, soul, and spirit. This absolute consecration to God (or "triune salvation") is the real secret to the successful Christian life and essential to becoming the habitation of God. The Bishop of London felt that John Lake's triune salvation teaching was so significant that he recommended its careful study to every priest.

John Lake was also an example of how the "signs of a true apostle" were manifested. Through him the Holy Spirit was able to heal the sick, cast out demons, save the lost, and manifest the nature and character of Christ with power—displaying that Jesus is the same yesterday, today, and forever. His unique ministry came from his lifelong search to know the resurrected Christ.[1]

6. Apostles are witnesses of His resurrection.

This is related to the last point, which is to have seen Christ in His resurrection glory, but it also speaks of proclaiming His resurrection. It is by seeing the glory of His resurrection that our proclamation is empowered.

In Acts 1:22 we see that the office of the apostle was given to be a witness of His resurrection. In Acts 4:33 we see that power was given to the church to be a witness of His resurrection. In Romans 1:4 we see that Jesus "was declared the Son of God with power by the resurrection from the dead."

The Resurrection was the central theme of the gospel preached by the first-century apostles. Yet Charles Spurgeon went so far as to say,

"There are very few *Christians* who believe in the resurrection." When I first read this, I thought that it was a misprint, but I went through my library searching for messages on the Resurrection by those who are considered some of the greatest men and women of faith since biblical times. I was astonished at what I found. Of the numerous volumes of teaching and insight from some of these men, they would only have a page or two on the subject of the Resurrection! Many of these were obviously just obligatory Easter sermons. How is it that this foundational truth could be so neglected? Is it not time to again recover the meaning and power of the Resurrection?

In my studies it became apparent why this message has been so neglected: in the early church, belief in the Resurrection caused not only faith and power *but also persecution.* Peter and John were dragged before the Sanhedrin because the rulers were "greatly disturbed because they [Peter and John] were teaching the people and proclaiming in Jesus the *resurrection from the dead*" (Acts 4:2, emphasis added). When Paul was later arrested and brought before this same board, he declared, *"I am on trial for the hope and resurrection of the dead!"*

Little that we do will bring persecution upon us faster than preaching the message of the Resurrection. This is because this message attacks Satan's strongest fortress, his most powerful grip upon this world and the church—*the fear of death.* This freedom is a prerequisite to complete freedom in any other area of our lives.

True faith is more than just an intellectual assent to certain facts. It is believing in our *hearts,* not our minds. If we really believed in our hearts, most of our lives would be radically different. We would not be as consumed with the tyranny of the temporary; instead we would be fully committed to the things that are eternal. What Spurgeon was implying is that we give intellectual assent to the fact of the *Resurrection* but go on living our lives as if it did not exist. As Paul wrote in 1 Corinthians 15:13–14, if we do not believe in the Resurrection, our faith is in vain.

But how do we get this biblical truth transferred from our minds to our hearts? The answer to this question is utterly practical: begin to develop a secret relationship with God. One can conform to all the characteristics listed above and yet still not be an apostle. The apostolic ministry requires a commission from God, and it requires genuine spiritual authority. True apostles will not offer theories, forms, recipes, and formulas but instead will offer an impartation of authentic church life. That is nothing less than to be the temple of God, to dwell in His presence, and to manifest everywhere the sweet aroma of knowing Him. Before the end of this age, such a church will again turn the world upside down, because God is with her.

If you meet the requirements of an apostle, then God will grant you the gifts needed to fulfill your purpose: apostolic vision, apostolic character, and apostolic resolve, which will also result in another great grace, the ability to endure apostolic persecution.

THE APOSTOLIC GIFTS

APOSTOLIC VISION

Moses was a man of vision. He actually saw the tabernacle in detail on the mount before he was able to begin its construction (Ex. 25:40). *True spiritual vision must originate with God;* it is not something that we create in our minds.

The prophet Haggai said that "the latter glory of this house will be greater than the former" (Hag. 2:9). He did not say that the house was greater, but that the glory in it would be greater. The apostolic goal is not focused on the house as much as on the glory of the One who is to inhabit the house. The apostolic call is to lead people to Christ, not just to church. If people are truly led to Christ, they will end up in church, but the reverse is not necessarily true. Many are drawn to the church for various reasons but never come to know the Lord. What good is the most glorious temple if the Lord is not in it? The great apostolic prayer was:

I pray that the eyes of your heart may be enlightened, so that you may know what is the hope of *His* calling, what are the riches of the glory of *His* inheritance in the saints, and what is the surpassing greatness of *His* power toward us who believe. These are in accordance with the working of the strength of *His* might. (Eph. 1:18–19, emphasis added)

This prayer does not say that we should come to know what is the hope of *our* calling or *our* inheritance. Neither will anything of true eternal value ever be accomplished by *our* power. One of the most subtle but devastating deceptions that we can fall into is the overemphasis of who we are in Christ in place of who He is in us. We do need to know who we are and what our calling is, but we must never allow that to eclipse our devotion to seeing Him.

APOSTOLIC CHARACTER

Since apostles are called to be God's master builders for His dwelling place, the church, we can see aspects of the character required for this task in the lives of all who were used to build His dwelling places in Scripture, like Moses and the apostle Paul. Of Moses, the first to build a dwelling place for God, it was said:

By faith Moses, when he was come to years, refused to be called the son of Pharaoh's daughter; choosing rather to suffer affliction with the people of God, than to enjoy the pleasures of sin for a season; esteeming the reproach of Christ greater riches than the treasures in Egypt: for he had respect unto the [spiritual] recompense of the reward. (Heb. 11:24–26 KJV)

Here we see that he chose *to sacrifice* the greatest of worldly opportunities to serve the purpose of God, refusing to be called the son of Pharaoh's daughter. The apostle Paul, as the archetype (model) of the biblical apostle, did the same. As a Roman citizen, Paul was obviously in a high position—a member of the aristocracy of the world's greatest empire. Yet, by his own admission he counted every such title and privilege "as dung." Just as the earth does not even register as much more than a speck of dust in the great expanse of God's universe, all of the riches of this earth could not be compared to a speck of dust in the eternal dwelling place of God.

Moses is also a "type" (forerunner) of apostolic ministry, as he was the first to build a dwelling place for God on earth, which is the primary apostolic purpose. Moses chose to suffer affliction with the people of God, esteeming the sufferings of Christ "as greater riches" than all the treasures of Egypt. Paul also walked in continual persecution, dangers, and setbacks, viewing all of them as greater opportunities for the gospel, and even as a basis for his authority. To suffer any kind of persecution for the sake of Jesus' gospel is a treasure far beyond any earthly wealth.

Moses rejected the temporary pleasures of sin. All of the apostles lived a life that was above reproach, sanctified and holy to the Lord. They were examples to the church, but they did not do this just to be examples. They dwelt in the presence of a holy God, and they could not really love Him without loving purity. Just as Moses *chose* to suffer affliction for the purposes of God, we, too, have a choice as to whether we sin or not. If we are to be an apostolic church, we must begin to choose to walk uprightly before the Lord.

Moses' vision was on the (spiritual) recompense of the reward. "For he [Moses] endured, as seeing him who is invisible" (Heb. 11:27 KJV). It is sometimes said that some people are so heavenly minded, they are not of any earthly good. Those about whom this is said may be close to being apostolic. (Who were more heavenly minded than the apostles?) Unfortunately, the reverse is true today: some are too earthly minded to be any spiritual good. Spiritual vision requires that what we see with the eyes of our hearts will be more real to us than what we see with our natural eyes. *We must see what is invisible to others.* Unfortunately, much of what is called apostolic today is really the building of earthly organizations more than the true dwelling place of God.

APOSTOLIC RESOLVE

Apostolic resolve is unwavering commitment to a goal, being so determined that failure or defeat is never considered an option. Jesus set His face "like a flint" to go to Jerusalem, knowing what awaited Him. Paul got up after being stoned and went back into the city. Apostolic resolve caused him to brave any consequence and refuse to be distracted by any problem when he was determined to get to Jerusalem. Apostolic resolve holds to the course and vision, regardless of opposition or problems.

A good historical example of this kind of resolve was Wellington when he faced Napoleon at Waterloo, one of the great strategic battles of history. There two armies of more than 150,000 men faced each other in less than three square miles of territory. Napoleon had nothing but contempt for his adversary, whom he called "the sepoy general." He seemed almost bored with the looming battle and was looking forward to dining in Brussels that evening. In addition to being scornful of his adversary's ability, Napoleon knew that he had significant numerical advantages in troops and cannons. He slept late, almost casually arrayed his troops, and did not begin the battle until after eleven o'clock. This poor timing was possibly the only strategic mistake Napoleon made that day, but it was all that Wellington needed.

Napoleon ordered his artillery to begin one of the greatest cannonades ever witnessed. But soon after its inception, a huge thunderstorm broke upon the field that actually drowned out the cannonade, disconcerting the French. (Natural phenomena, especially thunderstorms, had accompanied some of Wellington's most important victories; he testified that it was "the finger of God.") The deluge so softened the field that the cannonballs lost some of their deadly potential as the ground absorbed them. The mud also reduced Napoleon's maneuverability. This was just the beginning of a score of "miracles" Wellington would need, and receive, that day. But it was not just the miracles that saved him; he was brilliantly prepared to seize those miracles and derive every drop of help that he could from each one, his own version of apostolic resolve.

Wellington knew that the fate of Europe rested on his shoulders that day. Regardless of the crisis or disaster, defeat simply was not an option he would consider; his assignment was more precious than his life.

Throughout the day wounded allied soldiers poured into Brussels giving the same report—Wellington was beaten and the French were just behind them. Actually their reports were understandable. At any time during the day, one could have looked at the allied position and determined that it was hopeless. One general later reported, "From noon until the very last moment of the battle, it was one continuous crisis." But Wellington remained locked onto his one purpose—to stop Napoleon and save Europe.

Those without resolve or a clear constitution become confused under pressure, but under such pressure Wellington's concentration increased. He was always at the point of crisis, directing and rallying his men. He kept the big picture of the overall battle in mind, and he personally directed individual regiments. He seemed always to appear just in time, with just enough men, with just enough resolve, to barely escape disaster. After plugging one hole, he would gallop off to the other end of the field where he suspected another emergency, and would usually find it. It was said that a lesser man would have retreated or surrendered a dozen times that day. Napoleon brilliantly pressed every advantage but was repeatedly stopped by the narrowest of margins.

By midday Napoleon began to suspect that "the sepoy general" had some ability. That morning Napoleon had told his staff that the odds were 10 to 1 that they would be in Brussels by nightfall. By afternoon he acknowledged to those gathered around him that the odds were now only 6 to 4.

Finally Napoleon's General Ney overwhelmed the outnumbered allies to take strategic ground in the center of Wellington's position. This was the most terrible disaster that could have befallen the allies. Napoleon astutely followed up this advantage with what would certainly be the death blow: he sent his famous Old Guard into the gaping hole in Wellington's center. In their many battles, the Guard had never been repulsed or failed to hold a position. Both armies stood in awe as the Guard's massive assault crossed the field in parade formations.

At that point Wellington may have been the only one on the entire field who gave himself a chance, but he remained as confident and calm as ever. As the Guard approached Wellington's center, he waved his hand and a regiment rose from behind a stone wall to pour a deadly volley into the French. Then, to everyone's surprise, another allied regiment, Colonel Colborne's, emerged from a nearby cornfield, and Wellington told an aide to command Colborne to advance.

All day long Wellington had kept the position of every brigade and regiment, including Colborne's, in his mind. This battle for the center became a cauldron of death. The Old Guard felt Colborne's fire and faltered. At this point, Colonel Colborne, standing in the midst of the fray, heard a voice beside him saying, "Go ahead, press them. You're doing it, press them now." He turned to see who was speaking and was astonished to find Wellington himself.

The entire French army groaned as they beheld a sight never before witnessed—the Guard's perfect formations disintegrated as they fled from their positions in disorder. After being pressed to the limits all day, Wellington's most desperate crisis quickly became his one brief opportunity for victory—and he seized it with apostolic decisiveness. He ordered his few remaining reserves into action; in the most perfect timing the Belgian division arrived to help. Just a few minutes earlier the situation had appeared utterly hopeless for the allies; now the entire French army was collapsing in defeat. The Guard's reserves formed squares and took their stand to protect the retreat. After they were surrounded and were asked to surrender, their reply was to the point: "The Old Guard dies, but it never surrenders." But they died, and Napoleon's power over Europe died with them.

When the church, which has an infinitely more important cause, grasps her commission and destiny with the same resolve, we will not lose, regardless of the forces arrayed against us. One man with a commission from God who will carry it with apostolic resolve outnumbers all the armies on earth. No power in heaven or on earth can stop us *if we do not quit.* Like every other spiritual and military battle in history, there will be casualties. There is a great price to pay for every victory, but death is the path to life in Christ. Someone once said, "The seed of the church is the blood of martyrs."

We must take up our crosses every day, and like Paul, we must be willing to take beatings, stonings, and even death to fulfill our commission. The things that are eternal must be more real to us than the things that are temporary. The fate of the twenty-first century rests on our shoulders.

4

Israel
The Cradle of the Church

THE CHURCH WAS BORN AND NURTURED IN THE household of Judaism. Israel was the mother who carried and gave birth to Jesus Christ, the seed that became Christianity. This was God's purpose when He called Abraham and set aside a people for Himself. God married the mystical nation of Israel, and together they had a Son. This love story permeates the Old Testament. The culture and conditions in which people are born and raised will inevitably have a profound impact on the development of their character, and the paradigm from which they view life. Likewise, God obviously intended the culture in which the church was born to have a significant influence on its development.

The church was Jewish for the first seven years of its existence until the gospel was preached to the house of Cornelius. And the first disciples continued to follow the basic customs of Judaism, so much so that it has been said that a casual observer would have had trouble distinguishing the church from other Jewish sects of the time. In fact, for the first two decades of its existence, the apostles considered the church to be an extension of the nation of Israel rather than an entirely new faith.

About twenty years after the birth of the church, converts began to consider a significant distinction between themselves and the Jewish nation. This was accomplished mostly through the emergence of a new breed of apostles led by Paul, whose conversion required that he be struck blind so that he could see the truth.

Though Paul was healed of his physical blindness after three days, he spent fourteen years alone with God in the wilderness seeking healing for his spiritual blindness. During this time, he examined the Jewish traditions to a much greater degree than any apostles before him seem to have done. In some ways this strengthened his understanding of the Law and the Prophets as the foundation of the gospel. However, he was also able to see where the wrong interpretation of the Law and the Prophets caused the leaders of Israel to reject their Messiah and become oppressors of the truth. This enabled Paul to have compassion for his Jewish brethren who were still trapped in the darkness that had once driven his life.

This revolutionized Paul's paradigm for viewing truth, and ultimately resulted in his developing what is probably the greatest spiritual vision of all time. The most rigid, inflexible zealot became the greatest apostle of grace. His brilliant ministry and teachings helped make it clear that men could become Christians without passing through the door of Jewish rites. This is quite amazing since Paul had once been a Pharisee, one of the strictest Jewish sects.

A HOLY GRAFTING

Like the unfolding of Paul's vision, the transition of the church from being what was considered another Jewish sect to becoming a truly new creation was a gradual process. Even so, it is apparent that the break from its Jewish roots was never intended to be total. The book of Romans was Paul's masterpiece of theology and the clearest exposition of the New Covenant in the Bible. In chapters 9–11 Paul asserts that the hearts of Jews were hardened so that they would not accept the gospel until it was time for them to be grafted back into the tree that God had planted.

In Romans 11:28 Paul made a remarkable statement: "Concerning the gospel they [the Jews] are enemies for your sake" (NKJV). The Jews have historically represented the greatest test for the gospel, but it is for our sake. In a sense, Jews are the "acid test" of our message. Until the church comes to the spiritual stature where she provokes the Jews to jealousy, we have not yet attained that to which we have been called.

The Jews' hearts were hardened to make them difficult to reach. In this way, they have become the barometer of all humanity. When the gospel is preached so well that it grafts the "natural branches" back into the tree, the church and Israel will then be able to reach the whole world. This is why Paul said that the gospel should be preached "to the Jew first." In my opinion, he said this not out of favoritism, but because the Jew represents the greatest challenge of the gospel, and one that we must have. He also declared that if the cutting off of the Jews for a time resulted in blessings for the Gentiles, the greatest blessing of all would be when they were grafted back in, which is "life from the dead." This is nothing less than victory over the last enemy.

Understanding the place of "the natural branches" in the plan of God has been one of the great historic, and current, stumbling blocks in the church. Paul warned us in Romans 11:18, 21: "Do not be arrogant toward the [natural] branches . . . for if God did not spare the natural branches, neither will He spare you."

An arrogant attitude toward the Jews can cause us to be cut off from the grace of God. Even so, our relationship to the Jews is not meant to be a stumbling block but a stepping-stone. Because the Lord gives His grace to the humble (see James 4:6), the proper relationship to the Jews requires a humility that will propel the church to a higher grace and anointing. In like manner, for Jews to recognize the place of the church in the plan of God will require a profound humility, but one that will enable the great grace of God to be extended to them in unprecedented measure.

Replacement theologies in the church today promote an arrogance toward the natural branches, which have caused many to stumble. These replace *Israel* with the *church* in the plan of God, attributing all of the promises for natural Israel to the church. There are some obvious truths in these doctrines, and there is truth to the understanding of "spiritual Israel," those who are born after the Spirit. However, as Paul made clear in Romans 11, the promises made to natural Israel cannot be revoked without impugning the very integrity of God. These mixed theologies usually result in a blinding of the church to what is one of the most critical issues of our time—the grafting back in of the natural branches.

Counter-replacement theologies also have sprung up in reaction to the replacement theologies. These have Israel replacing the church in relation to the promises of God. (We will discuss this more fully in the next chapter.) This is just as spurious as the replacement theologies, sowing arrogance in the natural branches. Pride, regardless of its form, cuts us off from the grace of God.

VICTORY OVER DEATH

The historic church has wounded many cultures and nations. However, the greatest spiritual schism is not between Catholics and Protestants but between the church and Israel. The terrible attacks by Christians on the Jews were not limited to the Catholics. With the emergence of the Protestant church in the 1500s, theologies were also promulgated within that branch of Christendom that continued this persecution. Some of these theologies contributed to the Nazi-perpetrated Holocaust. The Jews have survived each succeeding, and seemingly more vicious, assault, but the wounds they have received from Christians over the centuries are deep. This has caused Israel to equate Christianity with the destruction of their souls rather than with salvation. It has understandably hardened them even more to the gospel. However, this schism between the church and Israel is now being addressed, and many Jewish people are finding an extraordinary grace for forgiving and trusting Christians. This is the beginning of the healing of one of the ultimate spiritual barriers.

AN ODYSSEY OF RECONCILIATION

God has begun the process of reconciling the strife between Christians and Jews, and this is not a recent occurrence. There have been many Christians, and Christian movements, who have befriended and risked their lives to protect Jews from the assault of other misguided Christians. Many Christians who tried to protect Jews from the Nazis died alongside their Jewish friends in the concentration camps.

One example of how individual Christians are helping to lay a foundation of reconciliation between Jews and Christians began in 1961 when Uli Eiwen, wife of Pastor Helmuth Eiwen of Wiener Neustadt, Austria, was sixteen years old. At that time she was watching a slide show on Israel while on a visit to Switzerland. A picture of Mount Carmel in Haifa suddenly touched her very deeply. It was like a voice inside her speaking, "This is your calling." She went to her room and knelt down and prayed, "Jesus, if this was from You, please give me something from Your Word."

Uli opened the Bible and her eyes fell on Ezekiel 2:3: "I am sending you to the children of Israel." As she continued to read what the Lord was saying to Ezekiel, verse 4 jumped out at her: "I am sending you to them, and you shall say to them, 'Thus says the Lord GOD'" (NKJV).

He also quickened to her a portion of chapter 3, verses 4–6, although the clarity of this message would not become evident until many years later. Verse 5 said, "For you are not sent to a people of unfamiliar speech and of hard language, but to the house of Israel" (NKJV).

Greatly in love with Jesus, Uli immediately said, "Yes! If You want, I will go." After this prayer she went to bed, and the next morning the presence of the Lord was in the room. She experienced a profound peace that she had never experienced before or since. It was so powerful that she was not able to move. When it subsided, a deep love of the Jewish people remained in her. Strangely enough, she had never seen or met one Jew in her life.

Because of that decision to go to Israel, Uli decided to attend a Bible school where she met and fell in love with Helmuth Eiwen, a student preparing for the pastorate. Helmuth had no real feeling for the Jewish people. "What shall I do as a pastor in Israel?" he asked her. "I have no calling to Israel and no real heart for them."

In 1980, after Uli and Helmuth had been married for ten years, a Messianic Jewish woman invited Uli and her husband, who was now a Lutheran pastor in a small city in Austria, to participate in a weeklong seminar in Switzerland. During this week both Helmuth and Uli received the baptism of the Holy Spirit. As the Spirit came upon them, Helmuth instantly fell in love with the Jewish people. Now he was able to join Uli in her calling.

Three years later Uli was receiving Communion at their Lutheran church where the people had formed a half circle at the altar. Uli was looking down at the floor, and suddenly she saw a swastika in stone on the ground. She was shocked! When she looked again, it was no longer there.

Shortly thereafter Uli had another vision. This time she saw the tower of their Lutheran church. It looked as if it were a prison, and on the top was another swastika! Uli and Helmuth felt the Lord was showing them something about their church, so they spoke to an elderly Jewish woman who was now a member of their church. This woman had been in that city during World War II, and she told them that Hitler had personally influenced some important people in this church with his anti-Semitic philosophy.

Helmuth and Uli joined with approximately ten members of their church who were part of a prayer group to see if something needed to be done about this. Together they went into the church building and closed the door so that no one would know what was taking place. At the altar they began to pray and confess the sins of the former church members. Some of the individuals in that prayer group were older and had lived during the time of the Nazis. They realized that there was indeed a spiritual blockade over this Lutheran church, and the Lord told them they would receive authority to break that barrier.

From that day on, the church started to change. City residents were converted, and members were transformed. Helmuth and Uli realized an incredible connection between the Lord's blessing on the church and its behavior toward the Jewish people. This event in 1983 was a preparation for the next step, which would take place in the city of Wiener Neustadt, just ten miles away.

In 1990 Helmuth and Uli founded a nondenominational fellowship, which they named Ichthys Church. This fellowship met for two years in a village about half an hour from Wiener Neustadt. When the meeting place became too small, they began to seek the Lord for a larger facility. He made it quite clear to them that they were to go to Wiener Neustadt and construct a church building. That was surprising, since only one person from their church lived in that city.

During the next two years the Eiwens learned that Wiener Neustadt was a spiritually dry place; other groups had tried to establish churches there and failed. Helmuth and Uli began to ask the Lord, "What is wrong with this city?"

During a time of prayer, the Lord told Helmuth and Uli that He wanted to lie upon this city in the same way Elijah lay upon the dead boy—hand on hand, mouth on mouth (1 Kings 17:21–22). They understood Him to mean that they should be the ones to lie upon this city, as the Body of Christ. "How do we do this?" they asked. "Lord, please tell us what is wrong with this city."

Then Uli saw a vision of a black book in such darkness that she could see only the edges. Suddenly a bright light illuminated part of the book. After a while she recognized a specific portion of the old city wall in Wiener Neustadt. The dark part around the book seemed to represent some evil in the city's history and the bright light was shining on this occurrence.

The next day Helmuth and Uli went to the place at the wall where Uli had seen her vision. There they found six Jewish tombstones, affixed to the wall as a monument. Next to them was the inscription: "These tombstones came from a Jewish cemetery in Wiener Neustadt that was closed in 1496."

They began to search the history of this year and discovered that at the time Wiener Neustadt was the second largest Jewish community in

Austria, a very beautiful place and the favorite city of Emperor Maximilian I of the Hapsburg Empire.

In 1496 Maximilian issued a decree saying, "All the Jews from Wiener Neustadt must leave the city and for all time and eternity they may not come back." For three hundred years after this decree, no Jew was allowed to settle there. Some Jews came into the city to work, but they were required to live outside the city walls. Within 150 years from the time of Maximilian's decree, the entire city suffered a cultural and financial demise. Pastor Helmuth and Uli then understood that a curse was on the city.

Only in the last century were any Jews allowed to return, and the Jewish community very quickly developed. Before World War II, twelve hundred Jews lived in Wiener Neustadt, which made it the fourth largest Jewish community in Austria. But in 1938 the Nazis again destroyed the Jewish community, sending many to concentration camps. Helmuth and Uli saw that this only strengthened the curse that was the root of the spiritual stronghold over their city.

Even though Helmuth and Uli called their leaders together and cried out to God for forgiveness, they sensed God telling them they had not done enough. They felt a need to do something visible—not something done privately in a room. Could they invite these Austrian Jews to come there so that they could ask their forgiveness directly? Then Uli had another vision that confirmed this thought: "I saw a tree on the city wall in front of the gravestones. The Lord said this tree is the 'Tree of Healing' for this city. The interesting thing about this tree was that it had very, very old roots. Within these roots there was a young tree that was planted. I could see life, as if blood was pulsing throughout the tree. We felt that the Lord was saying that these roots were the seed of Abraham that was sown 500 years before. The young tree was the Body of Christ in this city, and this tree will bring healing for the city and for the Jews."

In 1993 a friend with an established ministry visited Ichthys Church, bringing about twenty people with him. They all gathered together for a prayer meeting in the new, but unfinished, building. During this time of prayer, the man had a vision in which he saw delegations of Jews from all over the world coming to Wiener Neustadt. They were dressed as if they were going to a reception, and he saw them drinking juice in that very building. He said a word would come out of this city that would go to Jews throughout the world. This friend did not know the significance of his prophecy since Helmuth and Uli had not spoken to anyone outside of their close friends and congregation about Uli's vision.

For the first time Helmuth and Uli completely understood what the Lord was saying. They were to invite the Jews from Wiener Neustadt who had survived the Holocaust and were now scattered throughout the world to come back there so that church members could ask them face-to-face for forgiveness. Since all the survivors had been children in 1938, their names and addresses would be difficult to find. However, a miracle enabled them to get the address of the last head rabbi of the city.

Pastor Helmuth and Uli went to Israel and explained their idea to this rabbi, who told them that he had a list of twenty-five other Jews from Wiener Neustadt who were now living in Israel. He and nine other Austrian scientists had been invited back to receive an award from the Austrian government. The other nine had gone, but he had declined because the last words he had heard as he left Wiener Neustadt as a boy were, "You Jewish pigs, get out!" And the only word since then had been, "Come and receive your award!" He felt strongly that something was missing between these two statements.

However, he immediately arranged a meeting in Haifa for as many Wiener Neustadt Jews as were able to attend. In the following months the Eiwens planned a trip to Israel for their church, and 120 members registered to go. Not only did they want to tour the Holy Land, but they especially wanted to meet the Jewish survivors of Wiener Neustadt.

At that meeting Helmuth told the Jewish survivors that the church wanted to ask their forgiveness, but they replied, "If the mayor had invited us to come, we would have, but we're not willing to accept the invitation with money from private people like yourselves."

The Jewish people were seated throughout the room with people from the church in between them, and as the love of God flowed from the heart of the pastor, it also flowed from each one in his congregation. Suddenly, supernaturally, the heart of every one of those Jewish survivors was totally changed. They said they could see that what they were experiencing wasn't just the love of the Eiwens but that of the whole church. Because of this, they were willing to return to the city. It was then that Helmuth and his wife saw that the reconciliation of these Jewish people was so important to God that He had sent most of their church body all the way to Israel in order to bring these, His people, back.

During the last week of May 1995, thirty of the surviving Jewish people returned to the place of their birth, most of them for the first time in fifty-seven years. Some days before this the rabbi called to ask, "May I please bring my twelve-year-old grandson with me?" He explained that bringing his son and his grandson with him meant that the three generations of exiles would say prayers together in the Sabbath service there.

This service took place in front of the city wall in Wiener Neustadt, precisely the way Uli had seen it a year and a half earlier in a vision. "I was in a Jewish service," Uli said, "and at the front was a menorah with the candles burning. In the first row was an old man, and he stood up and turned around as if looking for somebody. He motioned to a twelve-year-old boy to come to him. The man picked him up in his arms and said, 'You can blow out the candles.' At that point the little boy began to blow, but he did not blow in the direction of the candles. He blew into the face of the older man. Then together the older man and the boy blew out the candles of the menorah. I heard a Voice that said, 'The breath of the Father gives the breath of the Son the authority to blow out the candles.'"

At that time Uli had received an interpretation of the dream: when candles are blown out, it means that something is coming to an end. The older man symbolized the Father; the child symbolized the Christians. God was giving them the authority to end this bad chapter in the city's history.

After the service a Sabbath meal was held in the hotel. An inexplicable joy suddenly broke out, like an explosion. First there was singing, and then men stood up and began to dance with one another. One of the wives said to Uli, "I have never seen my husband dance!" These people never imagined laughing in Wiener Neustadt. The windows were wide open because it was so hot, and the singing could be heard all over the city.

Since then Helmuth and Uli have issued two other invitations to the Jewish survivors of Wiener Neustadt. Each time the same manifestations of joy and healing took place.

Now Uli understood the meaning of those words from her vision at the age of sixteen: "For you are not sent to a people of unfamiliar speech and of hard language, but to the house of Israel."

The Jews who came to Wiener Neustadt spoke Austrian German, as did the church members. Uli says, "In January of 1997 we were in Israel, and we visited all of our new Jewish friends. They invited all of their friends and relatives, and we were together in homes with about twenty to thirty people. We spoke to them about their God, about the Holocaust, and about the things that will be coming in Israel. As we read the Word of God, you could have heard a pin drop. In the groups were nonbelievers and some strong orthodox Jews, but there was so much love there that they all were taken captive by the Word of God that they heard in the German language of their childhood.

"We are listening to hear anew from the Lord what the next step will be. We believe that in the meeting with our Jewish friends a new chapter has begun. An act of reconciliation has been completed. Now we look forward to a deepening relationship. May they know the love of their God in a more personal and intimate way. That is the desire of our hearts."

And that has happened. Upon visiting a large synagogue in Vienna, one woman was quoted as saying to the head rabbi, "After the Holocaust, I didn't believe that there was a God anymore. But during the week in Wiener Neustadt I have found my belief in God again." Many similar testimonies were heard after the meetings.[1]

Further reconciliation between Jews and Gentiles continues to happen in many other places and ways. That Israel has now exchanged ambassadors with the Vatican is a remarkable event. Evangelicals also have a Christian embassy in Jerusalem. However, we are still a very long way from the healing of the wounds. Even so, before this age closes, this dividing wall between Jew and Gentile will be removed—through Christ. When the "natural branches" are grafted back in, it will mean nothing less than victory over death. This is because it simply cannot happen until both the church and the Jews come to the place of ultimate humility whereby the ultimate grace of God can be extended to us.

I do not believe that the church can fully understand Israel's purpose until we are healed of the rejection we feel because the Jews do not accept us by not accepting Christ. The Jewish people certainly have far more to overlook and forgive toward Christians, even if most of those who committed the terrible atrocities were not genuine believers. We all have wounds that we must overcome if we are going to have understanding. It will take humility and forgiveness on the part of everyone, but isn't that the foundation of everything to which we are called?

The Power of a Healed Wound

Spiritual authority is actually released through our wounds. It is by the Lord's stripes that we are healed. In the very place that He was wounded, He received authority for healing us. The same is true for us. In the very place that we are wounded we can receive authority for healing others.

For example, if people have suffered sexual abuse and have forgiven their offenders and been healed, they will always have special compassion for others who have suffered the same wound. God is love, and all true spiritual authority is founded on such compassion. It was because of this spiritual principle of how our wounds can be turned into spiritual authority that Paul defended his apostleship by telling of the wounds that he had suffered for the sake of the gospel.

Therefore, the Jewish people, who have suffered the most unjust persecution at the hands of the Gentiles and the church, can have the greatest authority for bringing healing to both. When a people who have been so mistreated show forgiveness, mercy, and love toward the very ones who wounded them, as the Jewish survivors of Wiener Neustadt did, there is power. We must overcome evil with good, and what the devil has meant for evil will be overcome with good.

In a similar manner, the true church, which has been persecuted from the beginning by the whole world, can have power to release healing to the whole world. We all have much to forgive, and much to be forgiven for. Let us all determine now that we will forgive so that we can be healed of our wounds, releasing the "one new man" who will help bring healing to this wounded world.

For about two thousand years, God moved almost exclusively among the Jews. Then the Lord dealt almost exclusively with the Gentiles. Now we are coming to the end of about two thousand years of the time of the Gentiles, a time when our relationship with God contains all of the cycles of apostasy and restoration that ancient Israel experienced. Now, at the end of this age, we are coming to the time of the Jews and Gentiles together. It will take supreme humility on the part of each group to see God's purpose in the other, which was precisely God's point in requiring this joining together. Neither the church nor Israel can achieve their destinies and callings without the other.

Israel is now spiritually very far from her place of ultimate destiny in these last days. In many ways, the church is just as far. The Jews do not believe the doctrines of Christ, and the church has been deceived into thinking that believing them in our minds is the same as believing them in our hearts. This often causes our pride in doctrines to remove us from the very grace of God that we preach so that our lives manifest the truth that we profess.

The final joining together of both "into one new man" is not going to look like Israel, ancient or modern. Neither is it going to look like the church, ancient or modern. What is coming will be something entirely new—something only the truly humble will be able to perceive. This humility will release the supreme grace of God, resulting in the healing of all spiritual and cultural wounds. When the church and Israel have been grafted together through Christ, the time of the restoration of all things may begin, and the last enemy will have been overcome.

5

The Jewish Branches

The Messianic Movement

THE MESSIANIC MOVEMENT IS COMPRISED OF Jews who have come to believe that Jesus is the Messiah. This has been an enigma to both Jews and Gentiles alike. Just to survive, this movement has had to overcome some of the most unique obstacles believers have faced since the first century—Messianic Jews are rejected by their fellow Jews and misunderstood by much of the Christian church. Yet, this movement has survived its most difficult stages of growth and is now becoming a mature movement. What is the significance of the Messianic movement? What does it mean to the church? What does it mean for Israel?

First, let's look at the problems that have divided this movement from their fellow Israelites and the church.

PROBLEMS FOR MESSIANIC JEWS

Jews have difficulty accepting the Messianic movement because they do not believe that a person can embrace Christianity and still be a Jew. To religious Jews, Judaism is the essence of what it means to be a Jew.

However, most Jews throughout the world, and especially in Israel, are not religious. Their Jewish identity is related more to their ancestry than to their faith. Even so, this is a controversy that religious Jews have been able to maintain against the Messianic movement, even to the degree that they have prevented many Messianic Jews from immigrating to Israel.

It is also a fact that the greatest and most deadly persecution that Jews have suffered has come from the institutional church. For centuries Jews have been forced to convert to Christianity or lose their families, possessions, and even their lives. They have had their children taken from them, forcibly baptized, and then given to Christian parents to raise. Time after time the Jewish people have been driven from their homes and lands by those who called themselves Christians. The Holocaust took place in what claimed to be a "Christian nation." It is therefore understandable that Jews would think it impossible to embrace the religion that has been such a threat to their very existence and still remain a Jew. Some Jews do understand that some Christians do not have the same nature as their persecutors and that they are even true friends and defenders of the Jewish people. Even so, the Jews fear attacks from those who claim to be Christians every bit as much as they fear attacks from Muslims.

PROBLEMS FOR THE CHURCH

The Christian church has had a hard time understanding the Messianic movement because we feel that anyone who is a true Christian must be a part of the church. Yet, Messianic Jews remember that throughout history the church has sought either to convert the Jewish people or to destroy them. These Jews do not want to be so absorbed by the church that they lose their Jewish identity. Is this legitimate? The Scriptures teach that it is not only legitimate but necessary. Messianic Jews understand that there is a reason for the miraculous preservation of the Jewish people, and they are a part of that purpose.

The book of Acts makes it clear that there is no distinction between Jewish and Gentile believers concerning salvation and how we receive the grace of God (Acts 15:8–9). Even so, the Gentile "branches" were allowed to establish a church life that was profoundly different from that of Jewish Christians, just as the Messianic Jews have done today. This was done with the full blessing and encouragement of the original apostles, verified by the Holy Spirit, and established by the Scriptures. The first Council in Jerusalem (Acts 15) confirmed this and liberated the Gentiles from all rituals of the Law, concluding with:

> For it seemed good to the Holy Spirit and to us to lay upon you no greater burden than these essentials: that you abstain from things sacrificed to idols and from blood and from things strangled and from fornication; if you keep yourselves free from such things, you will do well. (Acts 15:28–29)

Something that is often overlooked is that this decree was issued specifically for Gentiles, and not for Jewish believers who continued to observe the rituals contained in the Law and Prophets. In Acts 21:17–26 we see that those who believed in Jesus from among the Jews were "all zealous for the Law," but the apostle James reaffirmed that this was not necessary for the Gentiles. Then we see Paul purifying himself and offering sacrifices according to the Old Covenant. Was he doing this to pursue righteousness according to the Law? Certainly not! No one understood the fallacy of this more than Paul. Instead, he was honoring his heritage and the Lord's own commandments. The Jewish people were commanded to do certain things throughout all generations, such as observing the Sabbath. Their rituals were kept as a celebration rather than for righteousness, as the epistle to the Hebrews makes clear. It is important for us to see that a distinction is made between what was required of Jewish and Gentile believers.

A primary stumbling block that keeps many from being able to see this is the concept that Judaism only represented the keeping of the Law for righteousness, which nullifies the grace that we receive through Christ. Many of the first Jewish believers, as well as even some of the

Gentile believers, also had a hard time making this distinction. Christians still do today. There have also been branches of the Messianic movement that have at times drifted into the keeping of the Law for righteousness, which is understandable for a young, maturing movement. However, they seem to have been well able to correct themselves to see the Law in the light that we must now see it—as a prophecy and reminder of the grace of God through Christ.

THE LAW AS PROPHECY

The church was called to be the possession of God—His dwelling place—and the Law was given to prepare His people for this. However, it did not prepare His people by making them righteous and holy. It prepared them by revealing the standards of God's righteousness and holiness, how unrighteous and unholy we are, and how desperately we need His salvation and His power in order to live a holy life. The Law compels us to flee to the cross for salvation. This is not just for forgiveness but for deliverance and for power so that we might live righteous and holy before Him. This basic truth is the reason Paul wrote the book of Galatians.

Even so, another purpose for the Law has seldom been understood. In Matthew 5:18 the Lord stated this purpose: "For truly I say to you, until heaven and earth pass away, not the smallest letter or stroke shall pass away from the Law, *until all is accomplished*" (emphasis added). He is not saying here that the Law would not pass away until we have kept all of the commandments, as that would be in conflict with the basic principles of the New Covenant. However, He was here explaining the Law's purpose in being a *prophecy*. This He also affirmed in Matthew 11:13 when He said: "For all the prophets and *the Law prophesied* until John" (emphasis added).

All of the rituals and feasts of the Law prophetically portrayed Christ. That is why both the Lord Jesus and the early church continued to observe them as a celebration of the reality that they were fulfilled in Christ. When the church was completely cut off from its Jewish roots, pagan rituals were substituted for those that really did speak of Christ, and the drift toward deep darkness ensued.

Modern Christians often forget that the Old Testament was the only Bible that the first-century church had, and that it was the foundation for the New Testament doctrines of the faith. The "Scriptures" that Paul referred to in Romans 16, and in all of his other letters, are what we call the Old Testament, which was the basis of all the early church's doctrines and practices, including their revelation of the grace of God through Christ.

We tend to think of the Old Testament as law and the New Testament as grace, but this is not necessarily true. The Old Covenant is the letter; the New Covenant is by faith through the Holy Spirit. If you read the New Testament with an Old Covenant heart, it will just be Law to you. If you read the Old Testament with a New Covenant heart, you will see Christ in all of it.

The terminology used in the New Testament to describe the place and ministry of the Lord Jesus is from the terminology used in the Law and the Prophets. He is called the High Priest after the Old Testament priest who was the mediator between the nation of Israel and the Lord. He is called "the Lamb of God" after the sacrificial lamb that according to the Law was to atone for the sins of the people. That is why Jesus made the astonishing statement in John 5:46–47: "For if you believed Moses, you would believe Me; for he wrote of Me. But if you do not believe his writings, how will you believe My words?"

We will indeed be foolish if we do not believe *all* that is written in the Law and the Prophets. A considerable amount of the foolishness that the church has fallen into can be attributed to our failure in this. We, too, need to keep in mind the exhortation that Paul gave in 2 Timothy 3:16–17: "All Scripture is inspired by God and profitable for teaching, for reproof, for correction, for training in righteousness; that the man of God may be adequate, equipped for every good work."

The Law and the Prophets were enough for the early church to turn the world upside down. Now we also have the New Testament. The

Lord really did save His best wine for last. Even so, the addition of the New Testament was never meant to supplant the purpose of what we call the Old Testament.

It should be noted that the writer of what is considered the deepest of the New Testament Epistles, the book of Hebrews, lamented that he could only give the readers milk because they were not ready for solid food! All that is written in this book about Melchizedek, the tabernacle, and the expansive overview of the purposes of God was still spiritual milk and not solid food! How many Christians today even know what the Melchizedek priesthood is? That is the priesthood to which we are called in Christ, so isn't it time that we get weaned from milk and go on to solid food? Much of that solid food is found in the Old Testament, which can only be digested when it is understood as prophecy.

Once we understand this, we can see that it was the clear intent of the Holy Spirit for the Jewish believers to keep alive the prophetic rituals and celebrations, just as the Gentile church was free to develop a style that was completely fresh and new. For as long as the Jewish and Gentile believers were linked in fellowship, the important moorings of the church in the historic path of God's redemptive purposes through Israel would be maintained through the Jewish roots of the church.

Another fact that made it clear that the Lord intended for there to be a distinction between the Gentile and Jewish believers was the appointment of an apostle to the Jews and an apostle to the Gentiles. It is also significant that Paul referred to the Gentile "branches," plural, indicating a diversity within the Gentile groups. With strong moorings to the Jewish roots there could be a considerable liberty in the expression of the faith through different cultures and races, while still maintaining knowledge of God's righteousness and holiness. And with the fresh, creative vitality of the Gentile branches, the Jewish root would not be as prone to fall back into the rigid inflexibility of the Law. Both are essential, but they had to remain linked to each other while being free to be unique and different.

Recognizing that there are to be some distinctions between Jewish and Gentile believers does present some theological problems.

Questions are raised from Scriptures such as Colossians 3:11: "There is no distinction between Greek and Jew, circumcised and uncircumcised, barbarian, Scythian, slave and freeman, but Christ is all, and in all."

We see this stated again in Galatians 3:28: "There is neither Jew nor Greek, there is neither slave nor free man, there is neither male nor female; for you are all one in Christ Jesus."

Do these texts really indicate that there is no need for a distinction between Jew and Gentile? No. If we were to conclude that, we would also have to conclude that there is no need for a distinction between male and female. The unity described in these texts is not a unity of conformity but a unity in diversity. The way I become one with my wife is not by making her into a man. Instead, we come into unity when we both recognize and appreciate our distinctions, seeing how they complement one another.

The God who loves diversity so much that He makes every snowflake different, who delighted in making people unique, obviously intended from the beginning for the church to reflect His glorious creativity. Though both the Messianic and Gentile congregations of today are still quite far from the apostolic model of the first century, they are moving swiftly toward what was intended in the beginning, and confirmed by the Council in Jerusalem.

A Further Source of Division

Still, two powerful theologies—replacement theology and counter-replacement theology, which I mentioned earlier—separate the church and the Messianic movement. Replacement theology promotes the belief that the church is the "spiritual Israel" and has replaced Israel as God's chosen people, assuming all of the promises that were made to the Jewish people. Some Scriptures, such as Philippians 3:3, seem to indicate this: "For we are the true circumcision, who worship in the Spirit of God and glory in Christ Jesus and put no confidence in the flesh."

However, this extreme interpretation is refuted by a host of other Scriptures, including the entire chapters of Romans 9–11. These can only be applied to Jews according to the flesh because in this text a clear distinction is made between them and Gentile believers.

As I stated previously, one problem that many Christians have had with Messianic theology has been the tendency for some of it to become another form of replacement theology, dubbed counter-replacement or "replacement, replacement" theology. This is the teaching that Israel will replace the church at the end. As with the original replacement theology, some Scriptures seem to support this view, if we overlook the Scriptures that refute it.

To understand God's purposes at the end of the age, we must see both His purpose for the church *and* His obvious purpose for grafting the "natural branches" (Rom. 11:24) back into His purpose. This is why the modern Messianic Jewish congregations now spreading around the world are so important. As Romans 9–11 makes clear, the resurrection will not happen until the Jewish people are grafted back into the root, which is Christ. In Ephesians 2:11–22, we see that these two groups will be joined together:

> Therefore remember, that formerly you, the Gentiles in the flesh, who are called "Uncircumcision" by the so-called "Circumcision," which is performed in the flesh by human hands—remember that you were at that time separate from Christ, excluded from the commonwealth of Israel, and strangers to the covenants of promise, having no hope and without God in the world. But now in Christ Jesus you who formerly were far off have been brought near by the blood of Christ. For He Himself is our peace, who made both groups into one, and broke down the barrier of the dividing wall, by abolishing in His flesh the enmity, which is the Law of commandments contained in ordinances, that in Himself He might make the two into one new man, thus establishing peace, and might reconcile them both in one body to God through the cross, by it having put to death the enmity. And He came and preached peace to you who were far away, and peace to those who were near; for through Him we both have our access in one Spirit to the Father. So then you are no longer strangers and

aliens, but you are fellow citizens with the saints, and are of God's household, having been built upon the foundation of the apostles and prophets,
Christ Jesus Himself being the corner stone, in whom the whole building,
being fitted together is growing into a holy temple in the Lord; in whom
you also are being built together into a dwelling of God in the Spirit.

Here we see that neither Jews nor Gentiles can fulfill their ultimate
purpose without the other. We also see that neither will fulfill their destinies unless they remain distinct.

"WOUNDED" THEOLOGY

If we are going to know the truth, and know our purpose, we must
rise above the tendency to create theologies from our wounds. This is
true of both the Messianic movement and the church.

I personally experienced some rejection by Messianic believers when
I was a relatively new Christian. They seemed to try to make Gentile
Christians believe that we were second-class citizens in the kingdom.
Immediately after this distasteful encounter with a Messianic group, I
was visited by some believers teaching replacement theology. Because of
my wounds, I honestly wanted to believe what they were saying, but I
have always felt an obligation to search out such doctrines in the
Scriptures. When I did this, I saw too many Scriptures that contradicted
this teaching, and so I rejected it.

My point is that one reason the devil is called "the lord of the flies" is
that flies swarm to wounds, and flies often represent lies in prophetic
dreams and visions. I believe the devil targeted me with his lies immediately after he saw me wounded because he knows that this is the best
time to introduce them. Martin Luther, for instance, formulated his diabolical doctrines about the Jews after his gospel was rejected by a group
of rabbis. He was obviously hurt, and through his wounds he released
errors that would ultimately be used to justify the Holocaust.

Likewise, even Jews who come to believe in Jesus as their Messiah have
a very difficult time with the church because of their great historic
wounds. Both must be healed. This is why the priests in the Old

Testament could not have scabs, which are unhealed wounds. Unhealed spiritual wounds will also disqualify us from our spiritual priesthood. We must be careful never to accept or formulate doctrines while we are still wounded. Until we have truly forgiven, we are prone to distort doctrines.

THE ROOT OF MESSIANIC BELIEVERS

Because Messianic congregations usually call themselves synagogues instead of churches, many Christians do not think of them as a part of the church. Likewise, many in the Messianic camp do not think of themselves as a part of the church. However, we must remember that the first Christians were the Messianic believers of the first century. Just as we see in the book of Acts, the primary issues of church doctrine that were to be the foundation of the church were decided by the leaders of the church in Jerusalem, who were all Jewish.

It was not until the destruction of Jerusalem in A.D. 70 that the spiritual center of the church was moved from Jerusalem. From there it shifted several times over the next few centuries. Then it divided, and the spiritual center of the Western church became Rome, and the center of the Eastern church was Constantinople, or modern-day Istanbul. During this time, many practices that were rooted more in the pagan cultures than in Scripture entered into church doctrine. To this day, it is easy to conclude that the foundations of modern church life and doctrine are still more rooted in Rome than in Jerusalem, despite the Reformation and the continuous moves of the Holy Spirit since that time. It is not likely that we will return to our true roots until we have come full circle and the Messianic movement takes its proper place as a leader of the church.

This is not to say that the Messianic movement is to become *the* leader of the church as it was before the Gentiles were introduced to the faith or before they had raised up their own mature leadership. However, in due time the Messianic movement must take its place as a leader, and the spiritual center of the faith will again become Jerusalem, as we see in many prophetic Scriptures. When the Lord returns, He will rule from

Jerusalem. Even so, His body will be the two, Jew and Gentile, becoming "one new man."

It is interesting that Rabbi Chernoff, who is considered by many to be the founder of the modern Messianic movement, married Yohonas Joyner, a Gentile. To this day, many Messianic leaders are married to Gentile wives, and a large number of the Messianic congregations have many Gentile members.

During my first contacts with the Messianic movement, I was surprised to find that the Jews who were in it were far more relaxed in their devotion to the Law than the Gentiles among them. The Jewish believers understood that this was to be done to honor their fathers and mothers and the customs of their heritage, not in place of the righteousness that comes only through faith in Christ.

Even so, at the time of my first contacts with the Messianic movement, I was simultaneously encouraged and discouraged by its condition. I was encouraged by their depth and faithfulness in spite of intense persecution from orthodox Jews and their seeming separation from the church. I was discouraged by the lack of respect that many exhibited for the church. Even then I could see that they had the answers to many of the church's basic problems, and the church had the answer to many of theirs. In the twenty years since my early contacts with the Messianic movement, I have become even more convinced of this.

A NEW MATURITY

I have watched the modern Messianic movement from afar, and I marvel at all that has been accomplished to this point. However, the movement is like a teenager who has matured in many ways, and probably has a vague understanding of his gifts and callings, but has not yet fully matured to be able to use those gifts. Even so, this movement has weathered the most confusing and tumultuous times in its development, and its vision and purpose will now become increasingly clear as it begins to enter its most fruitful period.

Though I was at first disturbed by the Messianic movement's determination to stay separate from the church, I now know this was right. As has been widely taught, there are three basic levels to relationships: codependence, dependence, and interdependence. In codependence, the lowest relationship level, the stronger personality usually swallows up the weaker one. Because of this, a person usually must go through the phase of independence in which he finds his identity and becomes secure in it before he can move to the highest level of relationship—interdependence. The Messianic movement seems to be coming to the end of its independence stage, as leaders are now seeking interchange with the church and encouraging their members to do the same. They are now mature enough to embrace the truth that God has composed all of His people to need one another so they can be complete in Him.

ANTIOCH BEFORE JERUSALEM

An overview of history shows the cutting-edge move of the Holy Spirit from Jerusalem to Antioch to Constantinople to Alexandria, and then to Rome. After the apostasies of the Middle Ages had run their course, the Holy Spirit moved through Germany, Switzerland, England, the Americas, and then Asia. In the twenty-first century, the Holy Spirit seems to be reversing this course at a rapid pace. While the nations and cities may not be exactly the same, the recovery of the truths they represent is. Before we return to our roots in Jerusalem, we must revisit our spiritual Antioch.

Antioch was unique in the early church. Apostles did not birth the church in Antioch, but that church gave birth to a whole new kind of apostle—the missionary apostle. These new apostles took the harvest to another level and spread the gospel throughout the known world.

After the cutting-edge move of the Holy Spirit departed from Antioch, the apostolic ministry actually faded out. A few centuries later, prophets were no longer recognized. Then evangelists were replaced by politics and the sword as the leaders of the church sought to take the world for Christ by might and power rather than by the Spirit. The teachers and pastors were displaced by priests who basically reduced Christianity to rituals in place of faith. This led to what many historians call the Dark Ages.

As truth has been recovered, we see the corresponding ministries also being reestablished in the reverse order in which they were lost. The first ministry lost—the apostolic ministry—will be the last one restored. Presently the prophetic ministry is still growing into enough maturity and credibility to be received back into the general ministry. After this is accomplished, we can expect the release of true missionary apostles. And following this, we can expect Jerusalem to become the spiritual seat of leadership of Christianity. Then we can expect this age to close and the Lord to return to set up His kingdom on earth.

In the next chapter, when we study the Crusades, we will examine more thoroughly the roots of the doctrines that released the tragic Christian persecution of the Jewish people.

6

The Gates of Hell and the Doors of Heaven

Spiritual Battles Yesterday and Today

IN THE YEAR 2000 AND BEYOND, WE ARE ENTERING the period when the gates of hell—the entrances through which evil gains access to this world—and the doors of heaven—the openings through which divine grace and truth flow to the world—will be fully opened. It is imperative that we recognize these and then use the authority given to us to close the gates of hell while opening the doors of heaven.

In this chapter I want to address how these spiritual gates and doors are often found in localities, especially cities. A striking example of this is Cologne, Germany, which has been one of the most influential cities in world history, though its influence has remained remarkably hidden. Some of the most deadly theologies and philosophies the world has ever known originated in Cologne. It is probable that more bloodshed has resulted from the influence of this city than any other city on earth.

These diabolical theologies or philosophies have not yet been overcome. They continue to sprout and cause rivers of death to flow in almost every new generation. At the beginning of this chapter, we will address some of these "doctrines of demons" by exposing their source. However, this is only the first step in a long and difficult march to defeat and close these gates of hell. Just winning battles against this darkness is not enough. Like Joshua at Ai, we must learn to hold out our spears until the enemy is completely destroyed. If we do not finish the job, the same deadly enemy will confront our children.

A Spiritual History of Cologne

The province of Cologne was founded at the very time of the birth of Christ. Emperor Augustus's niece Agrippina, who was said to be a descendant of Aphrodite, the goddess of love, married Germanicus, the conqueror of Gaul, in A.D. 15 in Cologne. In A.D. 16 in the Oppidum-Obiorum in Cologne (a Roman and Germanic cultcenter, which was situated exactly where the Cathedral of Cologne now stands), she gave birth to a daughter, whom she named after herself. This daughter became the mother of the Roman emperor Nero, one of the most cruel and demented of the emperors. It was under Nero that the Christians were first fed to the lions in the Circus Maximus. It was also Nero who condemned both Peter and Paul to execution in Rome.

Thus the first great Roman persecution against the church had its roots in Cologne. Owing to the fact that Nero's mother, and the subsequent emperor Caligula, both came from Cologne, the city became the capital of the Western Roman Empire, beginning in A.D. 69 and continuing for the next two centuries. Provinces governed from Cologne included France, Spain, Germany, and Britain. During that time Cologne gained considerable influence and became the host of every conceivable god and temple.

In A.D. 313, Emperor Constantine, who made Christianity the state religion of Rome, sent a bishop called Maternus to Cologne, Trier, and Tongern to destroy their idols and temples. However, not all of these idols were destroyed. In fact, some were actually used as building materials for the first Christian churches, a prophetic parallel of what was to come. Though the structures were meant to be Christian, some of the most anti-Christian evils the world would ever experience would arise from these cities.

THE CRUSADES

In 632, the Muslims began making advances into Europe and the Middle East. In 638, Khalif Omar conquered Jerusalem, which had been held by the Christian Byzantine Empire (which later developed into the Orthodox Church). Its capital was Constantinople. At the time people believed that this empire would never fall because it was Christian. Nevertheless, the Turks, led by Alp Arslam, destroyed the Byzantine army in Mantzikert on Friday, August 19, 1071, and took the Christian emperor of Byzantine, Romanos Diogenes, captive.

The Muslims then advanced deeper into European territory, targeting France, Spain, and the Balkans. As their progress began to threaten all of Europe, a letter from the Christian bishop of Jerusalem convinced the pope to devise a strategy for retaking the ancient city. This plan would also relieve the pressure on Europe, because the Muslims would have to return to defend their own lands. The pope mobilized sovereigns and knights as well as peasants, the homeless, and even prostitutes, who wanted to be free from the bondage of serfdom. The pope then claimed to possess a letter from heaven, which summoned him to call the European nations to liberate the Holy Sepulcher.

THE CRUSADERS MUSTER IN COLOGNE

In March 1096, Peter of Amiens (also called "Peter the Hermit") left on his donkey and arrived in Trier, Germany, just before Easter. On Easter Sunday, he marched into Cologne with about ten thousand men. He then sent out preachers to proclaim the gospel of the Crusades and to raise further support in the Rhineland area. Consequently, his army grew to a total of thirty thousand men. Peter was, therefore, given the credit for starting the Crusades that would change the known world, leaving some of the deepest cultural wounds among Christians, Muslims, and Jews, which remain to this day. He began the persecution of the Jews with doctrines that would lead to some of the worst atrocities in history.

Needing more money for their venture, the crusaders determined to force the Jews, who were the primary bankers of that time, to support their mission. Many of the knights financed their participation in the Crusades by mortgaging their estates to the banks. Then the crusaders decided that they did not want to pay the banks back, so they declared a divine mandate to turn against the Jews because "they killed Jesus on the cross."

Gottfried of Bouillon was the sovereign of Lower-Lothringen, which also included the Ardennes, present-day Holland, and the Rhine Provinces of Cologne. He issued a decree that all the remaining Jews in Lower-Lothringen should be killed in order to atone for Christ's death. The Jews in Cologne and Mainz gave Gottfried five hundred silver coins in order to buy their protection, which was used to pay for and arm his forces. This method of raising financial support quickly became popular throughout Europe. In this way the Jews found themselves not only loaning money to the crusaders but also paying ransom money to bishops and knights.

Even after they had paid for protection, Rhineland count Emmerich began killing the Jews in the region of Cologne. Peter of Amiens's army then attacked the Jews in Prague while Gottschalk, Peter's former pupil, massacred them in Regensburg. Thus began almost nine hundred years of the Jewish people being subject to continuous threats of annihilation at the hands of "Christians." In one of the greatest perversions of the Savior's message, those who claimed to be His ambassadors delivered some of the bloodiest attacks against the people through whom He came.

During the following centuries, Jews were periodically assaulted and robbed, and at times all the members of Jewish ghettos were massacred, with only those who would submit to baptism being spared. Many Christians took stands against this tragic intolerance, including Bernard of Clairveaux, who tried earnestly to protect Jews from the bigotry and fanatical violence of the church, but with little success.

Catholics weren't the only ones who attacked the Jews. As the Protestant church emerged in the 1500s, theologies within that branch of Christendom continued this persecution, and ultimately led to some of the worst atrocities of all in Nazi Germany. The remarkable Jews have survived each succeeding, and seemingly more vicious, assault, but the wounds these people have received from Christians over the centuries are deep.

THE CRUSADERS LEAVE COLOGNE

At the end of April 1096, Peter of Amiens and his army marched from Cologne. They arrived in Constantinople on August 1. Since an army of that size (which was also escorted by women and children) had to be fed and provided for, and because there was very little discipline, these soldiers left a wide trail of pillage and destruction. Soon they became odious even to the Christian cities they were supposed to be protecting.

Most in this first crusade had little or no military experience, so it was recommended that they wait in Constantinople for the better-trained army of knights, which was being prepared in Europe. However, because of the rising strife between the crusaders and the population, it was decided that the army should march from Constantinople as soon as possible. They left on October 21 and were quickly defeated by the Turks in Civitot. The entire army of thirty thousand, including the women and children, were killed. Only Peter and a few knights survived the massacre and escaped back to Constantinople.

Gottfried of Bouillon set off from Lower-Lothringen in 1096, about the same time that Peter of Amiens was arriving in Constantinople. After marching for several weeks along the Rhine and the Danube, he finally reached Constantinople at Christmas. By the most conservative estimates, his army numbered no less than 600,000. There, Peter joined him and took the lead of the new "Farmer's Army." At the end of April 1097, the crusaders set off from Pelecanum near Constantinople. They crossed the Bosporus in October and besieged Antioch, which fell eight months later on June 3, 1098.

A TRAGIC VICTORY

On January 13, 1099, the army started for Jerusalem and came to the city on June 7. At midday on Friday, July 15, the Holy City fell. When

Jerusalem fell to the Christians, what appeared to be a great victory became a tragedy that would live in infamy as one of the church's greatest errors.

The Muslim mayor had been relatively tolerant of all his citizens, including Christians and Jews. He allowed them their own places of worship and freedom to come and go as they pleased. He even took the gracious step of allowing the Christians in Jerusalem to go over to the side of the crusaders during the siege. When it was obvious that the Christians would prevail in the siege, the mayor and his subjects likewise expected a high degree of chivalry from their conquerors. They were terribly mistaken.

On the day the city fell, many citizens had gathered under a Christian banner, where they had been promised amnesty by the crusaders. But the crusaders shocked the world with their treachery when they surrounded these helpless people and slaughtered them all. Seeing this, the Jews of the city fled into the synagogue. With the Jews trapped inside, the crusaders torched the building, killing everyone in a gruesome spectacle. This was a deliberate strategy to eradicate all non-Christians so that Jerusalem could become a "true Christian city." The triumphant crusaders, many completely covered by the blood of their victims, gathered at the Holy Sepulcher. There, weeping with joy, they offered thanksgiving for their great "victory." Over fifty thousand Saracens alone were killed in this terrible massacre.

Gottfried of Bouillon, the first Christian sovereign and primary instigator of the massacre, died one year later on July 18, 1100. King Baldwin I became his successor. The kingdom of Jerusalem existed for eighty-seven years until the empire was conquered by the Muslim king Saladin. Crusaders repeatedly marched for the next two hundred years, but they never managed to retake the Holy City.

Unquestionably, many noble and courageous souls participated in the Crusades. Many were motivated by a sincere desire to recover the honor of the name of the Lord in Jerusalem. However, regardless of how noble our motives may be, whenever we use methods that are contrary to the fruit of the Holy Spirit, evil will be the result. From their beginning to their end, the Crusades released some of the most evil forces, philosophies, and theologies into the world, and their fruit has been that countless millions have been separated from the gospel by huge barriers of hatred and distrust.

THE SPIRITUAL ROOTS OF COMMUNISM

On July 23, 1164, Archbishop Reinald of Dassel brought to Cologne what were supposedly the bones of the three wise men who had sought the infant Jesus. Emperor Friedrichs Barbarossa had given them to the city as a reward for their archbishop's loyalty. In 1181, the golden coffin made to contain them was completed (it can still be seen in Cologne today). Consequently, many pilgrims from all over the Western world came to Cologne to worship the golden shrine and the bones. As the crowds of pilgrims became more numerous, a larger cathedral became necessary. On August 15, 1248, the foundation of the Cologne Cathedral was laid as a place of honor for the bones of the three wise men.

The building of this great cathedral continued for more than three hundred years and then was abruptly stopped. A remarkable legend recorded in the city's history says that the master builder had to make a pact with the devil to complete the project. The pact stated that an aqueduct had to be built from the city of Trier to Cologne so that a river of death could flow from Satan's throne, just as the River of Life flowed from the throne of God. Once this aqueduct was completed, according to the legend, Satan would allow the cathedral to be finished. This river would be a river of death, which would ultimately eclipse all of the previous spirits of death that had originated from Cologne, resulting in an estimated one hundred million killed in the twentieth century alone.

Amazingly, the work on the cathedral was stopped from 1560 until 1842. In 1818 Karl Marx, the founder of socialism and the world's most powerful atheistic system, was born in Trier. In 1842, he moved from Trier to Cologne, and work on the cathedral began again. It was finally completed in 1880. This was no coincidence; it appears that the pact with the devil had been honored.

From 1842 until 1843, Karl Marx was the chief editor of the *Rheinische Zeitung,* a newspaper published in Cologne, and he became publisher in

1848. It was from this position that he printed *The Communist Manifesto*. On May 6, 1849, his communist broadsheets were thrown into the crowd assembled in the Gurzenich Hall in Cologne, marking the birth of the communist movement led by Marx and Friedrich Engels. Other powerful communist leaders from Cologne included Ferdinand Lassaile, Andreas Gottschalk, and Matthilde Franziska Anneke.

HEAVEN AND HELL COLLIDE

As the birthplace of the mother of the first Roman persecutor of the church, of the Crusades, of the Christian persecution of the Jews, and then of communism, Cologne has been the womb of the greatest human tragedies in history. The river that has flowed from this "throne of Satan" is a river of death that has not yet been stopped. But the Lord shuts the gates of hell by opening a door in heaven. His strategy for Cologne is to make it a testimony of His power of redemption. God is going to raise up new armies of crusaders from Cologne and Germany with weapons that are not carnal but spiritual. They will bring life and healing to all of the places where they once brought death and destruction.

It is noteworthy that Cologne, the city where the most serious persecution of the Jews originated, is also regarded as a birthplace of Zionism, which resulted in the establishment of the modern state of Israel. Moses Hess followed Karl Marx as an editor of the *Rheinische Zeitung,* and he first published a pamphlet called "Rome and Jerusalem—the Final Question of Nationality" in the 1860s. In 1891, Dr. Bodenheimer of Cologne, who was one of the three major founders of Zionism, wrote his poem, *Vision,* which prophetically described the establishment of Israel. He began to correspond with Dr. Theodor Herzl in 1896, the year that Herzl wrote his landmark book, *The Jewish State.* Cologne then became the home of the global Zionist movement and the Jewish National Foundation, which began to purchase property in Palestine. When Herzl died in 1904, David Wolffsohn of Cologne succeeded him as the head of the Zionist movement, keeping its headquarters there.

After Wolffsohn died and Bodenheimer retired, Weizmann took over the organization and moved its headquarters to London. Karl Marx had also moved his headquarters to London after the Prussian government expelled him. It was nearly five centuries before this that William Tyndale, the famous English Reformer who first translated the Scriptures into the common language and is called "The Morning Star of the Reformation," had his first Bibles printed in Cologne.

As a token of the Lord's present work in this fateful city, the Christian Congregation of Cologne *(Christliche Gemeinde Koln)* had its opening ceremony in 1982. The only place that could be found to rent was an old building called Gurzenich Hall. Without knowing it, Pastor Terry Jones began his work from the very pulpit where Marx had first preached communism. After suffering almost continuous persecution, this little congregation is now emerging as one of the great churches in Germany, comprised of almost 2,000 members from 45 different nationalities. They have a special love for Israel and the Jewish people.

The Lord's door into heaven will not come through a single congregation, however. Instead He will raise up, through His church, a people who live by the opposite spirit from what has been manifested through the stronghold of Satan. The spirit of the world will assault that church with all it can hurl at her, but she will remain faithful.

Job is one of the great biblical examples of how the Lord uses His people as a witness to principalities and powers. The Lord actually asked Satan if he had considered Job, obviously drawing the enemy's attention to him. God then gave the enemy permission to assault Job, with the stipulation that he could not take his life. The Lord then used Job's faithfulness as a witness against the accusations of Satan.

Moses comprehended Satan's greatest accusation against God when Moses restrained the Lord from destroying Israel lest the whole world would say, "God can deliver His people from Egypt, but He does not have the power to bring them into the promised land." Satan's accusation against God with regard to the church is that He can redeem us but He cannot really change us—which means He can get us out of Egypt, but He cannot get us into the promised land. Just as Job stood the test, the

Lord will have a church that testifies to all of creation, through all of eternity, that God has the power, not only to redeem us, but to change us, and bring us into the promised land. Like Job, we may be a mess for a while, but there will be a church that remains faithful through all of her trials.

WE ARE ALL GUILTY

When we study church history, it is easy to judge all of our church fathers, whether they were Catholics, Protestants, evangelicals, or otherwise. We can even find cause to criticize the most recent spiritual movements that seem to have stagnated. However, this criticism only ensures that we, too, will fall short because such criticism disqualifies us from receiving the grace that we all must have in order to keep on the path of life.

We must consider the sins of the historic church, or the contemporary church, not as *their* problems, but as *our* problems. If we are ever going to receive deliverance from the sins that are passed from generation to generation, it will come when we identify with the tragic evils that we, the church, have committed. We must repent and seek the Lord for grace.

It is no accident that the great restoration ministries in Scripture, such as those of Ezra and Nehemiah, gave so much attention to repenting for "the sins of our fathers." They understood the biblical principle that the sins of the fathers are visited upon the children, generation after generation (Ex. 34:7). This is not for the purpose of punishing the children for what their fathers have done, but to heal the wound that sin creates. Contrary to popular belief, wounds do not heal themselves with time; they become infected unless they are properly dressed and closed through repentance, which releases the power of the cross.

The Scriptures declare that some sins will defile the land, not just those who commit them, and the Law of Moses held procedures for cleansing the land from such sins. We also have the example during the reign of David, when he inquired of the Lord, "Why has a famine come upon our land?" The Lord answered, "It is for Saul and his bloody house, because he put the Gibeonites to death" (2 Sam. 21:1). David then had to make restitution to the Gibeonites for the sins of Saul. He gave them what they asked for, Saul's remaining sons so that they could hang them on trees. Here we see that David had to complete the restitution even though he had nothing to do with these sins. Under the Law, restitution was "an eye for an eye, a tooth for a tooth," or as in this case, life for life.

As Christians we are no longer under the Law, since the Cross has made restitution for all of the sins of this world, including the church's tragic sins. However, sins still defile much of the land, and curses remain that give authority to evil principalities and powers to take dominion. Why? Because the Cross has not yet been applied to them. Jesus paid the price for the sins of the whole world, but the whole world has not been saved because it has not yet embraced the Cross.

It is our commission as priests, and ministers of reconciliation, to carry the power of the cross to this world. Because we are now in the "Age of Grace," the procedures of the Law will no longer cleanse the land. We do not appeal to the Law but to the Cross. Even so, if there is to be reconciliation, the Cross must be applied to every wound caused by sin, including these deep historic wounds, so that the power of the gospel can be released.

How is the Cross applied? Through the humility of repentance. Christians must repent for their sins against both Muslims and Jews, as well as against other people groups in history. Interestingly, Pope John Paul II seems to have embraced this truth with such zeal and humility that the whole world has taken note of it and begun to respond. Other great movements, such as "repentance walks" to retrace the path of the Crusades, the Trail of Tears, and other tragic events have had astonishing results in healing the wounds and building bridges of trust between offended peoples. There are still great cultural and racial hot spots such as Bosnia and Rwanda that desperately need healing and forgiveness or the bloodshed will continue. The Lord has also set Jerusalem as the barometer that in many ways measures the strife level of the whole world.

David was not allowed to build a permanent house for the Lord because he had shed blood. The permanent house that Solomon constructed was to be a representation of the permanent kingdom that would be established by Jesus, who did not come to shed blood but to give His own blood for our salvation. When Solomon's temple was dedicated, the Lord gave a promise that transcended the age of the Law and pointed to the kingdom of our Lord Jesus: "If . . . My people who are called by My name humble themselves and pray, and seek My face and turn from their wicked ways, then I will hear from heaven, will forgive their sin, and will heal their land" (2 Chron. 7:13–14).

The Lord's people can humble themselves, seek the Lord, turn from their own wicked ways, and the Lord will forgive the sin and *heal the land*. We can try to beat up principalities in order to bring revival, but sometimes the curses on the land give them the authority to be there. No revival will occur until these sins are repented of *by the Lord's people*. It does not matter who committed them.

Many believe that it is wrong to uncover the terrible mistakes made by the church historically, such as the Crusades. However, it is quite clear that the greatest mistake of all has come from trying to forget them. Just as the world shudders at the thought of Germany forgetting her tragic history, knowing that she could then repeat it, it also shudders at this same folly of the church. There are *good* reasons that the world is appalled by the thought of the church again asserting political power— our historic use of it has ended in the most horrible abuses and tragedies.

This does not mean that the church cannot use political power for good, but until we recognize our mistakes, *and understand them*, we are doomed to repeat them. No Muslim despot or ayatollah has been as ruthless and cruel as some leaders of the church during the Inquisitions. We may protest that this was the doings of the Catholics, but the Protestants were guilty of all the same errors. Forces are still working powerfully in the church to lay the same stumbling blocks before our generation.

Many "crusades" that the church has initiated since the Crusades have resulted in more being turned away from the Lord than are turned to Him. The crusaders claimed to carry their swords for the sake of the cross, the very symbol of salvation, yet they used them to hack men, women, and children to death. We have been given an even greater sword, the Word of God, yet we too often use it to wound and destroy the ones we want to save and heal. We may use God's Word to try to change laws, while at the same time we harden hearts and erect impregnable barriers to the gospel of salvation.

THE EVIL ROOT

One doctrine has proven to be the most devastating throughout history, and is still one of the most popular emphases in the church today. This is basically the delusion that we can accomplish the purposes of God by might and power. However, the prophets solemnly warned, "'. . . Not by might, nor by power, but by My Spirit,' says the LORD of hosts" (Zech. 4:6).

The Lord is called by many titles in Scripture, and each one is used strategically. It is no accident that He calls Himself the "Lord of hosts," or the "Lord of armies," in this text. His army does not use military might, or political power, but what is infinitely more powerful—the Spirit of Truth. The truth, spoken under the anointing, is more powerful than all the weapons and bombs this world can muster. Why is it that we, who have been entrusted with the most powerful weapons of all, continually stoop to those that are so inferior? As the apostle warned:

> For though we walk in the flesh, we do not war according to the flesh, for the weapons of our warfare are not of the flesh, but divinely powerful for the destruction of fortresses. We are destroying speculations and every lofty thing raised up against the knowledge of God, and we are taking every thought captive to the obedience of Christ, and we are ready to punish all disobedience, whenever your obedience is complete. (2 Cor. 10:3–6)

As this Scripture declares, when our obedience is complete—when we are completely yielded to the Spirit, learning not to war in the flesh but only according to His weapons—we will be ready to "punish *all* disobedience."

The Lord has given two different mandates to two entirely different forms of government. He has given a mandate to civil governments to keep order on this earth. They keep this order with "carnal weapons"—the sword. That is why Paul wrote:

> Let every person be in subjection to the governing authorities. For there is no authority except from God, and those which exist are established by God. Therefore he who resists authority has opposed the ordinance of God; and they who have opposed will receive condemnation upon themselves. For rulers are not a cause of fear for good behavior, but for evil. Do you want to have no fear of authority? Do what is good, and you will have praise from the same; *for it is a minister of God* to you for good. But if you do what is evil, be afraid; for it does not *bear the sword* for nothing; for it is a minister of God, an avenger who brings wrath upon the one who practices evil. Wherefore it is necessary to be in subjection, not only because of wrath, but also for conscience' sake. For because of this you also pay taxes, *for rulers are servants of God* . . . (Rom. 13:1–6, emphasis added)

This exhortation was written during the reign of Nero, one of the most wicked men ever to hold a scepter, and after the apostle had spent many years being persecuted at the hands of civil governments. He did not say that we were to submit only to righteous governments. There are obvious exceptions when mandates from a government are contrary to God's law, but even such civil disobedience should always be conducted with the utmost respect for authority.

All authority in both heaven and earth has been given to Christ, but He has not yet directly taken His authority over the earth, nor given it to us, because He has not yet manifestly set up His kingdom on the earth. However, He has *indirectly* taken His authority over the earth because there is no earthly ruler, or spiritual principality, that gains dominion without His approval—even the most wicked.

There are evil principalities ruling over the earth that no amount of prayer or spiritual warfare can bring down because Jesus allows them to be there. Some are there for judgment, some to discipline His people to prepare them for greater authority, and some because the earth over which they prevail has been cursed, and they will be allowed to remain until the curse is properly removed.

The church has also been given authority from God, which is *much greater* than that entrusted to civil authorities. Civil authority is temporary; ours as ambassadors for Christ is eternal. Secular leaders can change laws, but we can change men.

In contrast, true spiritual authority is as limitless as eternity, and it is not found in streetlights that keep men in check; it is the light in men's hearts that compels them to do right even when the lights go off and no police are around.

King David is one of the great biblical examples of a person who walked in true spiritual authority. He is also one of the great forerunners of Christ, who will one day exercise both spiritual and civil authority over the earth, along with His church. Even when David was unjustly persecuted by the civil authority of his nation, even when he had already been anointed to take Saul's place, David would not lift his own hand "against the Lord's anointed." His heart smote him for cutting off the edge of Saul's robe.

This great respect for every authority that God had put in place enabled David to have a throne that will last forever—as Jesus Himself is "seated upon the throne of David." One who walks in true spiritual authority will never take a position by his own hand but will patiently wait for the Spirit to make the way, even if it is a position in the realm of civil authority. If we aspire to sit with Jesus on His throne, it can only be this way.

Presently, the Lord is allowing His church, the ones who are called to rule with Him, to be subject to all of the tests that David went through to prepare him for the throne. The temptation of Jesus by Satan in the wilderness was basically an attempt to pressure Him to take His authority over the world prematurely, enabling Him to avoid the Cross. This is also Satan's primary temptation for the church. He knows that if he can get us to seize temporal authority before we, too, have been through the trials that are meant to prepare us for this rule, we will end up worshiping Satan by doing his bidding—and thus far he has been very successful with this temptation.

A number of Christians in history were called to take a position in the realm of civil authority, and they accomplished great things for humanity. William Wilberforce, the prime minister of Great Britain who abolished slavery in the British Empire, is one. But even this great accomplishment was just a superficial victory, as exploitation through colonization would continue for centuries, and economic oppression in many forms continues today. Even so, in the realm of human history, this was a huge step in the right direction for mankind, and the great evangelists John Wesley and George Whitfield had much to do with it.

However, whenever the church has left her realm of spiritual authority to impose her will in the realm of civil authority, she has fallen to tragic and even diabolical excesses. The key here is that these mistakes have taken place *whenever she has left her realm of authority to do this*. The church has been called to be the "light of the world," to be a force for good, and to uphold the standard of God's righteousness; but the trap that she has often fallen into has been to try to accomplish this from the realm of civil authority.

The church will never be the light because she excels at the ballot box. When the people came to make Jesus king, He fled to the mountains. The people's desire to make Jesus king seems very noble, but it was actually one of the most presumptuous acts in Scripture. The people thought they could make God king! However, He was born King! The source of His authority never came from the people but from the Father above. Likewise, the church's authority comes from above.

PROPHETIC AUTHORITY

The church is called to speak prophetically to governments, and that prophetic anointing is a foundation of our mandated influence with governments. Prophetic authority does not come from our ability to rally great numbers to the polls; instead it is the moral authority and power of the truth, clearly articulated and established by righteous living.

Leo Tolstoy, the author of *War and Peace* and one of the greatest novelists who ever lived, once said, "Prophecy is like a spark lit in a dry wood. Once it ignites it will burn and burn until all of the wood, hay, and stubble has been consumed." He gave as an example the history of slavery.

One of the great sparks thrown on the dry wood of slavery was Harriet Beecher Stowe's novel, *Uncle Tom's Cabin*. This novel so clearly articulated the evils of slavery that it became impossible for that great evil to abide any longer in the civilized world. When Abraham Lincoln met Mrs. Stowe during the middle of the Civil War, he exclaimed, "So you're the little lady that started this great war!" She was. Once the evils were truly exposed, the word spread like fire lit in dry wood. Within just a few years the world was aflame with this truth, and slavery, at least in its most blatant forms, was abolished throughout the earth.

One of the greatest demonstrations of prophetic power in the church age came through Martin Luther. Luther was just a monk, but when he nailed his ninety-five theses to the door of the tiny church in the obscure little town of Wittenberg, Germany, the whole world changed! Not only did he change the world in his own generation, but he also set in motion changes that have profoundly impacted every generation since. There has never been an emperor, king, or even a dynasty that has so influenced this world as this one monk.

Luther's prophetic stand is unequaled, except in the first century when those two poor, often beaten, always harassed apostles would limp into a city. Paul and Silas could cause the most powerful rulers of the most powerful empire ever to exist to tremble in fear, declaring in dismay, "These men who have turned the world upside down have come here!" (Acts 17:6 AMPLIFIED).

Sadly, Martin Luther later succumbed to the temptation to consolidate his great gains by using political power, and his fall can be traced to that point. Before his death Luther had committed many of the tragic errors for which he had so resolutely challenged Rome. While Luther was composing one of the greatest hymns ever written, "A Mighty Fortress Is Our God," he was having an Anabaptist starved to death in a dungeon because he would not conform to Luther's dogma.

Mahatma Gandhi was said to have had a genuine conversion experience. However, he refused to be baptized when he saw how the evangelist used this event as a spectacle for his own self-promotion. Nevertheless, Gandhi clung to many of Jesus' teachings. He was especially captured by the Lord's admonition to overcome evil with good, and to turn the other cheek when assaulted, and he determined to live by this code. Using these aspects of the Lord's message, Gandhi was able to bring the most powerful empire of his day to its knees, giving birth to a new nation. Gandhi refused ever to accept a political office, even though he could have easily been his nation's first prime minister. He said simply that he had found a power greater than any political office could ever give him. He was right.

If Gandhi could so change his world by living by such a small fraction of the gospel, what kind of power would Christians have if we all started to live by the entire gospel? If a pastor of a flock really understood the power with which he has been entrusted, he would never care to stoop so low as to become just a president, much less a senator or congressman, unless it was a cloak placed upon him by the Lord. I am not using the term "stoop so low" because these are dishonorable positions, but because being a pastor for the household of God is such a high calling, with the potential for so much greater authority to influence the present world as well as the one to come.

One of the greatest traps set for those with spiritual authority is the temptation to succumb to using their influence in the realm of secular, civil authority. It is possible to use our influence to do good there, but good is the worst enemy of best. I understand that some have been called to serve in political positions, but it is a symptom of our profound confusion to think of politics as an equal or higher calling than a position of spiritual authority. When we have truly come to see who Jesus is, and who He has called us to be, we will have the constitution of Elijah, who could stand before the king and declare: "As the LORD, the God of Israel lives, *before whom I stand* . . ." (1 Kings 17:1, emphasis added). Elijah was saying to Ahab, "I am not standing here before you. You're just a king, just a man. I don't live my life before men; I live my life before the living God."

Why should we even want to see the king, or president, or any other man unless we have a divine mandate? We can go directly to the King of the universe *anytime we want, with boldness.* If we have seen the King in His glory, how can we be impressed with presidents or kings from this earthly realm?

WE CAN WIN THE BATTLE BUT LOSE THE WAR

One of the great spiritual battles being waged by the church today is over abortion. The side that wins will have taken one of the truly important battles of our time, and it is right for the church to be fully engaged in this conflict. If there is a greater revelation of the debauchery of humanity than the institution of slavery, it is abortion. However, if we "win" with the wrong spirit, the consequences will have been just as devastating for the cause of the gospel as the Crusades proved to be.

Regardless of how many laws are passed legalizing this great evil, the laws of nature have already been passed, and nature itself reveals that abortion is probably the lowest level to which fallen humanity has sunk. Even animals will instinctively sacrifice their own lives to protect their young, but we have proven willing to sacrifice our own children for the petty reasons of convenience and selfishness. While we bemoan the extinction of whales and spotted owls, we massacre our own children, helpless and innocent, by the most cruel, torturous techniques. This is a tragedy of epic proportions, but how are we going to deal with it?

Revival is usually God's final attempt to show mercy instead of judgment. The last of the Great Awakenings this country experienced came just before the Civil War. That awakening was given by the Lord as a way to prevent the war. Had that revival continued on track, it would have abolished slavery while avoiding the worst bloodshed this nation has ever experienced. When the abolitionists, the political zealots of that time, turned the revival into a political movement, the fate of the nation was sealed and bloodshed was inevitable.

The abolitionists were some of the most courageous, truth-loving, and self-sacrificing people in the country. Most were Christians and true patriots. However, they were also driven to extremes and blown about by winds of impatience. Their goals were noble, but their means were the way of destruction, because they did not comprehend the nature of the "wisdom from above" as described by James:

> Who among you is wise and understanding? Let him show by his good behavior his deeds in the *gentleness of wisdom*. . . . But the wisdom from above is first pure, then peaceable, gentle, reasonable, full of mercy and good fruits, unwavering, without hypocrisy. And the seed whose fruit is righteousness is sown in peace by those who make peace. (James 3:13,17–18, emphasis added)

The abolitionists had the right goals, but they tried to achieve them by the wrong means, which was to stir up the passions of war instead of reconciliation. Whenever we do this, we will depart from the wisdom that is from above, and we will display a nature that is quite the opposite of the Savior. Zealotry is the wisdom of Judas Iscariot, who thought that he could force the Lord to take His authority and declare His kingdom. Such political manipulation comes from the spirit of the evil one, regardless of the motives. The kingdom of God will not come by might nor power, but by the Spirit.

The issue of abortion still has the power to divide this country like it has not been divided since the Civil War, and I believe the Lord will send a revival first to try to prevent this. The revival, if it is not sidetracked by the zealots, will have the power to abolish abortion and replace it with the greatest esteem for life that civilization has yet realized.

Paul explained to the Corinthians that he had been given a sphere of authority that he would not presume to go beyond (2 Cor. 10:13–14).

The Lord Jesus never once tried to use the civil authorities to accomplish the Father's purposes. Neither did the apostles or other leaders of the early church. They understood that to do so would have been to come down from the high position they were given.

Those who understand spiritual authority will be very conscious of the sphere that has been appointed to them, because to go beyond it invites disaster. Just as a policeman from Atlanta has no authority in Mexico City, and would probably get hurt if he tried to exert authority there, we do not have any spiritual authority beyond the realm that God has given to us.

THE BOOKS OF LIFE

The Books of Life are God's history books. They are very different from human histories. They contain the names of many the world has never heard of, but these praying saints had authority with God and accomplished much more for the human race, and the human condition, than any president, prime minister, or king. Praying saints have freed many more slaves than Wilberforce and Lincoln combined—and they did it with a freedom that was much greater! This is why the Lord said in Luke 10:18–20:

> I was watching Satan fall from heaven like lightning. Behold, I have given you authority to tread upon serpents and scorpions, and over all the power of the enemy, and nothing shall injure you. Nevertheless do not rejoice in this, that the spirits are subject to you, but rejoice that your names are recorded in heaven.

It is a wonderful thing to have been given authority over all of the power of the enemy, but it is an even greater thing to be found in God's history books. His history books tell of those who live by the authority of His Word, who walk by the power of His Spirit. What good will it do us to be known by all men but not to be known by God?

7

Team Ministry
The Apostolic Model for Today

WHEN I ASKED THE LORD TO GUIDE ME AS I considered the organization of our church in Charlotte, North Carolina, He led me to study more carefully the first-century church. It functioned so successfully that it spread throughout the Roman Empire—despite persecution—and influenced nineteen centuries thereafter.

THE ANATOMY OF THE EARLY CHURCH

John and Philip. Peter and Thaddeus. Matthew and Bartholomew. We know little of their backgrounds, except their occupations, which were so different. They had somewhat disparate training and different skills. Yet, within a short period of time Jesus molded them into a team that would change the world.

Church government under the original apostles was so unique, free, and yet effective that it defies definition. First-century church government was dependent not on form but on the anointing of the leaders who held positions in it. It was not rigid but flowed and matured like the new life-form that it was created to be.

The apostles did not have a constitution that gave them the authority to dictate policy. Their authority came from something much higher: they had been with Jesus, and He had anointed them. Their main function was to lay a solid foundation of doctrine and to establish a church government that promoted liberty, not just conformity. This freedom enabled the hearts of men to be converted by the power of truth, not by coercion.

The apostles' adherence to this course of leadership was in such contrast to anything that had been known before—and certainly to the culture of the times—that it constitutes the most extraordinary leadership ever exercised by any government at any time. Once the church drifted from the genius of this extraordinary style, oppression grew, and the power of truth was replaced with a terrible, barbaric force intended to compel men to bend their knees to the dictates of church leaders without bending their hearts to truth.

Five hundred years ago, when the church began the long process of returning to its original form of government, the immediate result was the birth of democracy in civil governments and a new esteem for human dignity. The great freedom movements that are still expanding around the world today and setting people free can all be traced to the teachings of the Reformers. Without question, religious liberty is the foundation for all true liberty.

In the twenty-first century the Lord is calling forth people to be joint heirs with Him. They will rule and reign with Him over the nations. In this great position He will only have those who come to Him because they love the truth, not because of political expediency or a lust for power. Instead, they will prove their love for the truth by taking their stand for righteousness when it is least expedient, even to the forfeiture of their lives. These leaders will come not out of compulsion but of something much deeper—hearts that love God and His ways above all else. The first Eve lived in a perfect world and chose to sin. The bride of the last Adam will live in a most evil world and choose to obey.

HIERARCHICAL OR DEMOCRATIC?

As much as we in the West may be repelled at the abuses of hierarchical forms of church government, and as much as this form of government has been used to stifle liberty, it was unquestionably an aspect of the New Testament church. In the first century, all authority in the church was derived from the apostles. However, the way that the apostles exercised their authority was to transfer it to worthy subordinates at every opportunity. And when the apostles instituted the position of deacon, they allowed the congregation to choose those who would serve in this honored position. Regardless of how we would like to view this, it was a remarkable example of democracy in church government. The apostles did not act as if they were lords of God's inheritance, but led by being examples to the flock (1 Peter 5:3). They took authority when it was needed, but they seemed always devoted to delegating it to the people when possible. If these people were to rule over angels one day, they must have reasoned, then they should be able to take responsibility in earthly matters.

Therefore, both hierarchical and democratic forms of government have biblical precedents and merit. We cannot say that either form is *the* apostolic structure. Even in our present church government, the Lord intended for us to have liberty and diversity. This may seem impractical to the natural mind, but it is essential for true spiritual development.

As we read the New Testament, it seems as if the form of church government used just evolved over time. The Lord was building His government in people, not trying to build people around structure. This is not to imply that the Lord did not know where He was going. When a group is young, they probably need more controls than when they are mature. And people who have lived under oppressive forms of government, such as communism, can have their own decision-making ability so broken by oppression (or so underdeveloped because of a lack of freedom) that too much liberty can be destructive or confusing to their walk in the Lord. In these cases liberty must be given gradually.

In some countries where liberty has bordered on lawlessness, almost any exercise of church authority will be viewed as an imposition. This will cause serious rebellions that could have been avoided if authority had been taken more gradually. In other countries where there has been a good balance between liberty and control (not a control spirit), very little government may be needed.

This is a very delicate balance, and we must remember that the Lord always works from the inside out, not from the outside in. If our overwhelming emphasis is on imposing a form of government, we are going to end up causing a lot of problems and a lot of pain. Government is important, since one of the great evils of the last days is lawlessness. Even so, how the government is imposed can be a great help or hindrance to the work. The counter to lawlessness is not a control spirit; it is a love for the truth that comes from the heart of the people.

In all cases church government is intended to help us grow in our submission to the headship of Jesus. Our goal should always be to promote the individual's personal relationship to the Lord, his or her ability to know the Lord's voice, and his or her commitment to follow Jesus, so that every one of God's people has the law written in his or her heart. This pattern was left to us by the first-century apostles.

THE IMPACT OF AN APOSTOLIC MINISTRY

In December of 1990, Bob Weiner had a vision of a strategy for helping to bring in a great harvest of souls in the Soviet Union. Starting with just twenty new Christians in late February of 1991, he sent them out two by two to three hundred major cities and universities throughout the country (more than 90 percent of these regions were without churches). Each team's assignment was to find one key believer with the potential for leadership in each of these cities and bring that individual back to Moscow for training.

A month and a half later, in April of 1991, three hundred of these potential elders were brought to Moscow for five days of intensive training. After being baptized and receiving the Holy Spirit, they were sent back to their cities to win ten more to Christ. Ten weeks later two thousand new believers who had been won to the Lord were brought to Moscow. These, too, were baptized in water and the Holy Spirit and were given five days of intensive training on how to win souls to Christ.

From 1990 to 1996, Bob Weiner held seventeen of these conferences, which were attended by a total of 16,000 young Russians. (Because many came to more than one conference, it is not known exactly how many different individuals were trained, but by a most conservative figure there were at least 6,000.) These Christians fanned out across the country, preaching the gospel and establishing more than 250 new congregations, some of which have surpassed 1,500 people.

During these training conferences Weiner Ministries International paid for 240,000 meals and 80,000 nights in hotels. They also gave away more than 200,000 Bible studies and more than 100,000 Bibles or New Testaments, as well as paying for transportation to and from the conferences for those attending.

Often with little or nothing in the bank, Weiner would commit himself to paying roughly $100,000 in expenses for each conference. This was very inexpensive because of the exchange rate during those times, but it was a lot for Bob. On several occasions he would have only a few thousand dollars just days before the conference, but the Lord would always supply the rest on time. Once he had almost $80,000 come from unexpected sources in the week just before the conference.

Much of the support for this ministry has come from the often maligned "faith teachers," who would personally hear from the Lord to send Weiner Ministries large sums of money for Russia (in one case, a single check for $60,000). Regardless of what is said and written about these teachers, many will obviously have a great deal of fruit waiting for them in heaven since thousands of young Russian Christians can thank them for their faith.

One of Bob Weiner's most fulfilling moments came during the coup attempt to overthrow Gorbachev in August of 1991. Hundreds of new believers from his conferences poured into the streets and risked their lives to take a stand for freedom and to resist the illegal takeover of the Russian government by communist hard-liners. The whole world watched as they stood before tanks waving their new Bibles and declaring, "Where the Spirit of the Lord is there is liberty."

An apostolic approach to ministry had again stood for freedom and influenced secular society. Weiner's success, like the apostles', was based on team ministry. He did not go to Russia to minister but to train up ministers. Those he trained took their authority and went forth to do the work of the ministry.

TEAM MINISTRY

The apostles were the first ministry established by the Lord, but as they laid a foundation in the church with their teaching and leadership, other ministries began to emerge. Some focused on evangelism, others on teaching, still others on the prophetic or on administration or healing. In this way the ministry that began with twelve grew throughout the expanding church, meeting the increasing needs. The Holy Spirit brought forth gifts and ministries in each Christian, so that every believer had a part in the overall ministry of the church.

As we read the book of Acts, it seems that all of this happened quite swiftly, but actually it took many years. For example, it was seven years from the day that the Holy Spirit was poured out on Pentecost until Peter first preached to the Gentiles in the house of Cornelius. And more than two decades elapsed between the outpouring of the Holy Spirit and the time when Paul and Barnabas were sent out from Antioch.

This unfolding definition of the church is a good pattern for church life today. When you have a baby, you may know that it is male or female, but you really do not know what that child will look like as an adult. The same is true of the church. Unfortunately, for centuries, unfolding movements have been forced to try to fit into the clothes that were made for them before they were even born.

Throughout the Lord's ministry on earth, He only mentioned the eventual church community very briefly and gave very little definition to what it would be like. And even though He spent many days after His resurrection sharing about the kingdom of God, He apparently gave His disciples very little practical guidance about church administration. He purposely wanted them to get that from the Holy Spirit, and the Holy Spirit seemed to give the wisdom only as they needed it. The brilliance of what unfolded was far beyond human genius and perfectly fit the needs at each stage of development.

As the ministries emerged, a comprehensive team began to form. Prophets began to work closely with apostles. Pastors and teachers worked together. The only evangelist mentioned in the New Testament, Philip, seemed to work alone, but apostles were sent to follow his work. Local elders were appointed in each congregation to provide guidance and protection in the absence of the apostles, which was most of the time. Together this structure of leadership soon became so powerful that its very existence challenged the most powerful institutions and governments on earth.

A number of examples in the New Testament Epistles show that at times the apostles dictated policy, or took severe action against sin or false doctrines that encroached on the church. Even so, when Paul issued instructions for disciplinary action to the Corinthian church, he addressed not just the elders but the entire congregation. Basically, the apostles treated believers as fellow heirs to the kingdom and priests of God.

At the same time, clear lines of authority were established in the first-century church, as we see in 1 Corinthians 12:27–31:

> Now you are Christ's body, and individually members of it. And God has appointed in the church, first apostles, second prophets, third teachers, then miracles, then gifts of healings, helps, administrations, various kinds of tongues. All are not apostles, are they? All are not prophets, are they? All are not teachers, are they? All are not workers of miracles, are they? All do not have gifts of healings, do they? All do not speak with tongues, do they? All do not interpret, do they? But earnestly desire the greater gifts. And I show you a still more excellent way.

Paul proposed a clear chain of authority at the same time that he told believers to desire the greater gifts. All do not have the same authority,

Paul said, but they could seek it. Just as the Lord had called Paul from being one of the greatest enemies of the church to being one of its greatest leaders, so the Lord seemed to delight in using his leaders as demonstrations of His power of redemption. The small and the weak, and even the base, were often qualified for service (1 Cor. 1:26–29). God's main purpose for the church was for it to be an instrument to redeem and restore the lost, and those most qualified to do this were selected.

ELDERS

The elders were the highest local authority in a church. This office was borrowed from the government Moses established in the wilderness. In Israel there were basically two classes of elders, those who were respected because of their age (the Law admonished Christians to honor their fathers and mothers, and other biblical passages called for respect of the aged) and actual governing elders. Just as Moses chose seventy men "from among the elders" (Num. 11:16) to exercise governing authority, governing elders in the church were distinguished from those who were simply due respect for their age and faithfulness.

After Israel entered the promised land and conquered the cities, a primary responsibility of the governing elders was to sit in the gates of the city. Here they acted as judges and determined who would be allowed to come in or go out. Each gate had a different function. Some were for merchants, some for soldiers, others for nobility, and so forth. Each elder could exercise authority over that particular aspect of the city's life.

This has an important application in the New Testament. Because elders are always mentioned as plural, some have assumed that elders were all equal in authority, but both Old Testament and New Testament examples indicate that this is not the case. Elders who sat in one gate did not have the authority to dictate policy over other gates. This may seem like a small point, but its application can have several consequences.

Consider, for example, the effect of choosing someone to be an elder because of his maturity (or the respect that he has in the church community), even though he does not have a specific function. Such a person could easily become a hindrance to the progress of the church, even if he has the best of intentions, just by feeling compelled to meddle in areas where he really has not been given any wisdom or anointing. Before someone is appointed a "governing elder," we should look for the evidence of God's anointing in a specific area. In the case of Moses, the Spirit came upon the elders and they prophesied. This may not be exactly how the Lord verifies every elder, but we do need to see a spiritual anointing. If we appoint people to this position just to honor them, we will probably pay a high price for it later.

Another important point is to determine just what "gate" the governing elders are called to sit in. Should one who is anointed to oversee the deacons have authority over the children's ministry, where he may have no anointing or experience?

Our presidential cabinet is a modern example of the presbytery of the church. Here the heads of the different departments sit in a council. The Secretary of Defense may in fact have some wisdom for the Department of Labor, but he does not have the authority to dictate policy there. Elders may have wisdom for other ministries in the church, but one who is an overseer of one "gate," or ministry, should not be able to dictate authority over someone else's sphere of authority.

Of course, important doctrinal issues may arise that involve the entire church, such as we see in Acts 15. Here the question of circumcision affected all Gentiles who had become Christians. "Could these converts be saved if they were not circumcised?" some leaders asked. An issue of this importance required a meeting of *all* the apostles and elders. After listening to testimonies and debate, James, who was recognized as the leading elder in Jerusalem, made the decisive statement that circumcision was not a criteria for salvation (verses 13–19). As this "seemed good" to the other apostles and elders, the council issued a decree to the churches.

Another sphere of authority for elders can be tied to geography. When Paul talked about his sphere of authority, it was in relation to geographical boundaries (see 2 Cor. 10:13–16). Because the Lord established cultures, races, and nations, He prepares special ministries to relate to them. And everyone in ministry needs to be sensitive to different ethnic groups, which is why Paul said that when he was in Rome he did as the Romans, or when he was with the Jews he became as a Jew. The gospel is a stumbling block, but we do not want our personalities to become *unnecessary* stumbling blocks to people who hear the gospel. Many unnecessary offenses that have come to Christianity have resulted because we have failed to walk in this wisdom or have tried to go beyond the realm of authority that was given to us geographically.

We should also recognize that when Peter and John referred to themselves as elders, they were not talking about being elders in a local church, or even in the foundational church of Jerusalem. Peter and John were both recognized as elders of the whole Body of Christ. Does this contradict the statement that the Lord alone is Head of the whole church? No, it does not. Some realms of authority are international, and some may even extend to the whole church.

Today we could include a few in this position, such as Billy Graham, David Yongi Cho, Paul Cain, Pat Robertson, and Jack Hayford. A host of emerging international leaders from Britain, Hungary, Sweden, Germany, and South and Central America will probably one day be considered elders of the entire church. And eventually some will also come from Russia, Asia, and the Middle East.

Being respected in such a capacity does not give one the authority to dictate policy over the entire church, but these men sit (or are beginning to sit) in spiritual doors that are ministering to the entire church. Many others have international ministries, and though some of them may have both age and longevity in that position, they do not carry the kind of authority that would cause us to recognize them as elders of the entire Body of Christ.

We can biblically recognize elders on the local church level and the international level, but do we have elders positioned in levels in between? Personally, I think that it is right to recognize elders on every level of authority, which would include recognizing those in specific positions within movements. We have the liberty to do that which does not specifically violate the Scriptures. This does not mean that anything is right, but that we are free to be led by the Holy Spirit in these matters.

In the New Testament a distinction exists between the authority of one of the equipping ministries (such as apostle, prophet, evangelist, pastor, or teacher) and the authority of an elder. You will also note that the ministry of the pastor is only mentioned one time in the New Testament (when listed with the others in Ephesians 4), and yet somehow this position almost completely dominates the ministry of the modern church! The pastor was obviously only intended to be one member of a team of ministries given for the equipping of the people, who were to do the work of the ministry themselves.

Was there meant to be a hierarchy among elders? The only hierarchy that is mentioned in Scripture is that the apostles had authority over the elders, and the elders had authority over deacons. The Greek words for *bishop* and *presbyter* (elder) are used interchangeably in the New Testament and obviously referred to the same office. The elevation of the office of bishop above that of presbyter was gradual and was not recognized in church government until sometime between A.D. 70 and 120.

Emerging movements today use a variety of titles for the same functions, ranging from "leading elder" to apostle. Biblically we cannot establish that anyone had extra local authority in the church except for apostles and prophets, or elders who sat in special councils with the apostles, such as we see in the Council in Jerusalem (Acts 15).

Once I applied this apostolic structure to MorningStar, I then asked the Lord how we could create a church or movement that would keep on moving. He told me that I needed to observe the wisdom of the geese.

THE WISDOM OF THE GEESE

Geese are remarkable birds. Each flock of geese has a form of government that is popularly known as "the pecking order." Those who try to rise out of their place in the flock will have to fight, and subdue, geese on a level above them. This may sound brutal, but it is in reality the way most human groups also act. While we are earthbound, there will always be bickering and infighting about the "pecking order," but as long as we are going somewhere, soaring above the earth, the leadership position will not matter to us.

I think this, too, is biblical. In the first century we see the leadership of the church going from Peter to James to Paul and then to John. In the church today we see ministries emerge that help take the whole church a little further, and then they seem to give way to another one.

When geese fly, they also fly in formation, but this has a very different purpose from the ability of one goose to dominate another. As each goose flaps its wings, it creates an uplift for the birds that follow. In flight, the lead goose must cut through the wind while all of the others are drafting behind each other. By drafting this way, the rest of the flock is using about 20 percent less effort than the leader. Therefore, the leader tires much more quickly than the others, requiring a change of leadership if the flock is to keep pace, which is frequently done.

By flying in a *V* formation, the whole flock adds 71 percent greater flying range than if each bird flew alone. Likewise, people who share a common direction and sense of community can get where they are going more quickly and easily because they are traveling on the thrust of one another.

When the lead goose tires, it rotates back into the formation, and another goose flies to the point position. Geese take turns being the leader. If geese did not do this, the whole flock would be greatly limited in its range and speed.

In a similar manner, New Testament leadership is meant to function as a team. I am the overseer of the congregation, but we have many outstanding preachers and teachers on staff who take turns in the pulpit. In almost every service we also give fifteen minutes to someone in the congregation or school of ministry to speak. These teachings have been so good that the congregation now has a genuine excitement when they see someone about to speak whom they have not heard before. All these changes have brought a freshness and vitality to the church that has enabled some of our local church meetings to exceed anything we have experienced in conferences.

We are also implementing this in every department of the church. For example, when our pastor of children's ministry began to get weary, we moved someone else into that leadership position, and the former pastor took his place behind the new leader. There was some resistance to this at first, but we saw an immediate acceleration in the children's ministry. Within weeks the former leader was thanking us. We have let all staff members know that once they are rested, and their vision renewed, they may lead again (unless the Lord directs someone else into the position). Everyone in the ministry, including me, knows that when we tire, and things begin to bog down, a change is coming. We must take time to rest and renew our vision if we are going to continue moving forward. True leaders who are *true servants* will always welcome this.

Isn't this the model given to us in the Levitical priesthood? They ministered in the tabernacle from the time they were thirty until they were fifty, and then they let the next generation take over. This kept the ministry fresh. Those who were removed from ministry at age fifty then entered some fruitful years discipling the emerging generation and taking their place as elders in the gates.

We need to allow those who are the freshest to lead, and let someone else take the point position for a while. By having the humility to do this, we will all go much further and faster, just like that flock of geese.

When a goose falls out of formation, it suddenly feels the drag and resistance of flying alone, so it quickly moves back in formation to take advantage of the lifting power of the bird immediately in front of it. As with geese, people are interdependent on one another's skills, capabilities, and unique talents or resources. We must be willing to accept their help and give our help to others.

The geese flying in formation honk to encourage those up front to keep up their speed. We need to make sure our words are also encouraging. A friend of mine once commented, "The best preachers in America seem to all be black." Another friend replied, "Black preachers aren't better; they just have better audiences." If you have ever spoken in a predominantly black church, you know what he meant. Of the ten most encouraging audiences I have ever spoken to, every one was a black church. It helps when people show their excitement by shouting, "Yes, brother. Preach it!" or by waving handkerchiefs, standing up, and dancing around in circles! You start drawing from depths you did not know you had. If a church seems too staid, the reason may be the lack of the parishioners' hunger or the lack of encouragement they give their leaders.

It is also noteworthy that when a goose gets sick, wounded, or shot down, two geese drop out of formation and follow it down to help and protect it. They stay with the goose until it is either able to fly again or dies. Then they launch out with another formation or catch up with the flock. If we have as much sense as geese, we will stand by each other in difficult times as well as when we are strong. One of the great tragedies of modern Christianity has been our tendency to shoot our own wounded or at least leave them to die while pretending not to be associated with them.

FRESH MANNA TODAY

Applying all these principles in the everyday functioning of a local church or a national ministry is not easy. Although the Lord revealed these principles to me, I continue to struggle with them myself in all areas of MorningStar, such as the worship ministry.

Worship is rightly emerging as one of the most powerful aspects of our church life. This is important because Jesus said:

> But an hour is coming, and now is, when the true worshipers shall worship the Father in spirit and truth; for such people the Father seeks to be His worshipers. God is spirit, and those who worship Him must worship in spirit and truth. (John 4:23–24)

The apostle Paul also said, "Now the Lord is the Spirit; and where the Spirit of the Lord is, there is liberty" (2 Cor. 3:17). Therefore, to worship in the Spirit of the Lord, which is what the Father seeks, there must be liberty in worship.

We have a reputation for having a lot of liberty at MorningStar, and I do think that we have attained some degree of freedom. In fact, in some areas we have allowed too much, and the enemy, or the carnally minded, have used it. Even so, I still think that we need more, not less, as long as we don't short-circuit a maturity process. When we do so, the immature, the selfishly ambitious, and the devil will take full advantage of it. We have certainly experienced this too!

For example, as a father I give my sixteen-year-old much more liberty than I give my six-year-old. When Anna was fourteen, I gave her permission to go on a mission trip to Indonesia with another family, and I trusted that she had heard from God about it. However, at the same time we did not let Sam, who was three years old, leave the yard without one of us with him. Our children's privileges are based on their overall level of maturity.

As a pastor, I am constantly pressed from many directions. When the worship team wants more freedom, it often translates into more time for worship. However, in a typical meeting, our teachers or guest speakers usually need more time too. We also have other ministry during the service that requires time. As I am pulled in these different directions, I try to find the mind of the Lord. I do not always do this perfectly, and I never do it in a way that pleases everyone. I think, however, that we are making progress. To show you how we are doing this, let me share my interaction with two of our worship leaders, Don and Christine Potter.

A LEARNING PROCESS

When I first met Don and Christine, I saw in them a deep and sincere devotion to the Lord. However, I also saw a tendency to see things in extremes, a quality that is often found in strong and gifted leaders. Even so, this tendency can make working with others as a team, which is essential for advancement, very difficult.

My trust in Don and Christine has grown, but there have been some "bumps in the road." The first time we asked Don to play in a little concert where we had six performers, he went so far beyond the time allotted to each one that we had to change the rest of the program. A couple of those who were going to follow Don took it well, even offering not to play at all. I also knew that Don had just lost his concept of how much time he was taking and was oblivious to what he had done. Even so, this is one of the most difficult problems for someone overseeing a program, and I marked it down as something that we would have to watch.

On a second occasion, my wife, Julie, asked Don to co-lead a little session with her, and they went so far past their time that I again had to change the rest of the program at the expense of the session's purpose. When we walked away from that meeting, I basically felt that it had been a waste of time. Even though this was not a main session, I felt a deep grief. Of course, there is no way that I would give up on my wife, but I felt like giving up on Don as a worship leader.

I did not realize it at the time, but Don was also struggling. As a professional musician in Nashville, he had worked with such artists as the Judds, Elton John, Steven Curtis Chapman, and Twila Paris, and received many accolades. Even in his home church, where he led praise and worship, the pastor gave him free rein. After all those "atta-boys," he was now faced with someone who was not impressed with his past.

Still, Leonard Jones, who was on staff with us, wanted Don to lead a session at the next conference. I was not enthusiastic about it, but I trusted Leonard, so I agreed to let Don lead a main session. I also went to Don and let him know that the worship should be thirty minutes, not thirty-one.

As the worship proceeded that day, it was okay, but not spectacular. Then, right at the end, the anointing fell and it seemed as if we were on the verge of something special. I saw Don look at the time and stop. He had been obedient, but I knew we had missed something, and I think everyone else knew it too. I walked away from that meeting feeling as badly as I had about the previous one where he had gone too long. I also realized that Don had a much more significant anointing for leading worship than I had realized and knew he could not help but be irritated by what had happened.

Now I faced a dilemma. I still felt that Don tended to be oblivious to the overall program, but at the same time, it seemed that he needed a lot of time to get going. This was very unlike Leonard Jones, who could get to a high level quickly, a level that was so intense it was hard to take more than thirty minutes of his music without being too worn out for anything else.

That is when we began to learn to work together. Where Don may have been less sensitive than he should have been regarding time, I am often less sensitive than I should be of people. Once I gave the worship leaders the freedom to go for as long as the Lord seemed to be directing, they became much more sensitive to timing. When we missed the Lord in this, they would feel even worse than I did. Then they started asking for more input, or for me to interrupt them if worship got off track, sometimes even asking us to interrupt them in order to preach or prophesy. One of them even told me that he needed more specific instructions from the pastoral team, especially concerning how much time he should take. I have tried to do this, but with the directive that if the Lord is really moving, they are to keep going. I still remember well the meeting when Don was shut down because I did not want him to go one minute over thirty!

Although I have never asked the worship leaders to stay, rarely will I see them leave a meeting after the worship portion. This gives them a vision for all that is going on and gives me much more confidence in them. I have been challenged by other leaders for giving our worship leaders too much freedom, but I know they have earned it, I know they are trustworthy and will never knowingly abuse it, and I feel they deserve more freedom, not less.

We now have three main worship leaders who I think could be classified as "chief musicians." We then have about a dozen who lead from time to time, and some of them could eventually be chief musicians. This has brought a vitality and diversity to our worship.

VITALITY AND DIVERSITY

When Leonard and Don came to me with the idea of having a conference dedicated mostly to worship, I was for it. In this conference, we would give worship the highest priority and we would teach or minister if there was time. We felt that the Lord gave us the name, "The Heart of David—Worship and Warfare." Then we had to go through difficult planning sessions about such things as buying expensive recording equipment and bringing in professionals to do the recording. Don was accustomed to spending hundreds of thousands of dollars for a project. At that time, spending twenty thousand dollars took a lot of faith for our ministry. It might even mean we would have to lay off some people if the conference was not successful.

To our amazement, the Worship and Warfare Conference was much better than we had ever expected. The last day we worshiped God for nearly a combined eight hours at a level that we previously had hoped to be able to sustain for half an hour. At the end the musicians were so exhausted that Leonard was lying on his back trying to play his guitar, and all of them had gone far beyond their natural strength. That is when a little cloud appeared on the stage. It looked like what I imagined as the pillar in the wilderness, moving across the stage. This was not a vision, as it was witnessed by over two thousand people who were still worshiping. I knew that something had been born that we needed to follow.

Now everywhere I go, people tell me about the impact of our music on their lives. I also frequently talk to pastors who say they want the same for their churches. Yet I have found very few pastors who are willing to pay the price for it. They all seem to want the mature product immediately. The grace of God is free, but it is not cheap! Even though we have now spent years seeking higher levels of worship, we are still having a great deal of trouble working with some of our worship leaders. I have met very few musicians who are not deeply wounded, or prone toward depression. I believe that this is because, as we see in the Scriptures, Satan was the worship leader in heaven once, and he seems to take special exception to anyone who seeks to take that place.

Worship leaders can be in one of the most vulnerable places of any position in the church. When adoration is being raised to God, it is hard not to take some of it, which is what obviously caused Satan to fall. I have watched as some of the best, and seemingly strongest, are repeatedly caused to stumble. We are still searching for answers, but we know that we must not give up this fight until there is a complete victory and recovery of true worship that can only come with true freedom.

Without question, if we really want to comply with the biblical models of church government, radical changes must come to most modern churches and movements. It is also obvious that they are coming. Many new movements are now sweeping across the church, coming with such life and vitality that they are forcing change by their very existence. The Lord is seeking to prepare a wineskin that is perpetually flexible enough to embrace the new wine.

8

Persecution

An Apostolic Heritage

IN THE FIRST CENTURY, CHRISTIANITY WAS A supernatural experience. The Lord Himself sometimes personally appeared to people. Interaction with angels was so frequent that Christians were exhorted to be careful how they treated strangers, because they could be entertaining angels (Heb. 13:2). The Lord was very close to His people, and the spiritual realm became familiar to all believers, which made it easier for them to endure the almost continuous opposition, persecution, and affliction.

The Scriptures make it clear that the end of the age will be marked both by an increase in the supernatural quality of Christianity and an increase in persecution, both of which characterized the church in Acts. As Paul explained to the believers, "Through many tribulations we must enter the kingdom of God" (Acts 14:22). This was a proven truth in the first century. The more the church was afflicted, the more spiritual authority she experienced. The early Christians quickly learned to be thankful for all such trials because they prepared them to be stewards of even greater power.

Everything about the young church seemed designed to draw wrath and opposition from the prevailing powers on the earth, since any group that represented change or that the religious leaders could not control threatened them. At a whim, the religious leaders could expel people from the synagogue, thereby making it impossible for them to trade or relate to anyone in the community, and the leaders often drove them from their homes, their families, and their country. The religious oppression of first-century Israel could be as stifling as the political and military oppression of Rome. The leaders used almost any means to silence someone who challenged their dominance, even hiring false witnesses to bring charges or turning Christians over to the oppressive authority of the hated Romans.

But proclaiming Jesus as Lord also incited the Roman officials, who considered Christians' primary allegiance to Jesus as an affront to the authority of their emperor. Ultimately this stand would release the cruelest persecutions against the young church that had ever been seen in the civilized world. Yet when someone became a Christian, the person joined a community whose courage was also unprecedented. Never had a people arisen who were willing to suffer so much for the sake of their beliefs. The truth they lived for was so great, they were also willing to die for it. For nearly three centuries, believing in Jesus meant risking your life every day.

The Lord Jesus had warned His disciples that this would be their lot:

Behold, I send you out as sheep in the midst of wolves; therefore be shrewd as serpents, and innocent as doves. But beware of men; for they will deliver you up to the courts, and scourge you in their synagogues; and you shall even be brought before governors and kings for My sake, as a testimony to them and to the Gentiles. But when they deliver you up, do not become anxious about how or what you will speak; for it shall be given you in that hour what you are to speak. For it is not you who speak, but it is the Spirit of your Father who speaks in you. And brother will deliver up brother to death, and a father his child; and children will rise up against parents, and cause them to be put to death. And you will be hated by all on account of My name, but it is the one who has endured to the end who will be saved. (Matt. 10:16–22)

As the book of Acts documents, the early church was born in persecution and, with the exception of some brief respites, grew and prospered in the midst of continual opposition. Diabolical rumors about Christians were devised and spread throughout the empire. Christian "love feasts" and celebrations of the Lord's Supper were declared to be a covering for the most hideous crimes. Misunderstanding the ritual symbolism of Communion as a partaking of the body and blood of Christ, slanderers reported that Christians would bind themselves into a criminal league by feasting on a slaughtered child and then giving themselves up to the most shameless forms of indulgence.

The rumor that Christians were cannibals persisted for centuries, and the Roman government used this charge as justification for feeding Christians to wild beasts. Popular animosity against Christian practices reached such a level that every public calamity was blamed upon them. Hideous tortures were devised as the Roman emperor Nero unleashed the full power of the imperial sword in an attempt to destroy the young church. Christians were hung on crosses, dipped in oil and burned, and sometimes even set on fire to be used as streetlights. Men were hung on low trees where bears were allowed to tear them to pieces before they expired.

To the great consternation of the Roman and religious officials, the more they afflicted the young church, the more it grew and spread. Every time a church was scattered, the people became like seed, and dozens of other congregations sprouted up. And when a leader was killed, a dozen others would arise to take his place. The Romans could defeat any army in the world, *but they could not defeat the truth.*

The more severe the persecution, the more grace the Lord extended to the church. The first Christian martyr, Stephen, was so enraptured by the glory of the Lord as he was being stoned that he seemed unaware of his mortal wounds. In the same way, many other martyrs who were tortured by the Romans experienced such a grace that they did not even seem to feel the pain of their afflictions.

The peace and the reflection of God's glory on the faces of these early martyrs were sometimes so great that their torturers were converted on the spot, choosing to embrace the same kind of death. And many who came to watch the Christians be devoured by lions were so stunned by their courage that the spectators could find no peace until they, too, embraced faith in Christ. Never had anything like this been seen anywhere in the world. It defied human explanation.

These persecutions against the church lasted not just a few months, or even years, but for nearly three centuries! The most intense persecutions of all occurred during the last ten years of this period. On February 24, 303, an imperial decree was issued requiring the destruction of all Christian property and all copies of the Bible. The civil rights of all Christians were revoked, and Christians were reduced to the status of slaves. More than that, the entire populace of the empire was given permission to attack and afflict Christians in any way they desired. Multitudes of Christians were slaughtered, and others were attacked and violated in every conceivable way. Many had their property confiscated. Yet, the faith continued to spread and prevail, and the faithful grew even bolder in their witness.

During the times of persecution, there were no false conversions! And because leaders became special targets, those who accepted leadership positions were not motivated by selfish ambition, only by a sincere love for the Lord and His people. Many of the petty issues that can cause division in times of peace could find no place for producing discord in the persecuted church. Persecution was the fire that consumed the wood, hay, and stubble and purified the gold, silver, and precious stones.

As Paul wrote to Timothy, his son in the faith, "All who desire to live godly in Christ Jesus will be persecuted" (2 Tim. 3:12). And Jesus had said:

Blessed are those who have been persecuted for the sake of righteousness, for theirs is the kingdom of heaven. Blessed are you when men cast insults at you, and persecute you, and say all kinds of evil against you falsely, on account of Me. Rejoice, and be glad, for your reward in heaven is great, for so they persecuted the prophets who were before you. (Matt. 5:10–12)

Persecution has a way of stripping away all the facades and pretenses, in order to reduce our faith and our life to what we truly believe and hold essential. The truth of the gospel *is* more important than this life. As a testimony to this, every one of the original twelve apostles, with the possible exception of John, died a martyr's death. The following accounts of their deaths were condensed from *Fox's Book of Martyrs*[1] and the writings of Jerome, Clement, and other early church fathers. These accounts are traditions passed down rather than eyewitness reports, but they are corroborated by so many it is likely that they are fairly accurate.

THE MARTYRDOM OF THE APOSTLES

After the martyrdom of Stephen, the next leader put to death was **James, the brother of John.** According to Clement, when James was brought to the tribunal seat, his chief accuser was so moved by remorse that he confessed Christ himself, and both men were sentenced to death. On the way to the place of execution, the former accuser asked James to forgive him for what he had done. James paused, then replied, "Peace be to you, brother," and kissed him. They were beheaded together in A.D. 36.

Thomas reportedly preached to the Parthians, Medians, Persians, Carmanians, Hyrcanians, Bactrians, and Magians. In Calamina, a city of India, he was slain with an arrow.

Simon, brother to Jude and James the younger and the son of Mary Cleopas and Alpheus, became the bishop of Jerusalem after James. He was crucified in Egypt during the reign of Emperor Trajan.

Simon the apostle, called Cananeus and Zelotes, preached in Mauritania, Africa, and Britain, where he was crucified.

Mark, the evangelist and first bishop of Alexandria, preached the gospel in Egypt. He was seized when Trajan was emperor and drawn with ropes, which pulled all his joints out of their sockets. Then he was set on fire.

Bartholomew reportedly preached in India and is said to have translated the gospel of Matthew into their language. In Albinopolis, a city of greater Armenia, he was beaten with staffs, crucified, and beheaded.

Andrew, Peter's brother, was crucified by Aegeas, a Roman governor, in the city of Sebastopolis. Andrew had brought so many to faith in Christ that the governor came to the province to compel the new Christians to sacrifice to idols and renounce the faith. Andrew challenged Aegeas to his face, told him to renounce his false gods and idols, and declared that the gods and idols of the Romans were not gods but devils and the enemies of mankind. In a rage, the proconsul ordered Andrew not to teach and preach, and warned him that if he did he would be fastened to a cross. Andrew replied, "I would not have preached the honor and glory of the cross, if I feared the death of the cross." He was immediately condemned.

As Andrew was taken to the place of his execution, he saw the cross in the distance and cried out, "O cross, most welcome and long looked for! With a willing mind, joyfully and desirously, I come to thee, being the scholar of Him which did hang on thee: because I have always been thy lover, and have coveted to embrace thee."

Matthew, also called Levi, preached in Ethiopia and Egypt. Hircanus, the king, had him run through with a spear.

Philip, the apostle, after he had preached the Word to some of the most barbarous nations of the time, was crucified and stoned in Heliopolis, a city of Phrygia.

James, thought to have been the brother of the Lord, was esteemed by all Jerusalem for his righteousness, being called "James the Just." When many of the chief men of the city believed, the scribes and Pharisees ordered James to stop proclaiming Jesus as the Messiah. During the Passover, they carried him to a battlement on the temple from which he could address the crowds below. When he began testifying that Jesus was the Christ who was sitting at the right hand of the Father, James was thrown from the top. He did not die immediately but struggled to his knees to pray for his persecutors. They rushed down and began to stone him. As Stephen had done before him, he continued his praying until he died.

Peter was preaching in Rome when he was urged to flee the city because Nero wanted to put him to death. As he was leaving through a gate, he saw a vision of the Lord coming to meet him. Falling to worship Him, Peter asked the Lord where He was going, and He responded that He had come to be crucified again. Peter understood that this meant it was his time to follow his Lord in death, and he returned to the city. When captured, Peter asked to be crucified upside down because he was not worthy to be crucified in the same manner as the Lord. His request was granted.

Paul, the apostle, was also martyred by Nero. Nero sent two of his own esquires, Ferega and Parthemius, to Paul with the declaration of his sentence of death. Paul prayed for them at their request and told them that they would believe and be baptized at his sepulcher. He was then taken out of the city and beheaded. The two esquires believed.

The persecution ceased under the emperor Vespasian, but began again under Domitian, the brother of Titus. In this persecution, the apostle **John** was exiled to the island of Patmos. After the death of Domitian, John was released. He then went to Ephesus, where he sat as an elder to the churches and wrote his gospel until the time of Trajan. There are accounts of John's ministry continuing until he reached the age of one hundred.

There are also several accounts of unsuccessful attempts by the Romans to kill John. In one instance before his exile to Patmos, he was boiled in oil without effect. Because there is no account of his death, some wonder about the Lord's statement to Peter concerning John:

> Peter therefore seeing him said to Jesus, "Lord, and what about this man?" Jesus said to him, "If I want him to remain until I come, what is that to you? You follow Me!" This saying therefore went out among the brethren that that disciple would not die; yet Jesus did not say to him that he would not die, but only, "If I want him to remain until I come, what is that to you?" (John 21:21–23)

It was obviously a blow for the young church to see her leaders put to death. Even so, she did not waver but continued to spread the gospel and grow stronger. Seeing that killing the leaders could not stop Christianity, the Romans then turned to a general persecution against all who called on the name of the Lord. In some cities it was reported that thousands were put to death every day. At times even the Roman officials were appalled at the slaughter, commenting that the Christians had done nothing to deserve such fierce persecution. With some intermissions, the persecutions continued until the year 311, and in the most eastern districts under the control of Maximin, until 313. Ultimately, persecution proved that Christianity was unconquerable.

Scripture says, "Precious in the sight of the Lord is the death of His godly ones" (Ps. 116:15). The apostle Paul frequently spoke of both the inevitability of persecution and the benefits that it would bring:

> But remember the former days, when, after being enlightened, you endured a great conflict of sufferings, partly, by being made a public spectacle through reproaches and tribulations, and partly by becoming sharers with those who were so treated. For you showed sympathy to the prisoners, and accepted joyfully the seizure of your property, knowing that you have for yourselves a better possession and an abiding one. Therefore, do not throw away your confidence, which has a great reward. For you have need of endurance, so that when you have done the will of God, you may receive what was promised. (Heb. 10:32–36)

Throughout much of the world today, Christians are under the continual threat of official government-endorsed or led persecution. During the past ten years, Christianity has experienced the greatest percentage of growth in nations where the persecution is the worst. In most of the world, Christianity is under assault—yet some estimates are that as many as 400,000 people per day are being saved!

Christianity is now growing three times faster than any other religion in the world, and even faster than the population in some countries. It is estimated that one-third of all the people who have come to Christ throughout church history have been saved during the past ten years! It can be said of Christianity as it was said of Israel, "The more they afflicted them, the more they multiplied" (Ex. 1:12).

When viewing the procession of Christians through history, it is apparent that persecution is the "normal" state of people whose faith is genuine. True Christianity has *always* been an affront and a threat to those who live by the pattern of this present evil world and those professing Christians who have compromised with the world. This should never be a shock or a discouragement to us; in fact, we should be more concerned when we are *not* being persecuted. The absence of persecution can be a sign that we are not really living godly lives in Christ Jesus and are therefore not a threat to the powers of darkness.

9

The Legacy of Constantine
A Blending of Church and State

No one in the Roman world had ever seen a faith like that of the early Christians. The church was a nation within the nations with a culture of its own. In spite of the almost continuous persecution by the most powerful forces on earth, the church continued to expand. Christians further astonished their enemies by returning good for evil and being so given to hospitality and caring for each other that very few of their people ever suffered want. When fathers or mothers were lost to the persecution, even total strangers would raise the orphaned children as if they were their own. Soon this subculture of faith was stronger in fabric than the mighty Roman Empire itself. As the empire began to unravel because of the corruption and ambition of its leaders, Christianity started to be perceived as possibly the only thread holding the Roman Empire together.

In A.D. 313, the Roman Empire's official persecution of Christians suddenly stopped. Then news spread abroad that Emperor Constantine himself claimed to be a Christian. To understand this radical change, we need to go back to 306, when Constantine became emperor of Rome.

This was a period of continuous civil war as several different claimants fought for control of the Roman Empire. Constantine sensed that his campaign against Maxentius, one of the contenders, would be decisive in who would be the sole ruler of the empire. The armies of the two enemies met at the Mulvian Bridge over the Tiber River near Rome.

Constantine knew that he needed divine assistance to win this battle. Rumors said that he was already sympathetic toward Christianity because his wife, Fauta, had converted to this faith. Constantine prayed for help, and God sent him a vision of a cross of light, bearing the inscription *"in hoc signo vinces"* (in this sign you will be victorious).

Constantine related that he also had a dream the same night. In the dream "the Christ of God" appeared to him with the same sign he had seen in the heavens and commanded him to make a likeness of that sign and use it as a safeguard in all engagements with his enemies. At dawn the next day, Constantine rose and communicated his dream to his comrades. Then he called together craftsmen and described the sign to them so they could reproduce it in gold and precious stones.

On October 28, 312, Constantine was victorious in the Battle of Mulvian Bridge. Afterward, he officially converted to Christianity and ordered the symbol of his Savior's name (the intersection of the Greek letters *chi* and *rho*) to represent his army.[1]

An understanding of Emperor Constantine's conversion and subsequent influence over the church is essential for having anything more than a superficial understanding of our world today. These influences are still having a major impact in religion, philosophy, and government.

THE MARRIAGE OF CHURCH AND STATE

Many historians have doubted Constantine's conversion. The popular Protestant position is that he simply viewed the seemingly indestructible Christian faith as the only method to bind his fast-crumbling empire together. Others believe that he was truly converted but that he was ignorant of the most important principles of the faith and wrongly used his influence as emperor to steer the church into the spiritual quagmire of the Dark Ages, even though he may have had good intentions. Of course, the Roman Catholic position is that his conversion was real and that his influence steered the church into its "golden age," when it was able to dominate the life, culture, and governments of much of the known world.

Whether or not Constantine was truly converted will probably be debated until Judgment Day. There is merit to both sides of this argument. My personal opinion is that if he was not converted at first, the influence of Christian teaching did change him, and I believe that he sought to use his influence as emperor to help the church as much as he tried to use the church to help the Roman Empire. As emperor it is understandable that he would use his power the way that he did, and that he would seek to institute some of the changes in church government. However, whether with good intentions or bad, these changes devastated the essential spiritual nature of the church. They also opened the door for some of the most diabolical influences, which are still causing division in the church, and the perversion of the church's witness to the world.

Many of the great debates of our time, such as the relationship between church and state, are rooted in the consequences of Constantine's influence in the church. To this day, Protestants, Catholics, and Evangelicals alike still grapple with the questions concerning the boundaries of the church's relationship to civil governments, whether hostile or friendly. Until A.D. 313 the church had never enjoyed even the friendship of a civil government, much less union with one. The basic teaching of the apostles was that Christians were to respect and obey governments but also to expect persecution from them. The Lord had said that His kingdom was not of this world, so there were no specific teachings or even a paradigm for understanding what Christians were to do if a government wanted to unite with the church. However, many biblical exhortations said that Christians were not to love the world or the things of the world and were not to be yoked together with unbelievers. It is unquestionable that both of these happened on a massive scale because of the influences of Constantine.

The simplest solution to this question of joining with earthly governments was to say, with all due respect, "No." The church had always been open for government leaders to join the assembly of faith, but to be joined to the powers of the present age in a relationship was a violation of her betrothal to the Lord. Jesus alone was to be the Head of the church and to give this position to any man, even an emperor, was to reject Jesus. However, in the intensity of the times, even the clearest biblical truths can become blurred. Rejecting the overtures of the emperor was not so easy to do after the intense persecutions the church had endured.

UNITY BY COERCION

The response of most influential church leaders was to unite with the Roman government because of the seemingly immense possibilities for Christianizing the world, even though some protested that this union was in conflict with the basic principles of Christianity. Constantine's obvious sincerity in promoting Christianity won over many of the first critics of this union, but not all. Soon the protesters were removed from positions of authority in the church, and a subtle persecution arose against them. Then Constantine did not delay in bestowing his greatest favors on the churches that embraced his leadership. Almost immediately the leaders of the church, who just recently had been hunted like animals, were held in high esteem. Soon government positions of influence, power, and prestige were offered to them.

In 321 all secular business was prohibited on the first day of the week to honor what had become the primary day of meeting for Christians. Even so, this day was decreed to be "the sacred day of the sun," instead of the Lord's day (thus the name given to it was Sunday). This compromise appeased many of the heathens in the empire but stunned Christians. Then Constantine decreed freedom of religion throughout the empire, writing, "Let no one molest another in this matter, but let every one be free to follow the bias of his own mind." Finally, he founded the city of Constantinople as a "capital dedicated to the Christian religion."

Without question, Constantine's conversion marked the most dramatic change the Christian faith has ever experienced. It was a change so swift and profound that Christians had difficulty understanding what it meant, much less how to navigate through the new spiritual landscape.

Author Wallis, in his *Revival and Recovery,* expresses his view of this union between church and state: "Instead of suffering the persecution of the state, the church now enjoyed the patronage of the state. She was taken off guard. The people of God, who had been watchful, prayerful, and faithful in the time of opposition were now lulled into a false sense of security."

As Edwin Orr said, "It is one thing for the ship to be in the sea, but a different matter when the sea gets into the ship!" Imperial favor brought the world into the church, and what Satan had failed to do by persecution he achieved by patronage.

From the beginning it was obvious that Constantine's favor toward the church meant favor toward those who embraced and supported him. He personally took the theological positions of Christian leaders who were friendly to him. At first the emperor sought to persuade those with differing views and to bring harmony to the doctrinal factions within the church. For this reason, he called the great Council of Nicea, which brought together the primary Christian leaders. This was certainly a noble endeavor, even if it was colored by his coinciding desire to use it to unify his crumbling empire.

A serious and lasting problem arose when Constantine took a position on what he considered to be the truth on the major issues discussed at Nicea, and then decreed that these issues, such as the Nicene Creed, would be the accepted position of the church, which the state would recognize. Believing this creed to be a reasonable statement of faith, Constantine banished any bishop who refused to sign the creed or who opposed the emperor's peace measures. Thus began the first official persecution of Christians by Christians.

Through this process Constantine had become the de facto head of the church. He changed or laid the foundation for changes in both church doctrine and government. The most devastating change of all was that men were now compelled to become Christians because of the political and other worldly opportunities that it afforded rather than conviction by the Holy Spirit. The might and power of the Roman Empire was enlisted as a much easier means to cause men to bow their knees, not to the truth, but to the official leaders of the church.

SUPERSTITION REPLACES TRUTH

Although he had assumed the position of a Christian emperor, Constantine did not receive baptism until just before his death in 337. This was done because of his superstitious belief that baptism was a means of magical absolution, which of course, replaced the Cross. He felt that this absolution would be received more safely near the end of life, when there was little time left for new sins. Eusebius, the first church historian and bishop who baptized the emperor, wrote that Constantine was "firmly believing that whatever sins he had committed as a mortal man, his soul would be purified from them through the efficacy of the mysterious words and the salutary waters of baptism."

This seems typical of the kind of superstition and ignorance that Constantine's leadership was to release into the church, which would dominate it for centuries to come. Decisions were based on political expediency instead of biblical truth. Doctrines that would dictate the course of the church for more than a thousand years were based on the obscure writings of long-dead former church leaders instead of Scripture.

REMOVING THE SCRIPTURES

The Scriptures are the most powerful weapon against evil the world has ever known. It is through them that the truth of God's redemption through the cross of Jesus is revealed. Because the Scriptures were the greatest threat to the diabolical superstitions that were gaining an increasing dominance over the official Christian religion, the church itself was to actually wage war against the sacred writings. This, of course, is certain proof of apostasy.

Because those who read the Scriptures would easily see the contradictions between the emerging church doctrines and those of the apostles, soon only church officials were allowed to possess the Scriptures or read them. It was promoted that this was necessary because the common people did not have the capacity to understand them. This opened the door into the church for the single most powerful tool that Satan has ever had at his disposal—ignorance.

As the Lord declared in Hosea 4:6, "My people are destroyed for lack of knowledge." Ignorance is darkness, and that is the dwelling place of Satan. During this period literacy was uncommon, except among the Jews, and books almost nonexistent. The Bible was kept under lock and key by the Roman clergy, and when it was read to the populace it was read in Latin, which few if any of the common people understood. Soon it became a crime punishable by death for any unauthorized person to be caught with the Bible. For a time it was even difficult for a priest to get such authorization.

This policy was contrary to the teachings of the Lord Jesus Himself. As we read in Luke 10:21: "At that very time He rejoiced greatly in the Holy Spirit, and said, 'I praise Thee, O Father, Lord of heaven and earth, that Thou didst hide these things from the wise and intelligent and didst reveal them to babes. Yes, Father, for thus it was well-pleasing in Thy sight.'"

The Greek word that is translated *rejoiced* here is *agalliao* (ag-al-lee-AH-o), which means "to jump for joy, to express exceeding joy." The inference is that such a joy is near to uncontrollable ecstasy. The Lord was not just a little bit happy that "babes" could understand the truths of the kingdom—He was ecstatic. According to the Lord's own statement, a humble baby will discern God's truth before the wise and intelligent. This is not to infer that wisdom and intelligence are not to be sought, but we must not take pride in our own wisdom and intelligence, or use them to displace our dependence on the Holy Spirit to lead us to the truth.

Since the first century there has been a continuing battle between the "wise and intelligent" and the understanding of the "spiritual babes." However, we should never consider ignorance a blessing. Peter warned early Christians about this when he discussed the way some were misinterpreting Paul's writings in 2 Peter 3:15–16:

And regard the patience of our Lord to be salvation; just as also our beloved brother Paul, according to the wisdom given him, wrote to you, as also in all his letters, speaking in them of these things, in which are some things hard to understand, which the untaught and unstable distort, as they do also the rest of the Scriptures, to their own destruction.

Ignorance will always be an enemy of the truth. The untaught and unstable are likely to distort the Scriptures. However, the remedy for this is not to hide the Scriptures from the people but to teach them, which will help them become stable. We must also keep in mind that, regardless of how much knowledge we have, we should always approach the Scriptures with the humility of a child, whose basic characteristic is to be teachable. When we cease to be teachable, we cease to be disciples.

In Constantine's drive to establish unity in the church he released forces that made official Christianity the religion of ignorance. He did this by shutting off debate to all but his views of what Christianity was to be like. Very little attention, or reference, was given to Scripture, but to what desperate human minds perceived to be best able to achieve this unity.

Finally Constantine passed a law that no one should take the office of a teacher without a permit from the government, thus establishing imperial, bureaucratic control of schools and closing this vocation to any Christians who were not loyal to him. In this way his view of Christianity was stamped upon the future generation of intellectuals and officials. Opposing views were eliminated by not being available to anyone who wanted an accredited education, which was required for positions within the government or the church.

THE TEST OF ABUNDANCE

When Jesus walked the earth, He never compelled men to accept Him, or His teachings, by pressure or force. He did not want men to accept Him for any other reason than because they loved God and loved the truth. He allowed His church to suffer continual persecution as a means to purify His people's motives and character. Not all passed this test, but many did and became worthy to reign with Him as members of His own household. However, just as the apostle Paul learned to remain steadfast whether he had much or little (Phil. 4:12), the church also needed to pass the test of keeping the faith and character when it flourished. Unfortunately, very few passed this exam.

As stated, the Lord did not put the Tree of the Knowledge of Good and Evil in the Garden to cause Adam and Eve to stumble, but so they could prove their love and obedience to Him. There could be no true obedience from the heart unless there was the freedom to disobey. Like the bride of the first Adam, the church, the bride of the "last Adam," would be offered the fruit from the deadly tree. Like Eve, she ate. The church that was called to be the pure, chaste virgin espoused to Christ not only had an affair with the Roman Empire, she married it. The church and state became so merged and intertwined that the distinctions of each were to become almost completely blurred.

Constantine was prone to seek a consensus with the bishops, at least those who were favorable to him, but subsequent emperors asserted their own will in ecclesiastical matters, even to the point of issuing decrees in their own name on questions of dogma. The church that had been the light of the world was now easily used by Satan to lead to a most terrible age of spiritual darkness, aptly referred to by historians as "the Dark Ages." Considering the effects of these dark times, it is clear why the founding fathers of the United States were so adamant in maintaining a separation between church and state. To find the proper balance in this has been a running debate and, at times, conflict, but the principle itself is truly for the protection of everyone.

TWO MANDATES

The Scriptures teach that both the church and state have mandates from God. These mandates are different and were always intended to be distinct. Whenever the state has tried to fulfill the mandate given to the church, tyranny has always been the result. Whenever the church has tried to fulfill the mandate given to the state, tyranny has also been the result. Even so, the church and state do not have to be enemies—and should be friends—but the union of the two is strictly forbidden, as the church is to be united to Christ alone.

The church has a power much greater than the state because it is the custodian of the truth that can set men free, change their hearts and character, and lead to eternal life. This is the power of the Holy Spirit to convict us of sin, lead us to truth, and testify of Jesus, who is the consummation of all truth. When the church seeks to compel men to accept truth by force or law, it may compel men to do what is wanted, but it will not change their hearts.

In the New York City blackout of 1977, people robbed and plundered without restraint until the lights came back on. They did this because the light that controlled them was external. If the light had been in their hearts, they would have behaved rightly, regardless of whether the streetlights were on or not. It is the church's job to impart that light so men will do what is right even when no one is looking. It is the job of the state to keep the lights on to control the behavior of those who do not have that light in their hearts.

The laws of the state cannot change or save a single soul, but they can help to restrain corruption and keep the peace. A nation that encourages the fear of the Lord and is devoted to justice will prosper. However, the state does not have the authority from God to dictate policy in matters of doctrine or faith in the church. Whenever government authorities have tried to do this, the result has been devastating for both the church and the state. It is in the best interest of both the church and state to have a relationship of mutual respect, which seeks the good and prosperity of the other without sacrificing the independence of either.

However, this separation is between the church and the state, not Christians and the state. It is important for Christians to participate in the responsibility of citizenship, and even seek public office when called to do so. It is also just as important that we do this as citizens, not as official representatives of the church. This does not mean that we do not do it to help preserve Christian morality, values, and even the interests of the church, but we must always keep in mind that the greatest power on earth is the power of the truth. And the greatest power over the earth is prayer. Prayer can accomplish much more than any congress or international tribunal, because prayer can move the hand of God.

When the church married Rome, all of the ways of Rome poured into the church, while the church had very little sanctifying effect upon Rome. The worldly ways of Rome quickly flooded the church in four primary ways:

1. *A multitude of unconverted men and women poured into the church.* This was fueled by the prospect of imperial favor and worldly promotion. Eusebius, the church historian and friend of Constantine, even decried "the scandalous hypocrisy of those who crept into the Church, and assumed the name and character of Christians." This almost immediately diluted the discipline in Christian morals, devotion to doctrinal truth, and even monotheistic faith as many brought their former gods with them. The attempt to "Christianize" these other gods led to an idolatrous veneration of Mary, the mother of Jesus, and the saints.

2. *The lure of the temporal eroded the devotion to the eternal purposes of God.* Bishops and other church officials suddenly found themselves being awarded great wealth, worldly honors, and power in exchange for their favors or endorsements. Soon it was said that the feasts of the bishops surpassed that of kings. In a candid acknowledgment of this, Gregory Nazianzen stated in his farewell address to the council at Constantinople, "The people seek now not priests, but rhetoricians; not pastors of souls, but managers of money; not those who offer with pure hearts, but powerful champions." Of course, the same could be said of many of our churches today.

3. *The leadership of the church ceased to be servants of their flocks and became their taskmasters.* In one generation the general leadership of the church turned from the ways Jesus led to the ways of Rome, and a new hierarchy rose within the church that was built on pride and subservience.

4. *Religious freedom was abandoned.* Increasingly severe penalties were levied upon those who presumed to depart in even minor ways from the

dogma and practices of the official church. In Scripture excommunication is the most extreme penalty the church is authorized to levy. In its marriage with the state the church quickly began to employ secular means to enforce its will on believers, and then on the general population. Soon teaching any doctrine that was not in agreement with the official church position was branded heresy and led to banishment, then prison, and finally the ultimate penalty—death. For a period of centuries even to be caught with a Bible without authorization from church authorities was an offense punishable by both torture and death.

The writings of Augustine were used to justify the official church's drive to establish the kingdom of God on earth by might and power rather than by the Spirit. Augustine had penned one of the most concise statements concerning the means of power that the church was called to use when he wrote: "Nothing conquers but truth; the victory of truth is love." However, later in his life he publicly changed his opinion when he failed to convert the Donatists by logic, and saw them subdued by the power of an imperial edict. He then wrote:

> Originally my opinion was, that no one should be coerced into the unity of Christ, that we must act only by words, fight only by arguments, and prevail by force of reason, lest we should have those whom we knew as avowed heretics feigning themselves to be Catholics. But this opinion of mine was overcome, not by the words of those who controverted (challenged) it, but by the conclusive instances to which they could point.

These "conclusive instances" were the subjection of the Donatists by imperial force.

As renowned church historian Henry C. Sheldon wrote:

> This revised theory was supported by Augustine with unhesitating zeal. Persecution, he argued, gains its character from its source and aim. For the good to persecute the wicked in order to make them good, serves a beneficent end. In the former age, Christianity suffered persecution from the ungodly; now it is her prerogative. A theory was asserted and

founded by Augustine, which, although ameliorated in practice by his pious and benevolent disposition, contained, nevertheless, the germ of the whole system of spiritual despotism, intolerance, and persecution, even to the tribunal of the Inquisition.

The same evil deception that resulted in the torture and deaths of millions who refused to bow the knee to the official church of the Middle Ages can be found at the root of authoritarian church leadership that has wounded so many in our own generation. The sources of other vices and corruption are the same, whether they are used to destroy a great spiritual movement or a home prayer group. If we do not understand the schemes of the enemy, we will continue to be subject to them.

Likewise, victories over these evils have been accomplished by great souls from among our spiritual ancestors. In each generation, as the enemy came in like a flood, the Lord would raise up those who would become a standard against it. The recognition of sound, biblical truth sets us free. Continuing to walk in this truth keeps us free.

Many of the present doctrines and practices of even the most recent Christian movements still have their roots more in Rome than in Jerusalem or Antioch. Some of these are rather harmless, and some are great hindrances to further spiritual advancement—the preparation of the bride for the coming King and her witness to the world of His return. We can weigh these doctrines and practices against the Scriptures and view them in history to recognize their fruit.

10

Our Fall from Grace

Current Practices That Have Come from Rome

THE MIDDLE AGES ARE THE DARKEST AND MOST difficult period of church history. However, as I stated earlier, it is not possible to understand fully where the church, and indeed the world, is today without having a general understanding of this period. Even so, this period is a spiritual minefield. You do not wander around in a minefield. You carefully move through it as quickly as possible, and that is what I intend to do.

Before we proceed I want you to know that I have spent many years digging in this minefield. I did not come out without injuries, but I now know where many of the mines are hidden. My goal is to help you navigate through this period without any spiritual wounds; therefore, I want to interject into this chapter where some of them are.

THE MAP

The Lord was gracious to give us a map through this period, since the great events of this time were prophesied in both the Old and New

Testaments, along with the reasons that they had to happen. Our primary goal is to gain understanding, not just knowledge of the facts. Therefore, in this chapter we will look at some of these prophecies and their fulfillment.

First, we must understand why the book of Revelation, which is the "revelation of Jesus Christ," contains so much about the Antichrist. The Antichrist is also called the "man of sin" in Scripture because he is the personification of the sin of man. When we view the evils of the Antichrist, we see the true nature of every man who is not transformed by the saving power of the Cross. In a sense, *the man of sin is all of us without Christ.* There is so much contained about him in the "revelation of Jesus Christ" because the Antichrist shows us how desperately the world needs Christ.

As the apostle John wrote in 1 John 4:3, the spirit of the Antichrist was present in the first century and thereafter. Each antichrist is a revelation of the increasing depravity of man who tries to live apart from Christ. However, some of the most diabolical antichrist figures in history lived during the Middle Ages, and they did their evil in the name of Christ! Just as was prophesied, this man, or system of men, took its seat in the very temple of God, the church, and declared itself to be God (see 2 Thess. 2:1–4).

Some of you may have already recoiled at the sight of this huge mine. Am I calling the Roman Catholic Church during this time the Antichrist? No, though that was the position of the Reformers. However, as we study this period we must conclude that just as Paul wrote to the Thessalonians, the antichrist spirit did for a time take its seat *in* the "temple of God," the church, but it was not the church itself.

The antichrist spirit has seldom come in blatant opposition to Christ but rather as a substitute for Him. This happened at times in the Roman Catholic Church during the Middle Ages, and it has happened, to some degree, in almost every church movement since. That is why we must understand it. Not to point a finger at the Roman Church, but to identify the spirit that still seeks entry into our churches today.

At times in history this impostor has seemed to be in almost total control of the church. Then there is a battle against it, the false spirit is revealed and removed to some degree—until later when it comes back stronger and more deceitful than ever. This cycle will obviously continue until the end. As we see in the Scriptures, we can expect the ultimate evil—the real Antichrist—to be revealed then. However, the church's greatest glory will also be at the end of time, as the bride of Christ is made pure and spotless. This purity will probably come, at least to some degree, by the conflict of the times.

But how can both of these events, the purifying of the church and the revealing of the man of sin in the church, happen at once? This is an understanding that we must have.

THE TREE OF GOOD AND EVIL

To understand almost any spiritual principle, we must understand its foundation. We must therefore understand that since man partook of the Tree of the Knowledge of Good and Evil both of these forces have existed within us, and both struggle for control. The good from this Tree is a pseudo-good, not reaching for God but for self-righteousness or self-redemption. Therefore the "good" side of this tree is just as deadly as the "evil." No one in this struggle can understand this until the person finds the Tree of Life, which is Christ. Therefore, our quest through history is not just for "the good in man" but for what God does through men.

There is some good in the worst of people, and some evil in the best of them. Some church leaders in the Middle Ages promulgated the most diabolical deeds but also some of the kindest and most generous.

Is this not what happened to Peter? After Jesus congratulated him for receiving the revelation that Jesus was the Christ straight from above, He rebuked Peter for accepting influence straight from hell. What he spoke, Jesus said, came straight from Satan (see Matt. 16:15–23). If it happened to Peter, it could happen to any of us.

Let us also keep in mind that during times of war and conflict all governments become paranoid. During war, treason is usually punished with death. The greater a nation's jeopardy, the more this paranoia grows. In severe crisis even perceived or suspected treason is met with swift death, with little or no jurisprudence. This paranoia came upon the

Roman Empire, and the state church of Rome, and it led to some of the greatest human cruelty.

As we study this terrible period for the church, we must keep in mind that during this time Christendom was threatened by powerful enemies—without and within—and the most cruel reprisals were committed against those suspected of heresy. Heresy does not just mean to understand a doctrine wrongly but to cause division. Those who caused division from within were viewed as greater enemies than the enemies outside. This is hard to understand for many of us who live in relative peace, but those who have experienced the most terrible judgment of all—war—will tend to be more understanding. During wartime many casualties come from "friendly fire" because in the heat of battle you sometimes mistake your friends for your enemies.

We judge unrighteously when we think we are any better than our ancestors. The revelation of this sin is the revelation of the sin that is in all men, you and me included. Had we been in their place, it is very unlikely that we would have done any better. We do not want to look at this history to condemn those of this period, or the historic institutions that arose through them, but rather to humble ourselves and pray for mercy so that we don't repeat their errors. Until we take a hard look at what happened here, and how the same things can happen in the smallest congregation, if only to a lesser degree, we will not be able to stop the perpetuation of these unnecessary spiritual wars.

I learned most of what you are about to read during the first five years of my Christian walk, which began thirty years ago. As I studied, I became outraged, then bitter, and finally proud because of my knowledge. Then I went on to commit mistakes that were rooted in the very same evils when I was asked to pastor a small congregation. Of course, I did not kill anyone, but the Lord said that if we were angry with a brother, we were guilty of murder. I went beyond anger. I did all I could to kill my adversaries' reputations and to abolish those who disagreed with me from the fellowship of the church. Finally I realized that if my anger had been in the hands of one with more power, that power would have been used to destroy those whom I perceived to be my greatest threats.

We must recognize that fear, and especially the extreme fear of paranoia, are the most deadly enemies of the church and of truth. There are many today who promote extreme fears, which lead to extreme accusations, against fellow Christians. Some of these have a significant influence in the church and are used to do more damage than all of the cults combined. However, I went through a period when the same things gripped me, so I am not trying to cast a stone at any fellow believers who are now so bound by the enemy. This revelation about myself caused me to lay down the ministry and go through seven years of soul-searching in a spiritual wilderness. I did not even do that successfully, and in some ways I felt I came out of this wandering no better than I went in. Then the Lord had mercy and showed me the way to my deliverance. He simply told me to agree with my accuser! Now, when an accuser comes to tell me how terrible I am, I quickly agree. I know that there is no good thing in me, that is, in my flesh. However, my righteousness is in the cross of Jesus Christ. Only His cross could deliver me from this "body of death." We are all carrying around the same baggage, but we also have the same escape—simply abiding in Christ. I have therefore determined not to consider any man my enemy, as we do not war against flesh and blood.

As we proceed into these dark times, we will also see the glory of the Lord. Even so, our main goal is not just to see the darkness or the glory then, but now. How does the same darkness have a grip on our lives? How do we behold the glory today of the One who is the same today as He was then? How can we displace the antichrist spirit that still manifests itself in our churches?

WE SEE IN PART

We must also keep in mind that looking back at history is sometimes as obscure as looking ahead into the future. There are as many different explanations, interpretations, and insights into the events of the Middle

Ages as there are historians who wrote about them. I studied many accounts of this period, from as many different perspectives as possible, and my understanding of them is a composite. Even so, I know I only see many of these events in part, and only understand them in part.

I am a Protestant, evangelical, Pentecostal/charismatic/Third Wave believer, who has learned to love and respect Catholics. However, I still consider many Catholic doctrines and practices to be in basic conflict with the Scriptures, and I do not expect ever to be able to embrace those doctrines. I am also very grateful for the Catholic leadership in standing against some of the great evils of our own times, such as abortion and communism.

Even though I try to be objective, I cannot presume that my perspective of history is uncolored by my background. I have studied a number of Roman Catholic histories and have found merit to some of their perspectives as well. I think they also contain insights that are badly needed by anyone who seeks to have an accurate perspective of history. However, the conclusions I drew from my studies overall are generally the same as the most classical Protestant historians.

Someone might ask, "If you think Protestants are prone to make the same mistakes as Catholics, why do you embrace the classical Protestant view of history?" As the saying goes, "Just because someone is paranoid does not mean that someone isn't chasing him." Likewise, just because someone is judgmental and does the same things does not mean that his judgments are inaccurate. I have corroborated most of what I am sharing with secular and Catholic historians. However, I do not look at these as Catholic or Protestant mistakes, but as *our* mistakes. This man of sin, or *the sin of man*, has been revealed in the church, and it will continue to be until we, the church, understand that it is us—and we repent of it.

FUTURISTIC AND HISTORIC ESCHATOLOGY

Many of the events that we are about to study were prophesied in specific, accurate detail in Scripture. We will examine some of these prophecies and how Christian historians felt they were fulfilled. For those of you who have been brought up with the futuristic view of Bible prophecy, you are about to have some of your beliefs challenged. If you are afraid of this, please consider that fear never leads to truth. We must have more faith in the Holy Spirit to lead us into truth than we do in the devil to deceive us.

I, too, still hold to the futuristic view of many biblical prophecies. However, the futuristic view of some prophecies can only be held by those who have an almost complete ignorance of history, as they were so clearly fulfilled in history. Every book I have read on end-time prophecies that held to the futuristic view exclusively had glaring contradictions, or seriously twisted some Scriptures to make them fit. The same is true of those who seem to hold to an exclusively historic view of their fulfillment. It seems obvious that the truth is found in some combination of these two great prevailing views.

Even so, my reason for doing this study has never been just to find out what has been fulfilled, but why these things happened, or why they continue to happen. That is why there seems to be a need to fit both the historic and futuristic views together. Some of the prophecies seem to have been fulfilled repeatedly, almost with every new generation. For this reason, even the things that seem to have been fulfilled very specifically and accurately in history may yet be fulfilled again in the future.

With all this in mind, let us look at the church in the Middle Ages.

A GATE OF HELL OPENED

Paul made it clear that the Lord would not return until the apostasy came and the man of sin took his seat in the temple of God, displaying himself as being God (2 Thess. 2:3–10). Because the temple of God is no longer one made with hands, but the church, the early church fathers understood that this man of sin would seek to take his place in the church.

As the apostle Paul wrote, the mystery of lawlessness was already at work in his own time. In 2 Thessalonians 2:3 he boldly stated, "Let no one in any way deceive you, for it [the coming of the Lord] will not come unless the apostasy comes first." We must not be deceived into thinking that the Lord is about to come until we can clearly establish that the apostasy has come and the man of sin has been revealed.

Before continuing, let us carefully examine the text of 2 Thessalonians 2:3–10 so that we can understand why most of Protestant Christianity believed that it had been fulfilled:

> Let no one in any way deceive you, for it will not come unless the apostasy comes first, and the man of lawlessness is revealed, the son of destruction, who opposes and exalts himself above every so-called god or object of worship, so that he takes his seat in the temple of God, displaying himself as being God. Do you not remember that while I was still with you, I was telling you these things? And you know what restrains him now, so that in his time he may be revealed. For the mystery of lawlessness is already at work; only he who now restrains will do so until he is taken out of the way. And then that lawless one will be revealed whom the Lord will slay with the breath of His mouth and bring to an end by the appearance of His coming; that is, the one whose coming is in accord with the activity of Satan, with all power and signs and false wonders, and with all the deception of wickedness for those who perish, because they did not receive the love of the truth so as to be saved.

Before the Lord can come, the apostasy *and* the man of sin must come. Classical Protestant theology and eschatology state that both did. If that position is true, the Lord can return at any time. If it is not true, we must expect both a great apostasy and the man of sin. This is a basic issue that we need to settle to understand where we are now.

THE CLASSICAL PROTESTANT VIEW OF THE APOSTASY

The classical Protestant view is that the apostasy did come very soon after the death of the apostles in the first century. They believed that the apostles were the restraining force that Paul said would hold back the apostasy until they were taken out of the way (verse 7).

As we studied in previous chapters, the church endured centuries of almost continuous persecution. At the same time it had to battle subtle and deceptive doctrines that were constantly trying to seep into the church, which sometimes carried many believers into serious errors. Embattled within and without for centuries, as we just studied, the persecutions ended when Constantine claimed to become a Christian and Christianity was elevated to the state religion. The tables were turned so quickly that even the noblest leaders were left reeling, trying to figure out what was happening and what direction they should take. During this time of disorientation, the Roman emperor quickly stepped into the vacuum of leadership to give direction to the church. One of the ultimate questions that still separates Protestants and Catholics is, Who gave him this authority?

Constantine's conversion brought about such drastic change that some with opposing views considered him to be the man of sin who took his seat in the temple of God, the church. He was displaying himself as God, they said, by actually taking authority as the head of the church, which should only be given to Jesus. Regardless of whether he was the man of sin, from this point the flood of corruption that had perpetually assaulted the church increased to a tidal wave that crushed all remaining resistance.

As soon as Christianity was established as the state religion, it became fashionable to claim belief, then essential for political influence. As the authority of the church formed into a more rigid hierarchy, the leading positions soon attracted the most ruthless and ambitious political operatives, causing a veritable meltdown of the standards of truth and morality that had been held until this time.

When the church was persecuted, it was honorable to want to be a leader. Leaders were special targets of the persecution, and the life expectancy of elders was usually very short, which helped maintain a high degree of purity in their motives. When Christianity became the official religion of the state, positions of authority in the church were soon sold to the highest bidder because of their enormous power over both the government and commerce.

It was not long until the church rivaled the government as the true power over the empire. During this period, if a person was excommunicated from the state church, no one could hire him or do business with him, effectively banning the person from being able to buy, sell, or trade within the empire. At the time this was the equivalent of a death sentence.

When the church allowed imperial endorsement to determine first its doctrine, and then its leadership, a terrible corruption entered the church. This corruption would eventually erode and obscure even the most basic Christian truths, such as the Cross and the place of Christ as the Head of the church. Immediately the church began its descent into the Dark Ages, and the light of true Christianity was almost extinguished.

THE HARLOT CHURCH OF REVELATION?

First, imperial power established the state church. Over a relatively short period, however, the true seat of power shifted from the state to the church. From the beginning protesters preached vehemently, to the risk of their lives, that the bride of Christ was called to wait for her King who was "not of this world." They believed that this union between the church and state was spiritual adultery. This caused the church to become the power behind the throne, and she was now using both the wrong power and the wrong throne to gain influence for her message. Protesters saw this as the fulfillment of the prophecy in Revelation 17 about the great harlot who committed acts of immorality with the kings of the earth. They argued that this great harlot had to be some form of the church, as the church alone was betrothed to the Lord, and no earthly or secular system would be considered a harlot as they were from the world, and therefore already married to the world.

Let's look at a few of these verses to see why they felt that way. Revelation 17:9 states, "Here is the mind which has wisdom. The seven heads are seven mountains on which the woman sits." Because the city of Rome is built on seven mountains, it is believed that this specifically spoke of the Church of Rome. Almost the entire empire at the time when John wrote the book of Revelation referred to Rome as "the city on seven hills."

Then verse 18 states, "And the woman whom you saw is the great city, which reigns over the kings of the earth," which at the time was Rome. For more than twelve hundred years the church's political power was so great, no king could be crowned on the continent who did not submit himself to the church; therefore she did rule over the kings of the earth.

IDOLS IN THE TEMPLE

In the book of Revelation, the Lord warned the church of Thyatira: "But I have this against you, that you tolerate the woman Jezebel, who calls herself a prophetess, and she teaches and leads My bond-servants astray, so that they commit acts of immorality and eat things sacrificed to idols" (Rev. 2:20).

As Jezebel refers to the woman spoken of in 1 Kings who persecuted the true prophets and seduced Israel to worship idols, this could be attributed to the church. After Christianity became a state religion a flood of practices that must be considered idolatry were released into church services in an attempt to compel those of other religions to embrace the state religion. In his *Essay on the Development of Christian Doctrine,* Cardinal Newman, of the Roman Catholic Church, says:

> Confiding then in the power of Christianity to resist the infection of evil, and to transmute the very instruments and appendages of demon worship to an evangelical use . . . the rulers of the church were prepared, should the occasion arise, to adopt, to imitate or sanction the existing rites and customs of the populace, as well as the philosophy of the educated class.[1]

For example, most of the heathens throughout the Roman world worshiped some form of a fertility goddess. Church leaders took some of these popular rites and included them in the holiday established to celebrate the resurrection of Jesus. Even the name of this holiday was changed to Easter, which is believed to have derived from the name of the pagan god Ishtar.

As the general populace of the empire was used to having many deities, Christian saints were also elevated in stature and authority so that they became mediators with Christ, in clear contrast to 1 Timothy 2:5: "For there is one God, and one mediator also between God and men, the man Christ Jesus."

One of the most destructive practices that crept into the church was the substitution of rituals for reality, which took many forms, each of which seemed profoundly to undermine the greatest truths of the biblical gospel.

RITUALS REPLACE TRUTH

Instead of Communion being a "remembrance of the Lord," as a means of communing with Him, the ritual itself began to be the supposed source of power. Then the doctrine was formulated that the bread and wine actually became the literal body and blood of the Lord after a priest recited a special incantation over it. This became known as "transubstantiation."

As the doctrine of transubstantiation grew, it was taught that the sacrifice of Jesus was made for the sin of Adam, and that for the forgiveness of their sins, the faithful had to partake of this ritual, which only an authorized priest could offer. In this way the priest offered Christ anew for each sin. This doctrine became the special target of a large section of the Reformation, since this put the priest in the place of Christ as mediator. Many Reformers actually believed this doctrine was "the abomination of desolation," or as it could have been literally translated, "the abomination that desolates."

Transubstantiation made the ritual of Communion a "substitution for the cross of Christ," and presumed the authority of a mere man to offer up Christ again, both of which many of the Reformers considered ultimate abominations. They also believed that this one doctrine did the most to desolate the church by removing the power of the cross from the life of the individual and instead putting a man in the place of Christ to forgive daily sins, which blatantly contradicts Hebrews 7:25–28:

Hence, also, He [Christ] is able to save forever those who draw near to God through Him, since He always lives to make intercession for them.

For it was fitting that we should have such a high priest, holy, innocent, undefiled, separated from sinners and exalted above the heavens; who does not need daily, like those high priests, to offer up sacrifices, first for His own sins, and then for the sins of the people, because this *He did once for all* when He offered up Himself. For the Law appoints men as high priests who are weak, but the word of the oath, which came after the Law, appoints a Son, made perfect forever. (emphasis added)

When used properly to highlight and emphasize important truths, Christian rituals do have a powerful place in the lives of believers. However, it does not do us any good to *take* Communion if we do not *have* communion with the Lord and His body, the church.

It should be noted that some of the most effective Reformers, such as Martin Luther, continued to embrace the doctrine of transubstantiation. Others who rejected this doctrine sometimes became overly committed to other rituals that displaced Christian truths. Even so, possibly the greatest agitation for all non-Catholic Christians was for the pope to be proclaimed the "head of the church," which was the designation of Christ Himself.

THE ANTICHRIST?

During the Middle Ages, Catholic writers, theologians, and some popes actually gave the pope all of the titles, and in some cases even the attributes, of Christ Himself. This caused many to proclaim the papacy (the office of the pope) to be *the* Antichrist, *the* man of sin, of Bible prophecy. Virtually all of the prophecies in Scripture seemingly fit what this system had become, not only in doctrine but also in practice. The ruthless persecutions of the Roman Church against heretics during the Middle Ages has been estimated to have claimed as many as fifty million lives.

This extraordinary number is verified in *Halley's Bible Handbook*, which states, "Historians estimate that in the Middle Ages and Early Reformation Era, more than 50,000,000 martyrs perished" under the persecutions perpetrated by the Church of Rome.[2] A similar number is collaborated by many secular and church historians. When the stories of these persecutions are studied it seems likely that they are not inflated but may actually be conservative.

Concerning this period, Professor Alfred Baudrillart, rector of the Catholic Institute of Paris, acknowledged:

> The Catholic Church is a respecter of conscience and liberty . . . She has, and loudly proclaims that she has, a "horror of blood." Nevertheless when confronted by heresy, she does not content herself with persuasion; arguments of an intellectual and moral order appear to her as insufficient, and she has recourse to force, to corporal punishment, to torture. She creates tribunals like those of the Inquisition, she calls the laws of the state to her aid, if necessary she encourages a crusade, or a religious war, and all her "horror of blood" practically culminates in urging the secular power to shed it, which proceeding is almost more odious—for it is less frank than shedding it herself. Especially did she act thus in the sixteenth century with regard to the Protestants. Not content to reform morally, to preach by example, to convert people by eloquent and holy missionaries, she lit in Italy, in the Low Countries and above all in Spain, the funeral piles of Inquisition. In France under Francis I and Henry II, in England under Mary Tudor, she tortured the heretics, while in both France and Germany during the second half of the sixteenth and first half of the seventeenth century if she did not actually begin, she at any rate encouraged and actively aided the religious wars.[3]

The most terrible tyrants of modern times cannot be compared to the horrors that faced those who refused to bow the knee to them during these times. Human imagination was pressed to its limits in devising more horrendous tortures for those considered heretics, which was anyone who did not fully embrace the dogma and authority of the Church of Rome. To be burned at the stake was soon one of the fastest and easiest ways to die.

At the peak of the Inquisitions (the tribunals established for weeding out heresy in Christian Europe), the New World was discovered. Many of the colonists who first came to America were fleeing religious persecution in Europe. Protestants considered this immigration to be the fulfillment of Revelation 12:13–16:

> And when the dragon saw that he was thrown down to the earth, he persecuted the woman who gave birth to the male child. And the two wings of the great eagle were given to the woman, in order that she might fly into the wilderness to her place, where she was nourished for a time and times and half a time, from the presence of the serpent. And the serpent poured water like a river out of his mouth after the woman, so that he might cause her to be swept away with the flood. And the earth helped the woman, and the earth opened its mouth and drank up the river which the dragon poured out of his mouth.

The Protestants considered themselves to be the true church, and the Roman Church to be the harlot church, as well as almost every other synonym for the devil in Bible prophecy. That the earth "opened" and swallowed the flood was considered to correspond to the earth opening with the discovery of the "New World," which came during the peak of the persecution against Protestants. The "wings of an eagle" were to carry her off to a wilderness, the New World. When the United States was birthed as a nation fundamentally committed to religious liberty and the separation of church and state, and then took on the symbol of the eagle, this seemed further to establish this nation as the fulfillment of this prophecy.

THE FATAL HEAD WOUND

One of the prophecies many Protestants could not fit into their scenario of the papacy as the man of sin was Revelation 13:3–4:

> And I saw one of his heads as if it had been slain, and his fatal wound was healed. And the whole earth was amazed and followed after the beast; and they worshiped the dragon, because he gave his authority to the beast; and they worshiped the beast, saying, "Who is like the beast, and who is able to wage war with him?"

Then came Napoleon, who seemed especially dedicated to humbling the Roman Church, if not destroying it altogether. At his coronation as emperor of France, he did not allow the pope to crown him as was customary; instead he took the crown out of the pope's hands and placed it on his own head, essentially declaring that the pope had nothing to do with the emperor's authority.

Then Napoleon fined the pope huge sums that obviously were designed to bankrupt the church. To the astonishment of the world, the man who was considered to be seated on Christ's own throne, above every other power and dominion, paid the fines. Then Napoleon actually had the pope imprisoned, which seemed to be the fulfillment of Isaiah's "Taunt against the King of Babylon," a title many Protestants used in reference to the pope:

> How you have fallen from heaven, O star of the morning, son of the dawn! You have been cut down to the earth, you who have weakened the nations!
>
> But you said in your heart, "I will ascend to heaven; I will raise my throne above the stars of God, and I will sit on the mount of assembly in the recesses of the north.
>
> "I will ascend above the heights of the clouds; I will make myself like the Most High."
>
> Nevertheless you will be thrust down to Sheol, to the recesses of the pit.
>
> Those who see you will gaze at you, they will ponder over you, saying, "Is this the man who made the earth tremble, who shook kingdoms,
>
> "Who made the world like a wilderness and overthrew its cities, who did not allow his prisoners to go home?" (Isa. 14:12–17)

When the pope died in prison, Napoleon would not allow another one to be appointed, so for several years there was no pope. One of the heads had been slain, and it did not look like the Roman Church would ever recover from the mounting assaults on its legitimacy from both the secular and religious powers. This changed when Napoleon had a son, and he began to see the need for a historical perspective to justify his son's succession as the emperor of the Holy Roman Empire. Therefore he allowed the appointment of another pope so that the divine right of kings could be bestowed on his son as his successor. This so shocked the world that soon the papacy quickly recovered extraordinary influence. To the Protestants this was the healing of the fatal head wound, which caused the whole world to marvel and follow after the Antichrist.

The evidence seems to be quite overwhelming that this period known as the Middle Ages, or Dark Ages, was indeed the apostasy prophesied in Scripture. However, we should keep in mind that the man of sin, or the sin of man, was to take his seat in the temple of God, displaying himself as God. This does not mean that the temple—the church—became the man of sin. The church during this time was deceived, and then used by the spirit of the world, but she was still "the temple of God." This seems to parallel the times in the Old Testament when Israel fell into apostasy and the temple of the Lord in Jerusalem was desecrated. However, even during these times of apostasy the Lord continued to refer to it as His temple.

There were also times during the Middle Ages when the church fell into such terrible depravity and spiritual adultery that spiritual "Josiahs" arose to ignite great movements that brought cleansing to the church. Through them millions have turned from spiritual corruption and idolatry, and great renewal movements continue to turn the tide of iniquity. We must understand the roots of this deception, because the same ones continue to assault every new movement and advance of the gospel. Once they gain entry they can either quickly, or very slowly, divert these movements from their purpose.

SIMILAR ERRORS IN THE CHURCH TODAY

As I spent years immersed in studying those times, I became convinced that the Roman Church was the one prophesied in Revelation. Even so, it was the Roman Church that stood almost alone against one of the greatest threats to all of Christianity, Islam. Some papal administrations were some of the most cruel and evil of any power ever established on the earth; then others would arise to do great good. During the Reformation there was also a Counter-Reformation in the Roman Church that addressed many of the errors and excesses of previous administrations.

The Catholic Church today is not the same as it was then, and neither are the Protestant churches. Both were used to do great good and great evil, and both today are experiencing powerful renewal movements. The outpouring of the Holy Spirit within the Catholic Church has resulted in there now being nearly one hundred million born-again Catholic charismatics in the world. Because of this, we must come to the conclusion that Peter did in the house of Cornelius: Can we say that they are not a part of the church to whom the Lord has given the Holy Spirit?

We may be repulsed by the idea that any man would claim to be the head of the church, but in practice it seems that almost every congregation has a man or woman who is standing in that place, even if the person has not been honest enough to state what he or she is doing.

We may be repulsed at the way Catholics have allowed the intended veneration of Mary to become a worship that eclipses their devotion to Christ, but how many of us have not allowed our veneration of the church to eclipse our devotion to Him?

We may be repelled by the way priests are elevated to the status of intercessors and the people are compelled to pray to dead saints, but have we stopped making pastors into mediators, and elevating other spiritual superstars to the place where we do not even wait for them to die before giving them our worship?

We can condemn the Catholic Church for selling indulgences, but it is hard to turn on Christian television without seeing an evangelist who claims that if people will just give to his ministry they will receive special blessings from God. Is this not the same abomination of selling the grace of God?

I could go on with how we continue to persecute any who will not

bow down to our elevated positions or our perspective on certain doctrines. Which church is not guilty of substituting the great rituals of the
faith for the realities they represent?

To his great credit, Pope John Paul II has repeatedly highlighted
church mistakes in history, and apologized for them. This is unprecedented. Such humility and devotion to truth build trust and should bring
conviction on our Protestant and evangelical counterparts. This is certainly a positive step toward helping the whole church get out of this
deadly minefield. However, our only escape from this corruption is the
transforming power of the Cross. When rituals and false doctrines
remove the truth of the Cross from our lives, then religious men seem
to be the most prone to the most diabolical evils, just as the most religious men of the times crucified the Lord Himself.

11

The Blessings of Sacrifice and Perseverance

Apostolic Travail Through the Ages

POSSIBLY THE GREATEST DEPARTURE FROM APOSTOLIC Christianity has come because of our failure to understand one crucial truth about the faith: Christianity was founded upon sacrifice, and the true faith is perpetuated by sacrifice. Whenever the sacrificial nature of Christianity has been compromised, apostasy has always been the result.

In Galatians 4:19 Paul wrote, "My children, with whom I am again in labor until Christ is formed in you." The apostolic travail Paul endured so that Christ would be formed in the church literally translated means "to be in pain." When the Lord called Paul, He said, "I will show him how much he must suffer for My name's sake" (Acts 9:16). Later Paul wrote, "For just as the sufferings of Christ are ours in abundance, so also our comfort is abundant through Christ" (2 Cor. 1:5).

The true apostolic ministry is a life of sacrifice, which requires that in everything we live for the Lord and others, not ourselves. As Paul also wrote: "But we have this treasure in earthen vessels, that the surpassing greatness of the power may be of God and not from ourselves; we are

afflicted in every way, but not crushed; perplexed, but not despairing"
(2 Cor. 4:7–8).

The apostles had the power to impart spiritual life to the degree that
the dying of Jesus worked in them. Jesus warned His disciples, "If anyone
wishes to come after Me, let him *deny himself,* and take up his cross, and
follow Me. For whoever wishes to save his life shall lose it; but whoever
loses his life for My sake shall find it" (Matt. 16:24–25, emphasis added).

To deny oneself is almost unheard of in modern Western
Christianity. This is an increasingly foreign mentality, but if we are going
to be true followers of Christ, it must be our nature. The principles of
sacrifice that we see attributed to biblical apostles were the same for all
believers. However, the apostles, as leaders, had to be the first to lay
down their lives as a living sacrifice. As Paul wrote to the Romans:

> The Spirit Himself bears witness with our spirit that we are children of
> God, and if children, heirs also, heirs of God and fellow heirs with
> Christ, *if indeed we suffer with Him in order that we may also be glorified with
> Him.* (Rom. 8:16–17, emphasis added)

If is one of the biggest words in the Scripture. *If* directs us to understand the condition that is attached to the promise. We are told here that
we are heirs of God and fellow heirs with Christ *if* we suffer with Him.
That is why Paul also wrote:

> That I may know Him, and the power of His resurrection and the fellow-
> ship of His sufferings, being conformed to His death; *in order that* I may
> attain to the resurrection from the dead. Not that I have already obtained
> it, or have already become perfect, *but I press on in order that I may lay
> hold of that for which also I was laid hold of by Christ Jesus.* (Phil. 3:10–12,
> emphasis added)

Amazingly, Paul wrote this near the end of his life. Having endured
so much, and having accomplished so much, he was still pressing on, not

feeling as though he had yet accomplished this great goal. *Perseverance* and *sacrifice* are two words that may have most epitomized Paul's life, as well as the lives of all the true apostles of the first century. These are also characteristics of anyone who aspires to that great calling today. As Paul told the Roman Christians:

> We also exult in our tribulations, knowing that tribulation brings about perseverance; and perseverance, proven character; and proven character, hope; and hope does not disappoint, because the love of God has been poured out within our hearts through the Holy Spirit who was given to us. (Rom. 5:3–5)

How often do we start feeling content after just a few accomplishments, and begin to rest more on what we have done rather than pressing ahead until we have fully completed our course in victory? We may never know the value of our lives and our sacrifice during our lifetimes, but we must remain faithful to our calling to serve God. One of the great examples of how we may never know all that we can accomplish through our life of faithfulness is Elizabeth Anne Everest. She was just a nanny, one of the thousands in Victorian England who quietly spent their days caring for other people's children. Elizabeth never knew the impact her life would have on England, and even the whole modern world, many years after her death.

Elizabeth Everest was a Christian whose occupation was not a job, but a ministry. Maybe it was her faithfulness that compelled the Lord to trust into her care one rosy-cheeked baby boy named Winston Leonard Spencer Churchill.

There is a famous English anecdote that once a man with a tour group inquired of an old man in a village if any famous men had been born there. "Nope. Just babies," the old man replied. We never know when looking at a baby or young child what great destiny they may have. It seems that some with the greatest futures have the greatest obstacles to overcome when young.

Soon after taking the position of nanny for the Churchills, Elizabeth learned the immensity of her task. Even the boy's mother would warn visitors, with typical British understatement, that he was "a difficult child to manage." He kicked, he screamed, hid for hours at a time, and he bullied. The word *monster* was often used of him. Knowing of Mrs. Everest's Christian faith, young Winston once tried to escape a mathematics lesson by threatening to "bow down and worship graven images." It worked—for a while. But Elizabeth Everest was an exceptional woman. She knew how to enforce the boundaries she set, and from the beginning Winston held a grudging respect for this woman who seemed to know the reason for his rebellion.

To the neglect of their son, Randolph and Jennie Churchill gave themselves completely to their social ambitions. Of his mother Winston later wrote, "I loved her, but at a distance." His father thought Winston was retarded, rarely talked to him, and regularly vented his mounting insanity and rage on the child. Winston reacted predictably—with irritating behavior that served to hide his desperate longing for love.

Elizabeth Everest knew her Lord had not entrusted young Winston to her solely for the discipline she would enforce but for the vacuum she would fill in the life of this lonely little boy. Thus Elizabeth Everest— whom Winston came to call "Woom"—became not only his nanny but also his dearest companion. She was, after all, the stereotypical British nanny: plump, cheery, ever optimistic, always compassionate. The boy grew to love her completely. Of their special relationship, Violet Asquith later wrote: "Mrs. Everest was his comforter, his strength and stay, his one source of unfailing human understanding. She was the fireside at which he dried his tears and warmed his heart. She was the night light by his bed. She was his security."

She was also his shepherd. In the safety of their shared devotion, Winston first experienced genuine Christianity. On bended knee beside this gentle woman of God, he first learned that surging of the heart called prayer. From her lips he first heard the Scriptures read with loving devotion and was so moved he eagerly memorized his favorite passages. On long walks together they sang the great hymns of the church, spoke of the heroes of the faith, and imagined aloud what Jesus might look like, or how heaven would be. As they sat together on a park bench or on a blanket of cool, green grass, Winston was often transfixed while Woom explained the world to him in simple, but distinctly Christian, terms.

Though in early adulthood Churchill immersed himself in the anti-Christian rationalism that swept his age, he eventually recovered his faith during an escape from a South African prisoner of war camp. In this time of crisis, the prayers he had learned at Mrs. Everest's knee returned almost involuntarily to his lips, as did the Scripture passages he had memorized to the familiar lilt of her voice. From that time forward, his faith defined him, as it did his sense of mission. He came to see himself in much the same terms as those great heroes of the faith. He would then dedicate his own grandchildren, holding them aloft and tearfully proclaiming "Christ's new faithful soldier and servant."

So when his day of destiny arrived, Winston Churchill was ready to lead the world with a clear trumpet call of the solid faith he first learned from his godly nanny. In an age of mounting skepticism, Churchill proclaimed the cause of "Christian civilization." It was threatened from without, he believed, by "barbarous paganism"—like Nazism—which spurned "Christian ethics" and derived its "strength and perverted pleasure from persecution." Therefore, every Christian had a "duty to preserve the structure of humane, enlightened, Christian society." This was critical, for "once the downward steps are taken, once one's moral intellectual feet slipped upon the slope of plausible indulgence, there would be found no halting-place short of a general Paganism and Hedonism."

While other leaders of his age vacillated and sought the compromises of cowards, Churchill defined the challenges of his civilization in the stark Christian terms that moved men to greatness. Yet behind the arsenal of his words, behind the artillery of his vision, was the simple teaching of a devoted nanny who served her God by investing in the destiny of a troubled boy.

When the man some called the "Greatest Man of the Age" lay dying in 1965 at the age of ninety, only one picture stood at his bedside. It was a picture of his beloved nanny, gone to be with her Lord some seventy years before. Elizabeth Anne Everest had truly fulfilled God's plan for her life, even though she did not live herself to see the fruit of it. She had continually pressed on without knowing how influential her service would be.[1]

Our time in this life is not for our happiness but for the will of God. We can know no greater joy or peace in this life than that which comes from doing His will. If seeking our own satisfaction is the purpose of our life, we will not find it here on earth, and we will also sacrifice the greatest of satisfactions for eternity, just as Paul wrote in 1 Corinthians 9:24–27:

Do you not know that those who run in a race all run, but only one receives the prize? Run in such a way that you may win. And everyone who competes in the games exercises self-control in all things. They then do it to receive a perishable wreath, but we an imperishable. Therefore I run in such a way, as not without aim; I box in such a way, as not beating the air; but I buffet my body and make it my slave, lest possibly, after I have preached to others, I myself should be disqualified.

This text reveals the spiritual principle that to the degree that we live by the law of sacrifice in the flesh, we will receive and be able to give spiritual life, just as Elizabeth Everest did.

For if you are living according to the flesh, you must die; but if by the Spirit you are putting to death the deeds of the body, you will live. For all who are being led by the Spirit of God, these are sons of God. For you have not received a spirit of slavery leading to fear again, but you have received a spirit of adoption as sons by which we cry out, "Abba! Father!" . . . For I consider that the sufferings of this present time are not worthy to be compared with the glory that is to be revealed to us. (Rom. 8:13–15, 18)

Adam lived in a perfect world, yet he chose to sin, and the whole creation under his authority suffered because of his transgression. Since then creation has been waiting for those whom will live in the darkest of times, and yet choose to obey, and lay down their own lives for the sake of those under their authority.

The first Adam fell and gave his domain over to the evil one, whom he had obeyed. As the "last Adam," Jesus remained faithful and will return the domain of Adam to the Father. So did three great men who impacted the church as Peter, Paul, and John had done before them: Jan Hus, John Amos Comenius, and Count Nikolaus Ludwig von Zinzendorf. One planted the seed, one watered it, and one reaped the fruit. Through perseverance and sacrifice these three men changed the world.

Jan Hus (1369–1415) first prophesied that the message of spiritual reform would be "a hidden seed" that would fall into the ground and die for a season but would sprout again to bear much fruit. Hus's prophetic castigations of Roman Catholicism began the great spiritual earthquakes of the 1400s. Although the Roman Church dominated the religious and political life of Europe, the church had fallen into an unprecedented debauchery. Refusing to compromise his convictions, Hus was burned at the stake as a heretic in 1415, which was then the price for challenging the mighty Roman Church.

Church officials were convinced that Hus's message would die with him. To their dismay his heroic death seemed only to fan the flames of his message.

In 1627, John Amos Comenius, an educator and pastor, gave a remarkable and now famous prophecy, which echoed Hus's. As he and a small band of exiles left Moravia after the Catholics won the Battle of the White Mountain and declared Moravia a Catholic state, Comenius told his followers that God would preserve "a hidden seed" that would grow and bear fruit in a hundred years' time. He prophesied this—and lived with this hope throughout his life—despite the fact that he had lost his wife and his only child in the increasing violence and hunger after the war. He also lost his occupation when he was told that he could retain his school at Fulneck—only if he would renounce his Moravian convictions. He refused, and lost the school and his precious library and extensive writings on education.

To modern Christians who are so bound by the "tyranny of the immediate," a prophecy that our hope would not be fulfilled for another hundred years would seem most discouraging. Actually it had the opposite effect upon the Moravians. As a people devoted to self-sacrifice, they were honored to be able to help prepare the way for a future generation. This also enabled them to plan with such a long-term strategy and vision that it made some of their greatest contributions to the church and civilization possible.

Taking his own prophecy to heart, Comenius felt that the best way to plant this seed for future generations was to dedicate his life entirely to the education of the young, and one day, multiplied millions of the world's children would benefit from his plans.

Comenius believed that the wars, which had brought so much tragedy to his own life, were the result of basic human ignorance. He began to ponder the potential of schools for providing an education for all children, a novel idea at the time because outside of a few Christian and Jewish communities, education was almost exclusively limited to the children of the nobility, or merchant class, who were taught by private tutors. Comenius began to dream of schools for all children, which were founded upon the truth of the gospel. He believed that the knowledge of the Prince of Peace would be the agency for bringing peace among the nations.

John Comenius determined that to accomplish his goals he had to establish quality Christian schools. To do this he would have to provide excellent curriculum material and develop effective methods of teaching that not only imparted knowledge but stimulated a love for knowledge. He set out to find teachers who possessed above all things a deep love for God and were of strong moral character. He especially gave himself to the training of his teachers to impart that love of God and the reality that every child could have a close relationship with God so that each child would become "a creature which shall be the joy of his Creator."

In 1628 Comenius was able to establish a school in Lissa, Poland. In 1632 he was made the bishop of the scattered Moravian brethren. One of his educational treatises, known as the *Janua Linguarum,* was even translated by the Muslims into Arabic, then into Turkish, Persian, and Mongolian. His friends rejoiced greatly in this, believing that these translations would sow the seeds of the gospel among those nations.

In 1642 Comenius was invited to England by Samuel Hartlib, a friend of the renowned poet Milton. There he was persuaded to start his Pansophic College in London. Comenius's idea of pansophia was that the wisdom of God was sovereign over all things and that all things were connected within the circle of this knowledge. The Pansophic College would be a place where Christian educators could gather together from Europe and America to demonstrate that there was a unity of knowledge because in Christ "all things hold together" (Col. 1:17).

Comenius also believed that education established on this basic knowledge of Christ would bring unity to the Christian church. As Christians came into unity they would then be able to spread the gospel to all nations. This would result in the unity of all nations and an end to war. (A century later, this idea of taking the gospel of the unity in Christ to all nations would fire the heart of the young Count Zinzendorf and give birth to modern missions.)

With hopes running high just before the college was to open, the English Civil War broke out, making it impossible to proceed. Comenius again refused to be discouraged, remarking that "God has His own thoughts and seasons." He consoled himself with the fact that the Lord would not let David build His temple but did allow him to prepare the design and materials.

Comenius then left for Sweden, where he had a major impact on the Swedish educational system through his relationship with the brilliant Gustafsson Oxenstierna. In 1643 he returned to Lissa, Poland. He was then asked to be the first rector of the newly established Harvard University near Boston. He declined, deciding to stay in Lissa to face the rising storm clouds of war and obvious persecution. Even so, there he enjoyed a few years of peace before war would again strike a tragic blow to this great man of peace. In 1656 the Catholic Poles defeated the Lutheran Swedes who had occupied much of Poland. The Catholics then condemned Lissa as a "heretic's nest" and burned the town to the ground. Again Comenius's sacrifice was great: he lost all of his books and unpublished manuscripts.

Still Comenius persevered and refused to be discouraged, commenting that this must have been the will of God because when he rewrote his manuscripts they would be better. He moved to the Netherlands, where he spent the rest of his life. In spite of these almost continuous tragedies and opposition he wrote more than ninety books for publication. His works on education helped engender the modern democratic movements by empowering the common people with knowledge.

Satan thought the best way to deal with Jesus was to crucify Him. That plan backfired to his own destruction. He obviously also thought that the best way to deal with Comenius was with wars, tragedies, and the constant destruction of his work. Satan afflicted Comenius in every way, but he could not crush him. All that the enemy meant for evil was used to plant the seeds of an even greater vision in the heart of this gentle Moravian prophet. These seeds would one day result in some of the greatest revivals in history as well as some of the greatest advancements in the human condition.

Like his Savior, the great apostle Paul, and multitudes of faithful Christians since, Comenius died without having witnessed personally much fruit from his great labors. Still he had faith, "the assurance of things hoped for, the conviction of things not seen" (Heb. 11:1).

Those who trust their lives to the grace of God, regardless of problems, are always used as vessels of resurrection power. The hope that we have in resurrection overcomes the enemy's greatest weapon against us—the fear of death. When the fear of death is conquered, all of his other yokes and devices are powerless. Those who live in the hope of the Resurrection will always prevail, and not only will they prevail, they will sow in the earth seeds that cannot die.

That was true of Comenius. One hundred years later, just as Comenius had predicted, Count Nikolaus Ludwig von Zinzendorf was studying in a library at Zitau when he happened upon Comenius's writings. Zinzendorf was a member of one of the leading families in Germany and had already sacrificed his position on the court of one of the great thrones of Europe to pursue the pastorate. The count was stunned by how accurately Comenius's writings articulated some of the deepest burdens of his own heart. Five years earlier, in 1722, Zinzendorf had allowed a few Moravian refugees from the movement that Comenius had perpetuated a haven on his estate.

The count was amazed when he realized that Comenius was a spiritual ancestor of these refugees. He knew beyond question that these immigrants were a people of divine destiny.

Before this time Zinzendorf must have had questions. By 1725 the Zinzendorf estate had become a small city. Sympathetic Catholics had heroically aided the escape of many believers from Moravia, blessing them for the journey to their promised land at Herrnhut. Along with the Moravians, Lutheran Pietists, former Catholics, Separatists, Reformed and Anabaptists had also found their way to the new community, all seeking the fellowship of others who were pursuing "a heavenly city whose architect and builder was God."

As could be expected, trouble arose quickly. By 1726 a sharp disagreement had arisen between the Lutherans and the Moravians over the liturgy of the Sunday service. This was just the most visible of many other disputes that arose over doctrine, language, and the economic pressure of supporting a community that had swelled to more than three hundred. Every group was seeking to impose its own agenda on the entire community. A false teacher took an intense personal dislike to Zinzendorf, his benefactor, and began to preach that the count was none other than "the Beast" mentioned in the book of Revelation.

A lesser man would have simply driven the whole lot off his land, but the count was not one to abandon so easily his dream of a truly Christian community. Instead he ministered to this unwieldy bunch in the midst of this intense opposition. He moved from Dresden and set up residence in the academy building on the estate. With the love, patience, and authority of a biblical apostle, Zinzendorf began going from house to house, counseling each family from the Scriptures. Eventually love and a spirit of cooperation began to prevail. In May of 1727 the count established a set of manorial rules for Herrnhut.

That day in 1727 in the library at Zitau, as the count was studying Comenius's writings, he read a list of disciplines instituted by Comenius for governing the community one hundred years earlier, which almost exactly paralleled the list of governing rules that he had given to the Moravian refugees a few days prior. A spark was ignited in the young nobleman that would forever change his life and the course of the entire advancing church. Zinzendorf quickly encouraged the refugees with the words of Comenius.

This solidified the people into a prayerful, united community with faith in their calling and purpose. Not only were they growing in unity with each other, but the count's discovery at Zitau made them now feel a genuine link, and a sense of unity with the saints who had gone before them. As the community moved into increasing unity over the summer of 1727, an expectation of something wonderful began to permeate the Zinzendorf estate. The settlement *Diary* recorded, "There was evidence of the fire of love." On the fifth of August, Zinzendorf and a group of the brethren spent the entire night in prayer and sharing the wonders of the Lord. Anticipation was so great that many did not want to sleep for fear they would miss what God was doing.

On Wednesday, August 13, 1727, at the first Communion service of the reconciled community, the Holy Spirit fell upon the gathered believers with such power that historians have called it "the Moravian Pentecost." The day began with a message from Rothe, one of the elders, on the meaning of the Lord's Supper. Then, as the people walked the one mile from the settlement to the church at Berthelsdorf for the service, it seemed as though they were all enveloped in a cloud of love and mutual admiration.

Through the experience of the preceding weeks, all of the exiles had been humbled under an intense conviction of their sin and spiritual helplessness, which caused all to begin esteeming others more highly than themselves. This humility, combined with the deepening unity and mutual love that it precipitated, seemed to touch the very heart of the Holy Spirit so that He just could not resist pouring out His power on them.

As Rothe pronounced what was called "a truly apostolic blessing" upon two young girls who were being confirmed, the congregation knelt and sang, "My soul before Thee prostrate lies, to Thee its source, my spirit flies." Then prayers of great unction rose from the brethren as they interceded for each other and those who were still living under persecution in Moravia. The Holy Spirit swept across them in waves, as the passion of the Lamb and the benefits of His sacrifice became so real to them that this little band would prove willing to sacrifice everything for Him.

In the testimony of one Moravian, "We discovered therein the finger of God, and found ourselves, as it were, baptized under the cloud of our fathers, with their spirit. For that Spirit came again upon us, and great signs and wonders were wrought among the Brethren in those days, and great grace prevailed among us, and in the whole country."

After one hundred years the seed had sprung to life, just as Comenius had prophesied, and one of the great Christian movements of all time began. They called themselves "the Unitus Fratrum" or "the Unity of the Brethren," but they are still affectionately known throughout the church as "the Moravians."

The outpouring of the Holy Spirit at Herrnhut did not result in spiritual arrogance among those who received it but rather the opposite. It so branded the cross upon their hearts that they could no longer bear to go on living just for themselves, but would be compelled to "do all things for the sake of the gospel." Sacrifice and the laying down of their own self-interests would become as much a part of Herrnhut as the daily meals.

The spirit of sacrifice that was kindled at the Moravian Pentecost not only released the power for signs and wonders, it released the power for a humble group of exiles, led by an unlikely nobleman, to change the course of Christianity and the world. "The word of the cross . . . is the power of God" (1 Cor. 1:18), and individuals who embrace the cross will know the power of God in their lives.

Hus, Comenius, Zinzendorf, and the Moravians used their sacrifices and their perseverance to leave a legacy to us almost three hundred years later.

Paul exhorted, "Through many tribulations we must enter the kingdom of God" (Acts 14:22). This is a basic spiritual principle: we enter the kingdom through tribulations. We all want to claim "kingdom living," but are we willing to go through the gate? This principle applies to us as individuals as well as the whole creation. The kingdom age is going to be issued in through a great tribulation. We must therefore view tribulations as a blessing (a gate for entering into the full purpose of God), not as a curse.

One of the most important lessons for every believer to learn is not to waste his or her trials. Every one of them is an opportunity to enter the kingdom, just as it was for these three great men and the Moravians. As the apostle Peter stated:

> In this you greatly rejoice, even though now for a little while, if necessary, you have been distressed by various trials, that the proof of your faith, being more precious than gold which is perishable, even though tested by fire, may be found to result in praise and glory and honor at the revelation of Jesus Christ. (1 Peter 1:6–7)

If only we esteemed the dealings of God even half as much as we tend to esteem earthly riches, Christians today would again be turning the world upside down with the power of the gospel. Let us join with these pioneers of our faith so our lives will leave an eternal legacy to our children, not just a bank account.

12

Revival

The Fire That Ignites the World

MANY CHRISTIANS TODAY ARE EXPECTING REVIVAL. How many are expecting one so great that the NFL season is canceled because both the fans and the players won't leave the revival meetings? Who could imagine a revival that has such an impact on a nation that one of the greatest crises is trying to find work for the laid-off policemen who lost their jobs because there wasn't enough crime for them to have anything to do? Who could believe that the whiskey makers would empty all of their stores into rivers so that no one would drink it, being convicted that it was not right to sell? Or that the gambling ships would be turned into mission ships by their owners? Such revivals have occurred before, and they will happen again. In the next two chapters we will look at three of them: the Nashville Revival of 1885, the Welsh Revival of 1904, and the Azusa Street Revival of 1906.

These revivals were different from each other and were led by different evangelists, but the similarities of God's hand are also evident in each. In a special way they each contained seeds of that which is to come. There are great moves of God happening around the world at this time, but what is coming will sweep the earth like great tidal waves.

In each of these revivals devoted men of God were the sparks that were used to light God's fire. Sam Jones, now an almost forgotten evangelist, at one time was followed in the news like presidents are today. Reporters tried to catch every word he spoke, and they carefully watched everything that he did, simply because his impact on the nation was so great. Later Evan Roberts was treated the same by the international press. William Seymour was never given the credit in his own time for what he was being used to start, but his influence on the modern church and world may well be greater than that of the other two combined.

THE NASHVILLE REVIVAL

Sam Jones was born in Oak Bowery, Alabama—a little town that doesn't even exist today. When Sam was eight years old, the older students in the one-room school he attended were asked to recite speeches for the parents. Sam insisted on giving a speech as well. While Sam waited his turn, the heat and boredom lulled him to sleep in his mother's lap. When his turn came, his mother woke him and the teacher stood him on the top of his desk. Sam straightened himself and boldly declared:

> You'd scarce expect one of my age
> To speak in public on the stage,
> With thundering peals and Thornton tones
> The world shall hear of Sam P. Jones.

Little did anyone imagine that he was prophesying his future! If they had, they certainly would have lost faith during his younger years. Only a few months after his bold pronouncement, he received a harsh blow when his mother unexpectedly passed away. Sam's life continued its downward spiral when the Civil War broke out and his father joined the Army of Northern Virginia.

As a result of his father's absence and the disorder in their family, young Sam fell into the wrong crowd. Because of the strength of his personality, he became the ringleader of the delinquent and unruly young people in his community. Sam had physical problems and was encouraged to find "medicinal relief" from drinking whiskey. This led to alcoholism. Despite the addiction Sam followed his father's profession and graduated from law school. Even though he was for a time a promising young lawyer, he was already caught in a downward spiral of alcoholism. This led to physical fatigue, mental anguish, and spiritual bankruptcy.

As Sam drank himself *down* the ladder of success, his wife, Laura, with courage born out of her faith, asked God to do whatever was necessary to save him from sure disaster. His health was being wrecked by the sleepless nights, restless days, and the resulting depression. He was on his way to an untimely death.

Then, in August of 1872, Sam found himself standing at his father's deathbed. As Sam grasped his father's hand, the old lawyer looked his son in the eyes and simply said, "Son, promise you'll meet me in heaven."

Sam declared, "I yield, I yield," determining right then and there that every remaining step of his life would be an honest effort to fulfill that promise to his father.

THE CALL TO PREACH

After peace and pardon came to Sam's heart, he went to his grandfather's church for an evening service. Before the service, he told his grandfather that he felt God had called him to preach. Later that evening, his grandfather proudly stood before the congregation and announced that Sam had received "the call." Then the old man turned to his grandson and said, "Sam, if you are called to preach, come up here and do it!"

Sam was astonished, but he walked to the platform and nervously read a passage of Scripture. "I don't know much about what I have just read," he admitted, "but I will tell you what I do know. I know that God is good, and I am happy in His love." By the end of the clumsy message, people were in tears; when the invitation was given, many thronged to the altar to receive Jesus as Savior.

Although God used Sam to bless many that night, nearly everyone was in secret agreement that his newfound "call" wouldn't stick. One of the biggest skeptics was Laura, because by now she had heard too many empty "I'll do better" promises. Nevertheless, after the service Sam's grandfather laid his hand on Sam's shoulder and said, "Go ahead, my boy; God has called you to the work."

The next morning Sam went to Atlanta, Georgia, to petition for an appointment in the Methodist church. The Georgia Conference of the Methodist Church had lost many of its pastors to the Civil War, so even though Sam was not educated for the ministry and his personality was a little too crude and aggressive, they accepted him. Then they shuffled him off to the most destitute, obscure place they could send him: the Van Wert Circuit of north Georgia, mostly made up of widows and orphans of war.

Still Sam rejoiced all the way back home. In order to pay off their debts incurred because of his alcoholism, he and Laura sold everything. Sam arrived in Van Wert with his wife, one child, a bobtail pony, eight dollars in his pocket, and several hundred dollars in remaining debts. He found out from the head deacon that the last preacher was paid $65 for a year's work, and the deacon was charging Sam $120 a year for rent. Sam determined that if the Lord had called him, He would make up the difference, so he accepted.

Sam violently preached against drinking, profanity, gambling, and every imaginable sin that was plaguing the church and community. He used the Word as a sword and cut to the heart of hypocrisy and injustice. Once a prominent church member took advantage of an elderly widow in the church. The next Sunday while Sam was preaching—with the man sitting piously on the front row—Sam pointed at him and said, "You old hypocrite! You hired a poor widow to pick blackberries for you and then paid her with spoiled flour."

The man and his family stormed out of the church, and Sam later found them outside holding a caucus. When the man threatened to whip him, Sam said, "Shucks, I don't care about being whipped. I can whip any old fellow that would cheat a poor widow, and I can whip all his kinfolks too."

The man paid the widow what was due.

Sam's conversational style was such a radical departure from the typical nineteenth-century preachers that it created a peculiar sensation every time he spoke. "I can't really preach," Sam admitted, "but I can talk a little." Friends and enemies alike believed his abrasiveness would eventually destroy him. He hated hypocrisy and shams with a vengeance, and his abrupt and intense manner often divided the congregations where he spoke. The more the "Old Heads" tried to harness him and tone down his preaching, the more daring he became.

In 1885 Sam was invited to conduct a revival in Nashville, Tennessee. Upon receiving the invitation, he wrote back and consented, with one stipulation: that the Protestant Ministers Association provide a tent that would accommodate five thousand people. Sam felt that God desired to do a great work in Nashville, but the ministers thought his request unreasonable and arrogant. Sam challenged them to let him come and preach in three churches one Sunday in April; then decide whether or not the tent was a feasible idea.

When Sam showed up in April, those who had never seen him before were struck by how physically unimpressive he was. He did not wear a funeral frock coat or a clerical collar. Instead he typically wore a combination of stripes and plaid, an alpaca suit with a limp tie and a wilted felt hat. He never wore cuffs, and said he "hated starch of all kinds." When he walked up to the pulpit, his rumpled folksiness set him apart from the starchy leaders on the platform, which in turn identified him more closely with the folks in the pew.

When Sam was introduced, he ambled up to the podium, closed his eyes, and asked God not to convict a single sinner at that service, because "the company in the church ain't good enough for them yet." He opened his eyes and quoted Acts 17:16: "Now while Paul waited for them at Athens, his spirit was stirred in him, when he saw the city wholly given to idolatry" (KJV). That was followed by a series of lightning flashes of wit that captured every ear in the house. His humor, adorned with his down-home dialect and illustrations, was spellbinding.

Sam then completely turned the tide by declaring a ruthless rebuke, which convicted the entire assembly. He started with the church leadership, holding each of them personally responsible for the spiritual climate of the city. When one of the pastors reacted negatively to the onslaught, Sam insisted, "Whenever you see me with a grubbing hoe on my shoulder, I'm out after grub worms. If you ain't a worm, sit still—I ain't after you."

Sam continued, "Folks, if I throw a rock into a crowd of dogs, and one of 'em runs yelping, you know that is the one I hit. When I first started preaching, I was afraid I would hurt somebody's feelings; now I'm afraid I won't. The fact is, sixty-eight of the eighty-eight saloons in this city are owned by church members. Nobody but a scoundrel will sell whiskey, and nobody but a fool will drink it. That tells me that we have a church full of scoundrels and a city full of fools. And not one of you pastors has been brave enough to fight the battle at hand."

Though everyone was startled by Sam's message, they knew his harsh honesty was the truth. The anointing on his life arrested hundreds of hearts and brought them to repentance. Needless to say, Sam also stirred up a multitude of hornet's nests. Some wanted him tarred and feathered, while others wanted him to run for mayor.

The next day, the Nashville newspapers blasted him with every insult they could think of. The controversy hit the city in full force, not to speak of the resulting conflict in the ministers meeting. Some defended him and applauded his bravery and sincerity, declaring that God was giving Nashville an opportunity for true revival. Others branded him an embarrassment to the ministry. Nevertheless, he had created such a buzz that they felt almost forced to have him back. A local citizen made a demand to the ministers association, "If you don't buy the tent, I'll buy the tent." So the Protestant Ministers Association bought an eight-thousand-seat tent, and the following month Sam arrived back in Nashville.

REVIVAL AT LAST

More than ten thousand people gathered for Sam's first meeting, and he preached one of the most powerful sermons of his life. Thousands turned to God. At the end of the message, he challenged them to pray for their city and put feet to their faith. "God will do a great work," Sam declared.

As he closed the first service, Sam announced that he would preach at 6:00 A.M., 10:00 A.M., 2:00 P.M., and 6:00 P.M.—four times a day, two hours per service, with no sound system, to crowds of more than ten thousand. Soon the city was aflame with revival. The power of God moved through Nashville with such force that every citizen within a hundred-mile radius was impacted to one degree or another.

Churches became united in the effort to save souls. The revival had such an impact on the community that drunks and prostitutes were becoming choir members. Sam was an untiring circus in full swing, as the masses hung on every word, erupting in thunderous laughter one minute and uncontrollable sobs of repentance the next.

One night Tom Ryman, the most notorious saloon owner and riverboat captain in the city, came to the meeting. Ryman was there to execute revenge on Sam for turning his whiskey drinkers and gamblers into "Bible-thumpers." The loss of his clientele to some "rude preacher from Georgia" was more than he could tolerate.

Ryman showed up with a group of his thugs, intending to physically attack Sam and run him out of town. Through the grapevine Sam had been informed of the saloon owner's intentions. He announced at the beginning of the meeting, "I understand some fellers have come here to whup me tonight. I weigh 135 pounds, and 132 pounds of me is solid backbone." He invited the thugs to meet him outside after the message and said he would welcome the exercise.

At the end of the sermon, Tom Ryman walked down the middle aisle and stated, "Sam Jones, I came here to whup you tonight, but you have whupped me with the gospel." The captain gave his heart to God and expressed his allegiance to Sam as a lifelong friend. He walked out of the tent and immediately went to his saloon where he rolled all the whiskey barrels down the street and into the Cumberland River. He then ordered all whiskey overboard on his thirty-five steamboats and turned their gambling halls into floating missions.

Tom Ryman told Sam that if he would continue to come back to Nashville and preach, he would build him an auditorium to hold his meetings. True to his word, he built the Union Gospel Tabernacle, which for years was a spiritual lighthouse that beckoned hopeless and hungry souls from the East Coast to the frontier. When the captain died in 1904, Sam preached Ryman's memorial service at the tabernacle. Before the gathering of some four thousand people, Sam said he felt it would be pleasing to God if the name of the tabernacle would be changed to honor the captain, who had given so unselfishly to the purpose of spreading the gospel to the community. So they changed the name of the building to the Ryman Auditorium, which became the home of the Grand Ole Opry.

Nashville was the gateway to national acclaim for Sam, and his meetings there were a turning point in his life and ministry. As he went forth to conquer in other battlefields, he always spoke of Nashville as "that most memorable meeting." Sam recalled it as the place of his greatest persecution and the most remarkable work of God's grace.

After this, Sam went on to St. Louis, Cincinnati, Chicago, Toronto, Baltimore, Boston, and many other cities. Every one of these cities had two things in common: they were desperately in need of an earth-shaking revival, and when Sam Jones showed up they got it. In every city, the largest facility was filled with an overflowing mass of humanity. Special trains ran from all over the country, and the crowds in the streets often were logjammed for hours as people struggled to get to the meetings.

It was said that the secret of Sam's success was that no one in his generation hated sin more than he did, and no one expressed it with more fire and fury, and that no one loved the sinner more than Sam Jones, or expressed more kindness and compassion. Not only did he have a splendid intellect, but he was a man of deep conviction and unwavering character. Although Sam was continually criticized for his unorthodox style of ministry, he insisted on being himself rather than trying to fit into someone else's mold.

Sam once told Captain Tom Ryman, "If Nashville ever becomes cold and indifferent again, God will do a work of grace in another generation that will warm her to the boiling point once again."

Today Nashville is a collection of the unorthodox and the orthodox, the loving and passionate, as well as the critical and indifferent. It is a city dominated by a music industry whose foundation is often built upon self-promotion, insecurity, criticism, and greed. It is also home to some of the great churches, denominations, inner-city missions, and a growing throng of resolute men and women of God. Revival will visit Nashville again.[1]

As Sam Jones was finishing his course at the turn of the nineteenth century, another revival burst forth in Wales. The revivals of Sam Jones impacted the lives of all who heard him. The revival in Wales would so change the world that it would even touch millions who never heard of it, and its influence can still be seen in churches around the world.

13

The Welsh Revival

IN 1904 REVIVAL BROKE OUT IN WALES, A SMALL principality of the British Isles. It was for a time arguably the greatest revival that the world has ever known. It not only spanned the globe and touched millions, it had a radical impact on all of society. It seems that the Lord looked down upon Wales and said, "I am going to show the church and the world what I can do with just a handful of faithful saints who will yield themselves to Me." Even though it only lasted between two and three years, the reports of it still send shock waves of conviction and hope to all who hear the story.

Evan Roberts, the most popular evangelist of the Welsh Revival, is also one of the more enigmatic figures in church history. Roberts was not a dynamic leader of people; he did not come with new teachings, neither was he even considered a good preacher. His great strength was simply that he was a dynamic follower of the Lord. He listened to God and obeyed.

At this time the overall spiritual condition of Wales was as dark as it had ever been, and it seemed to be getting darker by the day. Bars flourished. Football (soccer), cockfighting, prizefighting, gambling, and prostitution seemed to have completely captured the soul of the working class. Murder, rape, and other violent crimes were increasing so fast that the authorities were close to losing control.

The dark tunnels of the Welsh coal mines seemed a fitting symbol of what was happening to the country. At the same time God was preparing a young, half-educated miner to be the outstanding voice to his generation. When Evan Roberts emerged from the mines to preach the gospel, Wales began to emerge from the dark pits of her sin. Soon this young miner, and his tiny principality of Wales, would cause the whole world to stop and take notice.

Evan began work in the mines when he was just nine years old after his father, Henry, broke his leg in the pit. Evan had to help him in his job, for which he was paid seventy-five cents a week. Later he learned the trade of a blacksmith, which he also did in connection with the mine. But Evan felt a burning passion to preach. Few who had other ambitions ever left the mines, even those who wanted to be preachers. Evan's pastor and friends encouraged him even though his lack of education made his prospects seem dim. At twenty-six years of age, he entered the preparatory school at Newcastle Emlyn to prepare himself for the Trevecca College entrance examination. Evan had determined to do all that he could and trust God to do the rest.

One midnight in the fall of 1904, Evan's roommate and closest friend, Sydney Evans, came into the room to find Evan's face shining with a holy light. Astonished, he asked what had happened. Evan replied that he had just had a vision of the whole of Wales being lifted up to heaven. He then prophesied, "We are going to see the mightiest revival that Wales has ever known— and the Holy Spirit is coming just now. We must get ready. We must have a little band and go all over the country preaching." Suddenly he stopped and then cried: "Do you believe that God can give us 100,000 souls, now?"

The presence of the Lord so gripped Sydney Evans that he could not help but believe. Later, while sitting in a chapel, Evan Roberts had a vision of some of his old companions and many other young people as a voice spoke to him saying, "Go to these people."

"Lord, if it is Thy will, I will go," Evan replied. Then the whole chapel became filled with light so dazzling he could only faintly see the minister in the pulpit. Evan was deeply disturbed and wanted to make sure this vision was of the Lord. He consulted with his tutor, who encouraged him to go. Evan would never finish school. The Lord did not need his knowledge; He only needed his obedience.

On October 31, Evan returned to his home and went straight to his pastor to ask permission to hold services for young people. On that night, after the adult prayer meeting, Evan asked the young people to stay behind because he wanted to speak to them. Sixteen adults and only one little girl stayed. After the initial blast of disappointment, Evan began to explain in a quiet voice his reason for coming home. He was simply obeying the Holy Spirit, he said, and here at Moriah large numbers of young people were going to be saved. A mighty revival was coming to Wales!

A cold spirit of unbelief was so thick it seemed to hang in the air. The results were so disappointing that Evan could not help but think that his visions were some strange delusion. He did not realize that this was a test much like the one the children of Israel endured after leaving Egypt. Would the young preacher believe the visions or the human voices that were now telling him he had been duped by illusions of grandeur? At this point many stray from the course that leads to the fulfillment of their callings.

But Evan chose to stand by the vision. The next day's services were held at Pisgah, a small chapel nearby, which was a mission of Moriah. This was a Tuesday night, and strangely the audience had significantly increased. Evan spoke on the importance of being filled with the Spirit. This meeting lasted until 10:00 P.M.

On November 2, back at Moriah, Evan spoke on "The Four Great Tenets."

THE FOUR TENETS

This sermon was to become the foundational message of the revival, later known as "The Four Points." These were the four essential conditions that

Evan believed were required before revival could come. They were:

1. *All sin must be confessed and repented before God.* The church must be cleansed; the Lord's bride should be without spot so there is no room for compromise with sin. "If there is anything in our lives about which there is even doubt as to whether it is good or evil—then cast it off!"

2. *There must be no cloud between the believer and God.* "Have you forgiven *everybody*? If not, don't expect forgiveness for your own sins. The Scripture is clear: we cannot be forgiven until we have forgiven. Unforgiveness separates us from God."

3. *We must obey the Holy Spirit.* "Do what the Spirit prompts you to do. Immediate, implicit, unquestioning obedience to the Spirit is required if we are going to be used by Him."

4. *There must be public confessions of Christ as Savior.* "This is not just a onetime incident after our salvation experience or baptism—for the Christian it is a way of life."

On Thursday, November 3, and Sunday, November 6, Evan again preached at Moriah. The next service was a Monday evening prayer meeting. Like most congregational prayer meetings, there were a handful of regulars and a few who might occasionally drop in. On Monday, November 7, the chapel was packed all the way back to the door. At eight o'clock Evan Roberts arrived, opened his Bible, and read from the last chapter of Malachi, "But unto you that fear my name shall the Sun of righteousness arise with healing in his wings . . . and ye shall tread down the wicked; for they shall be ashes under the soles of your feet in the day that I shall do this, saith the LORD of hosts" (4:2–3 KJV).

Then Evan astonished those in attendance by boldly declaring that this Scripture was going to be fulfilled immediately in Wales!

Almost everyone in attendance that Monday night was moved to tears; many cried in agony. By midnight the presence of the Lord was so intense it could hardly be contained. The people had never experienced such deep repentance, or such deep joy. Those crying in remorse for their sins could not be distinguished from those crying in ecstasy at the nearness of God. It was after 3:00 A.M. before an attempt to close the meeting was possible.

The next evening, Tuesday, November 8, the people crowded into the chapel early just to be able to get seats. Everyone was talking about another great awakening, maybe even another Pentecost! But that night the meeting was cold and lifeless. Evan and a few faithful remained until almost 3:00 A.M. agonizing in prayer. Why had the Lord departed so quickly? Near 6:00 A.M. Evan and his brother, Dan, finally left to go home.

After arriving they were jolted by their mother crying, "I'm dying! I'm dying!" Discouraged, she had left the meeting early the night before. Now she was crying out in agony, declaring that she felt the entire weight of Calvary on her soul. Later she explained that after leaving the meeting, she began to feel the agony of the Lord as He had endured the cold hardness of Gethsemane, which even His own disciples would not bear with Him. She felt that her leaving the chapel at such a critical time to go home and sleep had been the same rejection of an opportunity to stand with the Lord. She was devastated. Evan was wise. He did not try to comfort her; he tried to help her repent.

The Lord had been working on others in the community in the same way. In fact He had been at the meeting in a very special way, but one which the people did not recognize. The people of Loughor got the message quickly. By 6:00 A.M. the streets were noisy with crowds on their way to the early morning prayer services. The entire population of the town was being transformed into a praying multitude.

On November 11, the Moriah was teeming with more than eight hundred people trying to squeeze into the little chapel. A girl in her early teens seemed to capture the feeling when she cried out, "Oh, what will heaven be like if it is so wonderful down here!"

By the next day the prayer meetings had so overflowed the chapel that people were opening their homes for meetings. The people's burden for their unsaved loved ones was reaching a fever pitch. By early afternoon wagons and carts were pouring into the town from all over the countryside. By night even the home prayer meetings were overcrowded. The evangelists were running from chapel to chapel and house to house. The grocery shops were completely cleared of food as people who had come from long distances determined they were not going to go home. They had found the cloud of glory, and they were not going to leave it.

Sunday morning, November 13, Evan introduced his friend Sydney Evans to the throngs at Loughor and then without sleeping departed for Aberdare with five young women between the ages of eighteen and twenty to conduct revivals there. From Aberdare, Evan traveled to more than two dozen cities and towns throughout the principality of Wales.

Wave after wave of the Holy Spirit passed over the land. The move so affected the people that they gave up their favorite sport, soccer, without even thinking about it. Working-class men seemed to think and talk only about soccer. Gambling on the games was rampant, and at times it seemed that the whole nation would be in a frenzy over a game. Then the star players were converted and joined the open-air street meetings to testify of the glorious things the Lord had done for them. Soon the players were so captivated with Jesus, they lost interest in the games and the teams disbanded. The stadiums were empty!

This miracle could be compared to turning on your television one Sunday afternoon to watch an NFL game, only to hear the announcers trying to explain that none of the players had shown up for the game because they were all out evangelizing the city—and none of the fans had shown up because they were in revival meetings! No one preached against the sport; the people had simply become so passionate for the Lord that such games no longer interested either the players or the people.

THE COMMON DENOMINATOR

The conspicuous common denominator found wherever this revival broke out was that the Son of God was being lifted up and all men were being drawn to Him. Holiness and obedience were emphases, but this was primarily because Jesus was holy and everyone wanted to please Him. In fact, the presence of the Lord was so strong that no one could imagine speaking vile words or performing vile acts in His presence. James E. Stewart published many releases from a Welsh newspaper under the heading "Doings of the Churches" in his book, *Invasion of Wales by the Spirit*. One from Rhondda Valley tells a story that was recurring throughout the country:

RHONDDA VALLEY. A scene which may be witnessed any morning in dozens of pits in South Wales is carried out every morning here at 5 A.M. Scores of miners hold a service before going home from the midnight shift. The Superintendent starts a hymn and then the pit re-echoes the song. An old man whose gray head is tinged with coal dust falls on his knees to pray. Others do the same. The service attracts men from different workings and flickering lights are seen approaching the improvised temple. "Now, boys, those of you who love Christ, up with your lamp!" cries a young miner. In a second, scores of lights flicker in the air and another song of thanks sets the mine ringing.

The revival among the miners was so great that they stopped swearing. A glorious event, but it threw the mining companies into a strange turmoil. The horses were so used to hearing swear words as a part of their orders that when the men stopped swearing the horses did not know what they were saying. The mines actually had to shut down until the horses could be retrained.

Before the revival there had been almost a plague of drunkenness and gambling. During the revival, taverns were either closed or turned into meeting halls. Instead of wasting their earnings on drinking and gambling, workers started taking their wages home to their families. Because of the conviction of the Holy Spirit, restitution became a fruit of repentance, and thousands of young converts paid outstanding debts. These two factors alone resulted in a substantial economic impact on the whole community.

The famous Welsh singing festivals, which had been so popular, closed down during the revival because their famous vocalists, such as the Sankeys and Alexanders, were now singing hymns in the revival meetings. Many of the elected officials, even those from London, abandoned their seats in Parliament to participate in the meetings. Businesses founded upon honorable trades and products prospered. Those that traded on vice went out of business.

The Welsh Revival transformed society—and the world, as we will see in the next chapter.

14

The Legacy of Revival
Lessons for the Future

REVIVAL IS LIKE A FIRE THAT IS CARRIED BY THE wind—its sparks will ignite the dry wood and grass in every direction it blows. These sparks can be carried by letters, phone calls, or newspapers, but most of all by people. Localities that were far removed from the center of the Welsh Revival broke into revival just by hearing the news of what was happening in Wales. In many of these places the awakening seemed to be just as intense as in Wales. Without question, the spiritual temperature of the entire world was raised a few degrees by this great outpouring of the Spirit.

Visiting preachers and ordinary believers who had come to see "the burning bush" returned home to start fires in their own churches, mission fields, and cities. Christians all over the world became encouraged at the news, and nothing ignites evangelism like encouragement. The Welsh-speaking colonies in America and elsewhere were quickly set ablaze with revival. India was swept with the fire. All of Britain was touched, and the continent was invaded by wave after wave of evangelists, pastors, Bible teachers, and even new believers who could not sit still with the good news that was burning inside of them. In Scandinavia hundreds of churches still trace their birth to the Welsh Revival. Rees Howells, the great intercessor, was among the young evangelists who carried the fire from Wales to the mission field. Waves of evangelists and missionaries swept across the continents of Africa and Asia, saving souls and planting churches, Bible schools, and colleges.

As the news of the Welsh Revival spread around the world, some of the great preachers and spiritual leaders of the time came to witness it. Some called it a "Pentecost greater than Pentecost." Many of these leaders came thinking they could give direction and leadership to this new movement since some felt that mere "children" were running this great revival. Evan Roberts was only twenty-six at the time, and his brother, Dan, and Sydney Evans, had just turned twenty. Evan's sister, Mary, who was an important part of the work, was sixteen. The "Singing Sisters" who were greatly used during the meetings were between the ages of eighteen and twenty-two.

When the great and renowned preachers arrived, they were so impacted by the presence of the Holy Spirit, they sat dumb and mute before Him and the children He had chosen. This was to be a hallmark of the Welsh Revival. Great knowledge and eloquence bowed the knee to love and pure devotion, possibly as it had not done since the unlearned and untrained apostles stood before the Sanhedrin in Jerusalem. G. Campbell Morgan, one of the great preachers of that era, testified that he would trade all of his learning for even a small portion of the presence of God that accompanied the youthful leaders of the revival.

The fire of the Welsh Revival would also reach across the Atlantic Ocean to the United States. There it would directly affect those who would be used to ignite a new movement that would one day spread to every nation on earth, reaching more souls and releasing more missions and churches than any previous movement in history.

THE AZUSA STREET REVIVAL

On April 8, 1905, nearly ten thousand miles from Wales in Los Angeles, California, a young man named Frank Bartleman heard Dr. F. B. Meyer preach. As Meyer described the revival that was going on in Wales and his meeting with Evan Roberts, Bartleman wrote: "My soul was stirred to the depths, having read of this revival shortly before. I then and there promised God He should have full right of way with me; if He could use me." Later Bartleman and James Seymour read the book *The Great Revival in Wales* by S. B. Shaw, along with G. Campbell Morgan's tract *The Revival in Wales*. They were both stirred to seek the Lord earnestly for revival in Los Angeles.

In May they were sent five thousand pamphlets titled *The Revival in Wales*, which they distributed in the churches. Several letters were then exchanged with Evan Roberts himself. Bartleman and Seymour were unknowns ministering in a little mission on a side street in Los Angeles. Evan Roberts could not have known the impending spiritual destiny of these men, but he took the time to communicate with such hungry souls and history was changed. These great spiritual pioneers continually referred to their encouragement from Evan Roberts as they pursued the fullness of God's Spirit in their lives.

TWO WITNESSES

William J. Seymour and Frank Bartleman were different in many ways, but alike in one: they could not live without seeing the Lord's power restored to the church. Seymour was the unquestioned leader of the revival, and he had the authority on earth, but Bartleman was the intercessor who had authority with God. But before I tell their stories, we must go back a little farther.

THE SPIRITUAL GRANDFATHER

Charles Fox Parham (1873–1929) presided over a Bible school in Topeka, Kansas. He was a true spiritual father, and many consider him the father of the modern Pentecostal movement. Parham was constantly challenged by what he viewed as the great chasm between biblical Christianity and the state of the church. In the early hours of January 1, 1901, as he was keeping a New Year's Eve prayer vigil, he experienced the spiritual gift of speaking in tongues, or *glossolalia*, at the precise dawning of the twentieth century.

Speaking in tongues and the use of other spiritual gifts are by no means unique in church history. Many reformers and revivalists had such experiences. Even so, Parham's experience came at what could be called the "fullness of time," a moment that was ripe for the harvest of a recovered truth. His experience created a great deal of interest, mostly because of the dry and lifeless state of the church at the time. Parham was not known for emotionalism or exaggeration; he was conservative and resolute. This gave even more credibility to his experience.

A couple of years later, Parham's health broke down, and he was forced to move to Houston so he could stay with friends. His strength recovered, and he began another Bible school in the Texas port city. William Seymour became one of his students, but because he was black, and Parham was a strict segregationist, Seymour had to sit outside of the classroom and listen through a door that Parham would leave cracked open for him. Seymour wanted the Lord so much, he would embrace any humiliation to be close to what he felt the Lord was doing, and he was convinced that a new Pentecost was coming to the church.

REJECTION MARKS THE SPOT

In January of 1906, Seymour left Parham's school to pastor a mission congregation, without having received the baptism he had sought for so long. Just a week after arriving he was rejected by the mission's congregational leaders, who did not like his emphasis on the coming of a new Pentecost. One recurring theme in church history seems to be that most men and women of destiny arrive at their appointed place because of some level of rejection. We can see the same theme repeated in Scripture, such as in the lives of Joseph, Moses, David, and the Lord Jesus

Himself. A great disappointment with ourselves or men seems to be a prerequisite to being used by God in a significant way, especially to begin something new. It could even be said that learning to deal with rejection comes on the list of instructions for being a Christian. We should never be surprised by it but keep our trust and attention on the Lord. He will use everything that happens to us for His own good, as well as ours.

Seymour recognized the hand of God in the mission's rejection and was content to form a little home prayer group. They met regularly in a little apartment for several months. While in the middle of a ten-day fast, Seymour and the others in the group were dramatically baptized in the Holy Spirit, receiving the gift of tongues as well as other charismatic gifts.

Word spread like fire in dry wood. This could at least be attributed in part to the remarkable ministry of Frank Bartleman. He had written a stream of articles and tracts on revival. He constantly moved about the city exhorting churches and prayer groups to seek the Lord for a revival. Bartleman longed to see the Lord do in Los Angeles what He had recently done in Wales. After a time, he began to sense that Los Angeles would be different from what was happening in Wales, and he began boldly to prophesy "the coming of another Pentecost."

Soon large crowds of interested people descended on Seymour's little prayer group. To accommodate the large numbers, they were forced to rent a rundown old barnlike building in the middle of a black ghetto. The rent was only eight dollars a month, and it could hold as many as nine hundred people. Even so, services were soon going almost around the clock to handle the hungry multitudes that were coming. At the time no one imagined that the little street that it was on, Azusa, would soon become one of the most famous addresses in the world.

From the very beginning a remarkable characteristic of this revival was the diversity of the people who were drawn to it. The revival began with a few black men and women, but soon most of those who came were white. In one meeting more than twenty nationalities were counted. Fine ladies could be found lying prostrate on the floor next to domestic servants and washerwomen. Prominent churchmen and high government officials sat next to hoboes. No one seemed to care. Within a week even a prominent Jewish rabbi announced his full support. Soon astounding healings and dramatic conversions were taking place almost daily. Testimonies from the Welsh Revival had stirred many to seek the Lord for revival in America, and the deplorable spiritual state of the country made her ready for it. Because of this, the fire spread faster than possibly any previous or subsequent revival in American history.

Within weeks a steady stream of missionaries were coming from every continent on earth. Those who were on the front lines of the battle against the forces of darkness were the most acutely aware that they needed more power. They seized it like a drowning man grasps a lifesaver and soon gospel fires were burning brightly all over the world. In just two years the movement had taken root in more than fifty nations and was thought to have penetrated every U.S. town with a population of more than three thousand. Because missionaries were some of the first to come, missions remain a fundamental part of the spiritual genetic code of the Pentecostal movement—and one of its greatest strengths.

LESSONS FOR THE FUTURE

The first and most obvious question that researchers inevitably ask about the Welsh and Azusa Street Revivals is: Why did the Lord do it there? James E. Stewart concluded simply that God sends His fire where it is likely to catch and spread, and that "Wales provided the necessary tinder." This explanation applies to both revivals and provides at least a part of the reason, but it leads us to the question: *What is the necessary tinder?*

THE NECESSARY TINDER

The first logical answer to this question is that tinder is wood that is dry enough to burn easily. Both the Scriptures and history testify that a holy desperation precedes new beginnings. The intercessory ministry of the church before the Welsh and the Azusa Street Revivals was extraordinary. In Wales, thousands of believers, often unknown to each other, in small towns and great cities, cried to God day after day for the fire of revival to fall. This was not merely "a little talk with Jesus" but daily agonizing intercession. These devoted saints were so jealous for the name of their God that they agonized day and night because of the way Satan was being glorified all around them. They yearned from the depths of their beings to see the Lord's name lifted up in Wales. They constantly reminded God of what He had done in 1859, through the Second Great Awakening, and begged Him to pour out His Spirit again.

Evan Roberts captured the spirit of the whole revival with the theme: Bend the church and save the world. James E. Stewart claimed that this is the secret of every true awakening. Christians must humble themselves and get right with God so that the Spirit can break through in converting power. There must be no hypocrisy; the Christian must BEND to all the will of God for his life in perfect obedience before the Spirit of God is released. When we are bent to the will of God we will be intercessors, because as He "ever lives to intercede" for His people, we will do the same if we are abiding in Him.

Such a holy desperation also preceded the Azusa Street Revival. On the first of May 1904, a glimmer of revival broke out at the Lake Avenue Methodist Episcopal Church in Pasadena. Intercessors had been praying for revival to come there. Frank Bartleman visited the church and was deeply touched. That night he made a prophetic notation in his journal: "God has always sought a humble people. He can use no other. . . . There is always much need of heart preparation, in humility and separation, before God can consistently come. The depth of any revival will be determined exactly by the spirit of repentance that is obtained. In fact, this is the key to every true revival born of God."

On June 17 Bartleman went to Los Angeles to attend a meeting at the First Baptist Church, where they were waiting on God for an outpouring of the Spirit. Their pastor, Joseph Smale, had just returned from Wales. He was filled with zeal to have the same visitation and blessing come to his own church. Soon the revival spirit at Pastor Smale's church rapidly spread over the city. Devoted intercessors came from all over the region and represented almost all spiritual backgrounds.

At a tent meeting Bartleman met Edward Boehmer, who seemed to have the same burden of prayer, though he had just been converted the previous spring. They were immediately united in spirit and seemed to feed each other's fire for revival. Bartleman later said, "My life was by this time literally swallowed up in prayer. I was praying day and night."

Every significant outpouring of the Spirit seems to have been preceded by earnest, agonizing intercession, accompanied by a heartbrokenness and humiliation before God. Pastors and their flocks were deeply concerned about the terrible discrepancy between the heart-stirring record in the book of Acts and their present condition.

As James E. Stewart observed, "It is improbable that this revival, or any other, is of sudden origin. When the revival manifests itself in a mighty way it comes suddenly as in the days of Hezekiah, but even so, its origins begin with the Holy Spirit of God moving effectively in individual lives in private. Let no one pray for revival—let no one pray for a mighty baptism of power who is not prepared for deep heart-searchings and confession of sin in his personal life. Revival, in its beginnings, is a most humiliating experience. When one, like Isaiah, sees himself in the light of God's holiness he must inevitably cry, 'Woe is me!'"

Deep spiritual awakenings, whether in local churches or in whole countries, begin with desperate people. Frank Bartleman's zeal for the Lord was so great that his wife and friends began to fear for his life. He missed so much sleep and so many meals in order to pray, they did not think he could last much longer. His response to their pleas for moderation was: "I would rather die than not see revival."

Hannah, the prophet Samuel's mother, is a good example of those whom God uses to give birth to His purposes. Hannah became so desperate for a son, she was willing to give that son back to the Lord after she received him. That is one devotion the Lord must see in His people before He can trust them with true revival—we must be willing to give everything that is born back to Him.

The Lord has proven over and over that He will answer the prayers of desperate Christians. We must pray when we are sick of cold, mechanical services, heartbroken over the deadness of the church and over sinners who are eternally lost, or desperate about our spiritual condition. When the awakening does come there is surely "joy unspeakable and full of glory," but this has never been the case during the days preceding it. It seems essential to have days of no song before the songs of the Holy Spirit come, groans and mourning before the joy and laughter. And always there must be Hannah's devotion to give what is born back to God.

DID INTERCESSION CAUSE THESE REVIVALS?

One of the oldest, unanswered questions about revival is the degree to which intercession is required to bring it to pass. It does seem that no great revival has ever taken place without a preceding heaven-rending intercession on behalf of the lost and the condition of the church. But we must also ask the question: Did the intercession bring forth the revival or did the impending revival bring forth the intercession? We might rephrase this: Does the travail cause the baby or does the baby cause the travail? Obviously, it is the latter.

This is an important issue because many dear saints have expended much of their lives in spiritual travail never to see a spiritual birth. In the natural, there is such a thing as a false pregnancy: a woman who wants a baby badly enough can start to have symptoms of being pregnant, even gaining weight and carrying it like a baby, when there has been no conception. Travailing intercession does precede revival, but this is not just something that we can decide to do without the Lord initiating it, just as a woman cannot decide that she is going to be pregnant. Without conception she can go through travail, but there still is not going to be a baby. Neither can we just decide to bring forth revival.

Romans 10:6–7 states: "But the righteousness based on faith speaks thus, 'Do not say in your heart, "Who will ascend into heaven?" (that is, to bring Christ down), or "Who will descend into the abyss?" (that is, to bring Christ up from the dead).'" We cannot call God down or bring Him up, such as mediums try to do with their incantations to demons. The Lord is not at our disposal; we are at His. True spiritual travail comes from being united with Him; therefore genuine travail is not something we can decide to enter into. But when a spiritual birth is impending, we cannot keep from entering into it. Just as a woman who is not pregnant cannot simply decide to be pregnant, one who *is* pregnant cannot simply decide that she is not—there is a baby in her that *is* going to be born!

The whole world is in desperate need of revival and, before the end of this age, there is going to be one so awesome and universal that all of these other great revivals will be considered a mere foretaste. Before we begin to agonize in prayer for it, let us simply seek the mind and heart of the Lord that we might pray with Him, not just for Him.

I do not want to in any way distract from the importance of intercession, which is one of the most important functions of the church. But we must be sure that we are praying in harmony with God's purposes and not just for what we think we need. Elijah was obviously in touch with God, and he actually prayed *for* judgment to come upon his nation; then God's judgment *brought* the repentance that stirred the revival in his time.

Now that we have looked at the necessary tinder for revival, let's look at the components that have been part of the burning. Eight similarities can be seen in most of the revivals we have discussed in these two chapters.

1. Like Jesus, Revival May Be Born in Stables

In biblical times the stable was a most offensive place. The floors were composed of decades worth of impacted dung and other filth. The stench was so great that stables were placed as far away from other dwellings as possible. By today's standards, they would not even be fit for animals. That the Lord of Glory would choose such a place to make His entry into this world is one of the more profound revelations of His message to man.

We would do well not to miss His point in doing this as He has not stopped using such places to make His appearances. Just as the Lord chose Wales, the least of the principalities of the British Isles, He later chose the tiny little Azusa Street mission and a humble but courageous black pastor to change the face of modern Christianity. The building on Azusa Street even had a dirt floor and had once been used as a livery stable.

To see what the Lord is doing, we may have to go to places that require the death of our flesh and sometimes our reputations. We must have the heart of prophets Simeon and Anna, who served in the temple at the time Jesus was born. They could see the salvation of the world in a mere infant. We must not be discouraged if the fruit is not yet apparent but rather look for the seed that will become the fruit. This does not mean that He is only found in the poor and lowly, but that is where He is usually found. The apostle Paul knew this when he said, "But God has chosen the foolish things of the world to shame the wise, and God has chosen the weak things of the world to shame the things which are strong" (1 Cor. 1:27).

2. Lack of Organization: The Plan Was Not to Plan

A true move of God is not fueled by organization, money, or advertising. True revival only comes when the pillar of fire, the presence of God Himself, picks up and moves. To try to organize, promote, or sell a move of God can be profanity in its lowest form. Historians would later write that the most astonishing feature of the Welsh Revival was the lack of commercialism. No hymnbooks, no song leaders, no committees, no choirs, no great preachers, no offerings, no organization. Yet souls were redeemed, families were healed, and whole cities were converted on a scale that had not been seen before or since.

Just weeks before the Welsh Revival broke out in his home church in Loughor, Evan Roberts had planned campaigns throughout Wales with his brother, Dan, and friend Sydney Evans. Quickly he discovered that the Spirit had another plan, and His plans were much better. Evan soon developed a healthy fear of man's planning and organization in the midst of revival. He looked to the Holy Spirit for leadership.

It was also William Seymour's ability to discern and trust the Holy

Spirit that created the fire at Azusa. In spite of almost constant pressure from world-renowned church leaders who came from around the globe to impose what they perceived to be needed order and direction, Seymour held the course and allowed the Holy Spirit to move in His own, often mysterious, ways. As long as he did this the fire continued. Immediately when he gave in to the pressure to organize the new movement the Holy Spirit moved on. However, it is remarkable that Seymour was able to hold his course for as long as he did under the pressure he received from well-intentioned but misguided leaders.

Seymour and Roberts both believed that the Holy Spirit required the freedom to move through whomever He chose, not just the leadership. They both resolved to allow anyone to be used by the Lord, even the most humble believers.

Evan Roberts refused to allow his meetings or visits to a city to be announced until a day or two before he was to arrive. Even then he would only say that he hoped to be at a certain place at a certain time. When the campaign was finally organized for his visit to Liverpool, it was a good example of Evan's uncompromising commitment to walk in the way that he understood. The committee pressed him to state a definite time when he would come. He refused to do it. When he did eventually go, he gave the committee only four days' warning that he was coming. Even then, though 100,000 Welsh people in that English city were longing to hear him, he insisted that he could not know in which of the crowded chapels he would speak at a given time.

Dan Roberts and Sydney Evans followed the same procedure as Evan. They sought the Lord daily for His will and went where He told them to go. They knew that apart from the presence and power of the Holy Spirit they would accomplish nothing. When they arrived in a place, sometimes they preached and sometimes they did not. Sometimes they kept silent during the entire services, which often lasted for four or five hours.

Sometimes Evan Roberts would also enter a meeting and sit on the front seat and say nothing for three hours. Then he would stand up, preach and pray for some ten or fifteen minutes, and sit down. Sometimes he might preach the whole time, or pray the whole time. Sometimes he would sit silently through the entire meeting. Regardless of what Evan did, the people would carry on under the influence of the Holy Spirit.

There were soloists, duets, special singers during the revival, but they seldom announced where they were going to sing. Sometimes they went to a place expecting to sing, but the Spirit had other plans. Then they would keep their peace or they might just pray. Those who witnessed their ministry knew that when they did sing it was the Holy Spirit. This was a revival in which the Lord Jesus Christ Himself was the center and main attraction: it was noised abroad that *He* was in the house. The young workers knew that the Holy Spirit came to testify of Jesus, and if an evangelist or the team became the center of the attraction, the Holy Spirit would depart.

As the Lord Jesus explained to Nicodemus: "The wind blows where it wishes and you hear the sound of it, but do not know where it comes from and where it is going; so is everyone who is born of the Spirit" (John 3:8). The workers in the Welsh Revival came to understand that the Lord meant this literally. Finally they did not try to figure out where the Spirit was going next, they only tried to stay close enough to hear the sound of it.

It is noteworthy that few who have tried to duplicate this kind of ministry style have succeeded. Many succumbed to spiritual delusions, or suffered the shipwreck of their faith. Even the apostles to the early church often planned their missionary journeys and would announce their impending visits months ahead of time. They always remained open for the Lord to change their plans, but because they were growing and maturing, they did not always make the right decisions. At times, the Lord would correct their course with an intervention of divine guidance through a dream, a vision, or a prophet. We need to labor with the spiritual wisdom that has been given to us, but always be open for the Lord to intervene.

Even Evan Roberts did not try to imply that leadership and organization are not needed in the church, but when the Spirit is doing something new and fresh, the greatest gift is *not knowing how to lead, but knowing how to follow.* The attempts at organization during the Welsh Revival all proved futile, and at times a hindrance to the true work. In the first mention of the Spirit in Scripture, He is moving. He is ever flowing, going somewhere. He is also moving over something that is formless and void. It seems that every time the Spirit wants to move in a creative way, He still has to find those who are formless and void, or who are flexible enough to move with Him. The humility that comes from knowing you do not have all the answers stimulates a holy desperation for God in oneself. Those few with this humility seem to be the only ones who can ever be responsive to the Lord when He wants to do a new thing.

During times of a dynamic outpouring of the Holy Spirit, such as the Welsh and the Azusa Street Revivals, the Lord can only use those who will yield themselves completely to Him in order that He might do something entirely new. It seems that in every city the apostle Paul visited, the Holy Spirit moved differently from the previous ones. Paul moved with vision, strategy, and decisiveness, but also with a finely tuned sensitivity to the Holy Spirit and the willingness to yield to a different plan.

Many of the great missionary ventures in church history, such as William Booth's Salvation Army, were planned over many years, and they generally followed the plan. Those who might have worked with some of these missionary ventures would probably scorn the lack of organization of the Welsh Revival and Azusa Street. Similarly, those who were a part of these revivals would almost certainly reject the seeming overdependence on organization of such missionary societies. A great tribute to General Booth was that he visited the Welsh Revival, observed how it was functioning in almost the opposite manner in which he ran the Salvation Army, and was still able to recognize this as God's work. He then went back and continued to run the army just the way he had been, recognizing that God employs *different* strategies for different places or purposes.

We must realize that the God who makes every snowflake different seldom moves the same way twice. It is His nature to be creative and diverse. There are lessons for the whole church in the way the Lord moved in Wales and Azusa. Likewise, there are lessons for us all in the way that He moved through the Salvation Army in its early years. Both the Welsh and Azusa Street Revivals died when human organizations were able to take the reins of the revival, but many of the moves of God that have born lasting fruit could not have done it without organization and planning. True revivals are the high-water marks of history. Even so, as Vance Havner so eloquently put it:

> Revival does not have all of the answers. Such resurgences can be compared to a sale in a department store. The sale may be more spectacular, but the main business is done in the daily merchandising the year round. Pentecost was a great day, but the steady growth came as the Lord added to the church daily. Revivals make headlines, but when the books are added up at the last day, it will be found that the main work was done by the faithful preaching of ordinary pastors, the daily witnessing of ordinary Christians, the soul winning in home and church.

Let us continue to pray for revival. It is certainly coming, but let us not neglect the important work of the kingdom that is in our hand today. Let us use every day to do the work that is before us and to prepare for the coming revival.

After the Welsh Revival, churches that had struggled to keep the doors open for the few saints who would attend were now faced with the problem of how to contain the multitudes that were causing even the prayer meetings to overflow. No congregation in Wales was really prepared for the magnitude of this revival. Some of the pastors strove to serve all the new converts and see that they were properly incorporated into congregations, but to most the revival was "gloriously out of control."

Pastors quickly burned out trying to do too much. In fact, it is probable that the revival could have lasted much longer had the leaders paced themselves better; no revival can last if the workers do not learn to rest. True revivals bring many strains upon congregations and Christian workers that few are prepared for. Almost every church or mission in the country grew dramatically, frequently doubling or even quadrupling in membership, and many maintained these members for years afterward. But multitudes who were touched by the revival and had a genuine encounter with the Lord were also lost again because there were not enough workers to care for them spiritually. It is hard to take the time to equip other workers and ministries in the heat of revival. Had this been done before the revival it is certain that many more of those who committed themselves to the Lord could have been established in the faith and truly added to the church. The eternal record will almost certainly establish that the Welsh Revival, like almost every other revival in history, paid a dear price in lost fruit because of church leadership's failure to heed the mandate of Ephesians 4—that the ministry of the church is given to equip the members who are to do the work of the service.

Possibly for the first time in church history a great revival is now anticipated almost universally throughout the church. It is probable that the reason the Lord has given us such a warning of impending revival is so that we *will* prepare.

3. A New Song

Spontaneous worship that gives birth to a new expression is usually found in true revivals. This was also true of the Welsh Revival. Much of the contemporary style of worship that is now attributed to either the Pentecostal or charismatic movements actually had its origin in Wales. This revival was exploding there at the same time that the Pentecostal outpouring was beginning on Azusa Street. The leaders of these two revivals, William J. Seymour and Frank Bartleman in Los Angeles and Evan Roberts in Wales, wrote to each other during the revivals. There was also a great deal of other interchange between the revivals as people hungry for God rushed from one to the other seeking His presence. Naturally, they impacted one another. Possibly the great contribution of the Welsh Revival was the new spontaneous form of worship called "singing in the Spirit," which was to become a signature of the Holy Spirit's presence for decades to come. R. B. Jones, a leader in the revival, said of the music:

The fact is, unless heard, it is unimaginable and when heard indescribable. There was no hymnbook. No one gave out a hymn. Just anyone would start the singing, and very rarely did it happen that the hymn started was out of harmony with the mood at the moment. Once started, as if moved by a simultaneous impulse, the hymn was caught up by the whole congregation almost as if what was about to be sung had been announced and all were responding to the baton of a visible human leader. I have seen nothing like it. Such was the perfect blending of the mood and purpose that it bore eloquent testimony to a unity created only by the Spirit of God. Another witness testified: The praying and singing were both wonderful. There was no need for an organ. The assembly was its own organ as a thousand sorrowing or rejoicing hearts found expression in the Psalmody of their native hills.

4. Intercession

The Welsh Revival was initiated and carried by a devotion to prayer and intercession that also spread throughout the worldwide Christian community. Much of the fire that continues in some of the great prayer movements of today could likely trace its origin to a lingering spark from the Welsh Revival. The prayer and the praise mingled together in most of the meetings. James E. Stewart wrote:

It was praying that rent the heavens; praying that received direct answers there and then. The spirit of intercession was so mightily poured out that the whole congregation would take part simultaneously for hours! Strangers were startled to hear the young and unlettered pray with such unction and intelligence as they were swept up to the Throne of Grace by the Spirit of God. Worship and adoration was unbounded. Praise began to mingle with the petitions as answered prayer was demonstrated before their very eyes. Often when unsaved loved ones were the focus of the intercession, they would be compelled to come to the very meeting and be saved!

This further fed the fires of both the worship and the intercession.

5. They Saved Souls

Conversions in the Welsh Revival were not just statistics, they were genuine new births. Men and women were so radically changed that being "born again" was not just a cliché—it was a reality. The new believer's first encounter with the Lord was not the promise of blessings but a profound comprehension of his own sinful condition. When moved by the Spirit to come to the wells of salvation, converts did not just raise their hands in the back of the building to acknowledge their decision, they were racked with such a holy desperation for the mercy of the Savior, they tumbled to the floor as if in physical pain. Those under conviction would sometimes writhe in their own tears until they gained the assurance of forgiveness; then their grief would turn into a joy of an equal depth that would be impossible to contain. As the meetings began to disband, often at two or three in the morning, new converts just could not leave and would continue singing, praying, and at times laughing uncontrollably until the prayer meetings started at sunrise.

There can be no revival without soul winning. In saving lost souls the Welsh Revival must be considered one of the most intense and effective revivals of all time. This was not a program for a few preachers or a campaign to get church members testifying to the saving grace of the Lord Jesus. There were no classes on how to reach the lost. Believers simply could not contain their joy of salvation so every coal mine, tramcar, office, school, and shop became a pulpit for the gospel. The witness of the common believers led multiplied thousands to a saving faith in Jesus, more than the preaching. There was no set pattern of strategy for the witnessing; it was simply born out of an overflowing joy and faith.

The presence of the Lord was so intense in Wales that those who had traveled from the ends of the earth to witness it said that just being in one of the revival meetings was worth the whole journey, even if Evan, Dan, or Sydney Evans was not there. The people of Wales lost a lot of sleep because they were afraid that if they left the services they would miss something wonderful. The meetings carried on until two or three o'clock in the morning many nights and did not end until the people, sometimes including the entire population of a city or town, had marched through the streets singing the praises of the Lamb!

The outreach of the Asuza Street Revival was just as significant, if not more so. Even to call what began at Azusa Street just a revival would be to obscure its true importance. It was a revival, but it was a renewal and a reformation of the church as well. With the possible exception of Luther's Reformation, there probably has not been another movement in church history that has had a greater impact on the entire church.

This impact is not only continuing, it is continuing to increase. Through the Pentecostal Revival—and the subsequent neo-Pentecostal movements spawned from it, such as the Charismatic Renewal—more ministers of the gospel have already been ordained, more missionaries sent out, more churches planted, and more people brought to salvation than through any other movement in church history. If the present rate of growth is sustained, soon the numbers of those impacted by this renewal will eclipse the totals of all other movements together.

To understand how the essence of this movement has been able to mature, while at the same time staying responsive to new moves of the Spirit, is important for every spiritual leader. Many of its churches, and even whole denominations, have continued to reach for greater spiritual power while at the same time sinking their roots deeper into sound biblical truth, making necessary corrections and adjustments while maintaining a forward momentum. Of course, this should be the norm, but it has in fact been the exception to the nature of such movements.

As we read of the great impact of many of the previous spiritual movements, it is often hard to imagine that most of them lasted a very short time. Rarely has a movement stayed on the cutting edge of what God is doing for more than a decade, and more often it is but a year or two. Even the apostolic movement of the first-century church faded rapidly into an increasing apostasy shortly after the death of its first leaders. However, defying all of the previous norms for such movements, the Pentecostal movement has continued to keep moving for almost a century, and there is no end to its continued advance in sight. Taken as a group, the Pentecostal/charismatic movements are now the second largest category in all of Christianity. If their present rate of growth is sustained, they will, in just a few years, outnumber the rest of Christianity *combined*.

Of course, many individuals, churches, and even whole denominations that were birthed out of this movement have stopped moving. In many places one can only find the remnants of the past glory, with little or no continuing fire. Even so, around the world multitudes of Pentecostal/charismatic churches are ablaze with the presence and activity of God. In countries where the greatest advances of the gospel are now taking place, Pentecostals are usually found at the vanguard.

6. *One Man Lit the Spark*

Those who heard Evan Roberts that night in Moriah were challenged in the same way as the townsfolk in Nazareth who heard the Lord read from the prophecy in Isaiah in His own synagogue. The Lord spoke with an authority that required all who heard either to believe Him or to reject Him. They chose to reject the Son of God. Those who heard Evan Roberts were challenged in the same way. For a few brief moments this great move of God very likely hung in the balance. This young man they had known from childhood and had worked with in the mines was now declaring the Word of God with a boldness they had never before witnessed. The townspeople were either going to have to believe God for a marvelous and unprecedented display of His power or reject the messenger. They chose to believe. Another major hurdle was passed; the spiritual atmosphere in Wales had reached its critical mass. Now revival to at least some degree was inevitable.

Could it be possible that this entire revival depended on the reception of this one man? Yes! If we believe both the biblical and historical precedents, it is likely that the great Welsh Revival depended on the reception of the messenger the Lord had chosen to strike the match on the prepared fuel, just as the Nashville Revival depended upon the audacity of Sam Jones.

One of the greatest biblical revivals took place in the wicked, heathen city of Nineveh because sinners chose to believe the most unlikely wayward Hebrew prophet Jonah. Our reception of the grace of God is often dependent on our ability to let Him use the foolish to confound the wise, the weak to confound the strong. Before His departure, the Lord Jesus Himself declared, "From now on you shall not see Me until you say, *Blessed is He who comes in the name of the Lord!*'" (Matt. 23:39, emphasis added). By this He was declaring that from that time on we would not see Him unless we blessed those He sent to us.

There is a difference between spiritual idealism and revelation. Idealism, even spiritual idealism, is a subtle form of humanism and is a manifestation of human pride. It was reported and is probable that Jessie Penn-Lewis played a significant part in bringing the great Welsh Revival to an end, even though she seemed to have had the best of intentions. She supposedly persuaded Evan Roberts to withdraw from the revival because he was getting too much of the attention that should go only to the Lord.

As is the case with many great leaders, their strengths are also their weaknesses. Evan Roberts's great strength was that he dreaded publicity because he felt that it detracted from the One who was the true Source of the revival. He dreaded newspaper reporters. He dreaded adulation. Many times he withdrew himself from the meetings when he felt that the people were coming to see and hear him instead of coming for the Lord. In meetings where he felt he was the center of attraction, he pleaded with an agonized spirit that the people would look away to Christ alone, or else the Holy Spirit would withdraw Himself from them. Though Evan Roberts became the most publicized preacher in the world at that time, he repeatedly refused interviews with reporters who came from every part of the globe. He refused to be photographed except by members of his own family. He knew this awakening was of God and not from himself and that if people idolized him the glory would be withdrawn. He did not even answer the multitude of requests that came from publishing houses around the world seeking to publish his biography. He greatly feared that by doing this he might rob the Lord of even some of the glory that was due only to Him. Evan Roberts's determination kept the people rightly focused and helped them to maintain the blessing of the Lord's presence for as long as they did.

Evan Roberts so abhorred even the thought that he might be getting some of the attention that belonged only to his beloved Lord that in 1906 he followed Jesse Penn-Lewis's advice and withdrew—and the revival quickly died.

The idealist would contend that if it had been a true revival, then removing any man would not have made a difference. However, both Scripture and history testify differently. Because the Lord entrusted the authority of this earth to men, He always looks for men to stand in the gap when He wants to move on the earth. Only God can ignite true revival, but God will always move through men.

There must be the human side of revival; it was to be "The sword of the Lord—*and Gideon*." Many, seeking to duplicate historic revivals, have tried to completely remove human initiative so that what will happen will be solely of the Holy Spirit. But the Spirit does not work that way. The Lord always uses chosen vessels for His work. Evan Roberts is a classic study of the type of vessel He can use. Like John the Baptist, Evan Roberts was given to preparing the way for the Lord, pointing to Him, and being willing to decrease as He increased. However, it was important that John not decrease until the Lord increased; this is the point that many seeking revival miss.

The Lord gave John the Baptist an anointing that stirred an entire nation, such that the great and the small alike came to him. Only after he had the nation's attention did he point to the One who is greater. John had to allow the Lord to raise him up or he would not have been able to accomplish his purpose. It is true that many who reach this prominence prove unwilling to decrease as the Lord increases, but that does not negate the fact that many more never get to the place where they can point to the Lord because they are unwilling to be elevated to a place where this is possible.

God's purpose from the beginning has been to *use men to do His work.* The Lord planted the garden, but He put man in it to cultivate and keep it. No farmer has ever grown corn; he plants and cultivates it, but only God can cause the corn to grow. Still, God never planted a perfect field of corn without using a man. Of course the Lord could do it Himself, but He has chosen to work through men to accomplish His purposes on this earth. To be greatly used by God is not to steal His glory but to show it forth in a greater way—as long as we, like John the Baptist and Evan Roberts, keep pointing to Him.

It is usually an evil religious spirit that seeks to deny man this union with God in His work with idealistic delusions of man getting too much of the glory. It is right to acknowledge that man is but the "earthen vessel" and that the glory is all God's, but it is humanistic idealism that denies that the glory of the Lord should be in an earthen vessel. Many thought that it was unfair to indict Jessie Penn-Lewis for single-handedly stopping the Welsh Revival, even though many of Evan Roberts's friends and coworkers believed that she did. Evan Roberts left the work and went to live in the Penn-Lewis home where he effectively became a spiritual hermit, never again being used in ministry. Jessie Penn-Lewis was the equivalent of today's heresy hunters. As she wrote in her most noteworthy book, *War Against the Saints,* she considered the speaking in tongues that was starting to break out in the revival to be from the devil (later versions of her work have omitted this condemnation). Self-appointed watchmen and judges have been used to stop or sidetrack many great moves of God. That is why the Lord did not appoint heresy hunters in the church but elders. The apostles and elders of the biblical church gained their influence not by exposing darkness but by manifesting the light.

7. Emotional Fire

Few would question that some of the emotional demonstrations still found in Pentecostal or charismatic meetings are rooted in attention seeking and can sometimes be demonic manifestations. But those who condemn such meetings because of the outbreaks would have to condemn the Lord's own meetings when He walked the earth. Contrary to some popular teachings, *love is an emotion*. The Lord Jesus actually promoted emotional demonstrations of love for Him, such as the pouring out of costly ointment and even the washing of His feet with a harlot's tears.

What husband would want his wife to say that she does not feel anything for him anymore but serves him because it is her duty? What wife would care to hear her husband say that he loved her with the power of his will but he did not feel anything for her? Even though the marriage may still exist, the life is gone. Those who serve the Lord only by their will, and not with their emotions, also have lost the spiritual life. Do you think the Lord receives our hymns during worship if we are only singing out of duty? Such worship is vain.

When people have been subjected to nothing but cold, lifeless religion and are suddenly touched by the living God, they become emotional, and often go to the other extreme for a while. It is impossible to feel God's presence without *feeling* a passionate love for Him. Spiritual maturity is doing the right things for the right reasons—with the right feelings. If man is deprived of the ability either to reason or to show his emotions he has been deprived of half of his humanity.

Those who attack emotional responses to the Lord are trying to steal the life from our worship. If a man becomes more emotional at a football game than he does when worshiping the Lord, it is probable that this man loves football more than he loves Jesus. Emotions are not meant to be the thermostat of human personality, but they are a relatively accurate thermometer.

8. Unity

We know from the Scriptures that before the end of this age comes, the church will be unified. When the Lord looks down upon the earth,

He sees only one church. The many divisions were devised in hell, not heaven, and they will be overthrown before the end comes. We must have unity if we are going to be prepared for the great harvest that will mark the end of this age. The "nets" simply will not be able to hold the catch if we do not join together.

Many are trying to unify the church for the wrong reasons and under the wrong spiritual organizations. Some, overreacting to this, decry all unity movements. Others proclaim that only persecution can bring unity. History testifies that this is not the case. During the terrible persecution of the church in Uganda under Idi Amin, the church in that country did come into a unity; all denominational barriers melted and the church seemed to truly be one. But within thirty days after the persecution, all previous barriers were erected again and the spiritual infighting picked up right where it had left off. External pressures dictated their unity, not a true unity of the heart.

When the Lord came down to see the tower that was being built in Babel, He stated, "Behold, they are one people, and they all have the same language. And this is what they began to do, and now *nothing which they purpose to do will be impossible for them*" (Gen. 11:6). There is a power in unity that multiplies authority; one can put a thousand to flight but two can put ten thousand to flight. For this reason the Lord scattered the languages of the men of Babel so that they could not continue building their vain tower. The Lord declared, "If two of you agree on earth about anything that they may ask, it shall be done for them by My Father who is in heaven" (Matt. 18:19).

When just 120 believers were in one accord on the day of Pentecost, the heavens opened and the church age was born. On that day a sign was given, the gift of tongues, by which all men from so many different nations could understand what was being declared by God. These tongues were a sign that the church would be the antithesis of the Tower of Babel. Through the church, men would again be unified and would be able to make it to heaven.

The church will come into unity before the end, but there is a good reason that there has been so much disunity until now. There is a general, biblical principle that between the place where we receive the promises of God (Egypt) and the place of the fulfillment of those promises (the promised land), there is usually a wilderness, which is exactly the opposite of what has been promised. The church was promised that she would rule with the Lord over the nations, but for nearly two thousand years she has been ruled by the world. She was meant to have a unity that would cause the whole world to believe in Jesus—but has probably been more divided than any other religion or philosophy.

Israel left Egypt overnight. It took forty years in the wilderness to get the Egyptian influence out of Israel and make her fit for the promised land. At one point, when the Lord was about to destroy the whole nation and start again with Moses, he interceded for Israel with the argument that if the Lord destroyed Israel after bringing her out of Egypt, the whole world's testimony would be that the Lord could bring them out of Egypt, but He could not bring them into their inheritance (see Ex. 32:1–14).

That is precisely the world's present testimony concerning the church—the Lord may be able to take us out of the world, but He has not been able to take the world out of us, or bring us into our spiritual inheritance. Before the end of this age the Lord will have a testimony through the church to the entire world that He was able both to take us out of our Egypt and to bring us into our inheritance. At the end of this age the Lord's prayer for unity will be answered and the whole world will know it; the result is going to be an outpouring of a power and authority that no one in the world will be able to deny. The Lord is returning for a bride, not a harem!

15

Our Quest for the Future

The Truth of the Past That Prepares Us for the Future

THE MINISTRY THAT OPENED THE CHURCH AGE will be the one that closes it. Before the end of this age, there will be a movement to return true apostolic ministry to the church. This is our primary quest—to see true, apostolic Christianity restored to the earth. However, this should not be construed that we must return to the first-century application of this to the church community. It will be a twenty-first-century church, dynamic and modern, but built firmly on the solid foundation of biblical truth and the leadership of men and women who walk in authentic apostolic authority and integrity.

What does this mean? First, it means that Jesus will be in us to do the works that He did when He walked the earth. Second, it means that the church will accurately represent Him to the world, our present world. Our words must become His words, our works His works.

When all of the ministries are fully restored and functioning in the church, we will have the stature Paul described in Ephesians 4:11–16:

And He gave some as apostles, and some as prophets, and some as evangelists, and some as pastors and teachers, for the equipping of the saints for the work of service, to the building up of the body of Christ; until we all attain to the unity of the faith, and of the knowledge of the Son of God, to a mature man, to the measure of the stature which belongs to the fullness of Christ. As a result, we are no longer to be children, tossed here and there by waves, and carried about by every wind of doctrine, by the trickery of men, by craftiness in deceitful scheming; but speaking the truth in love, we are to grow up in all aspects into Him, who is the head, even Christ, from whom the whole body, being fitted and held together by that which every joint supplies, according to the proper working of each individual part, causes the growth of the body for the building up of itself in love.

As this text states, when the ministries are functioning properly and together in harmony, we will see:

- all believers adequately equipped for the ministry;
- the whole church come to the unity of the faith (which is much more than just a unity around doctrine);
- all believers come to the full knowledge of the Son of God;
- all believers grow to maturity;
- Christians no longer tossed about by the winds of doctrine and the trickery of men; and
- the whole church begin to function like one body, fitted and held together by the proper functioning of each individual part.

This is the apostolic commission, and it is far beyond human genius or ability.

When the real nature of apostolic Christianity is revealed again, it will expose every pretender. Like the early church, the last-day apostolic church can expect the worst persecution to come from those who claim to be Christians, who will claim vehemently to be the protectors of the truth. Good has always been the worst enemy of the best, and those who have settled for a good thing will be the most offended when something better comes. This persecution will help to separate the wheat from the chaff.

In the last few years I have received much insight into the unfolding of events at the end of this age. Even so, I can still only be dogmatic about one thing—I see in part and am still seeing through a glass darkly, even though some things have become a little clearer. We all see in part; therefore, we will all have to put our parts together with what others are seeing if we are going to have a complete picture. That is why, as we see in the text quoted from Ephesians 4, it is the ministry of the apostles, prophets, evangelists, pastors, and teachers *together,* working in harmony, that brings forth the fullness of what the church is called to be. We all need each other.

THE FALSE APOSTOLIC MOVEMENT

Over the last few years, there have been many groups and streams that claim to be apostolic. In most cases these are wonderful, devoted Christians who are doing great things. MorningStar Ministries has been asked to join some of these, and some have called our ministry apostolic. Though I greatly respect many of these people, I still am not comfortable that we are seeing anything that is of the biblical stature of authentic apostolic ministry yet. In fact, I think that this has become so trendy that it will eventually muddy the waters so much that most of the church will have a difficult time recognizing the real thing when it comes. This seems to be the pattern for ministries to be restored to the church. There is almost always a "Saul" before a "David."

The Lord had promised Israel a king through their father Jacob (see Gen. 49:10). They were feeling a need for a king, but they did not have the patience to wait for God's chosen one. Saul was "head and shoulders above the rest." He looked like a good king, but there were deep flaws in his character that would surface when he was given authority that he was not called by God to have. The Lord allowed Himself to be moved by the people so that He would even anoint Saul, and used Him as much as He could. But Israel would still pay a dear price for their impatience. All of the confusion only delayed their ability to recognize God's chosen king by many years.

Without an awakening to the shallowness of what is now being called "apostolic," the church is headed for just such a debacle concerning apostolic ministry. Just as the Lord commended the Ephesian church for putting to the test those who called themselves apostles and were not, we must not be afraid of testing those who make such claims. However, churches are flocking toward those who now appear to be head and shoulders above the rest. There will be euphoria, and these groups will win some battles for the Lord. He will bless them and anoint them as much as He can. However, they will not be able to bring the ark of God to its chosen place, or establish the kingdom that will not end. In fact, without a major change of direction the result will be that the whole church will have a hard time just hearing the word *apostolic* for a time, just as Israel did not want to hear about another king for a long time.

Even so, we must have a restoration of apostolic ministry for the church to be equipped for her end-time mission. This ministry will be restored before the end comes. In 2 Peter 3:12 we are told to be "looking for and hastening the coming of the day of God." It is remarkable to think that we could actually "hasten" the coming of the day of the Lord, but it is true. One way that we can do this is to refuse to accept cheap or shallow substitutes for the apostolic or any other ministry.

A CHANGE IN VIEW

We are now approaching the end of this age. I cannot say whether it will unfold over years or decades, but the Lord has shown me that if I am going to understand it properly, I must see the ending of this age as a beginning more than an ending. We are coming to the dawning of the Day of the Lord, the time in which Jesus Christ will return to establish

His kingdom and rule over the earth. However, to see this accurately we must understand what He said in Luke 17:20–24:

> Now having been questioned by the Pharisees as to when the kingdom of God was coming, He answered them and said, "The kingdom of God is not coming with signs to be observed; nor will they say, 'Look, here it is!' or, 'There it is!' For behold, the kingdom of God is in your midst." And He said to the disciples, "The days shall come when you will long to see one of the days of the Son of Man, and you will not see it. And they will say to you, 'Look there! Look here!' Do not go away, and do not run after them. For just as the lightning, when it flashes out of one part of the sky, shines to the other part of the sky, so will the Son of Man be in His day."

As stated before, Jesus' emphasis here is that the kingdom of God is not coming "with signs to be observed." This does not imply that there were no signs of the coming of His kingdom, as He Himself spoke of these signs, but it is clear they will be very subtle. This subtlety is explained in the last verse, which is stated slightly differently in Matthew 24:27: "For just as the lightning comes from the east, and flashes even to the west, so shall the coming of the Son of Man be."

The word that is translated "lightning" in both of these Scriptures is the Greek word *astrape*, which could have been translated more accurately as "a bright shining." Lightning does not always come out of the east and flash to the west, but the sun does. It is apparent here that the Lord was not speaking about lightning but about the sun rising. If we are going to see His kingdom coming, we must be awake early enough and be looking in the right direction.

The first indication that the sun is about to rise comes when you see the morning star, which is actually the planet Venus. Psalm 19:1 says, "The heavens are telling of the glory of God; and their expanse is declaring the work of His hands." Satan has tried to pervert almost every one of these "signs in the heavens," which tell of the glory of God and the work of His hands. Satan named this planet after the false goddess of love, but the morning star, Venus, actually represents the passion of God's heart and the preeminent work of His hands, the church. She will rise far above the horizon before the end of this age, where she will be the greatest sign that the Day of the Lord is about to dawn, and His return is near.

Many have misunderstood the signs of their own times and wrongly thought that they were the signs of the end. This is because we tend to look for outward signs and events while we fail to look closely at the first place these signs will be seen—in God's people, the church. I do not believe that the kingdom will be fully established until the Lord's bodily return to the earth, but already great events are taking place that are preparing the way for Him. The greatest of all is what He is doing in His church. Just as the darkest, coldest part of the night is just before the dawn, which is when the morning star appears, during the darkest of times the church is going to arise as the glorious harbinger of the coming of the Lord.

His kingdom is even now being established in His people. That is why the Lord said right in the middle of the statement that we quoted from Luke 17, "For behold, the kingdom of God is in your midst." The first place to look for the coming of His kingdom is in His people, not the political, economic, or even great natural events of our times. When we see the church ascending, brilliant in the heavenly places, catching our attention as the brightest object to be seen by all who are awake, then we will know the dawning of the Day of the Lord is very near.

Has this happened? Has the church become the most brilliant body? One would have to be in great delusion to believe that what we are seeing today is the fullness of what the church is called to, but progress is being made. Before the end comes there will be a bride without spot or wrinkle.

The church's calling to be "the light of the world" involves having the answers to the world's problems, to show the way, and the church has been relatively successful in this aspect of her calling. Almost all of the great advancements in Western civilization can be attributed to the church, including many of those in science, government, law, and education. Today evangelical Christianity is growing at a pace of almost one million souls a week, far beyond any other religion or philosophy in the world, and it is growing fast in almost every region of the world. However, at the same time that the church is growing so fast numerically, there has been a virtual meltdown of morality among Christians in many parts of the world. This is about to change radically. Holiness will be popular again. However, it will not be the holiness of legalism but the passion of a bride that is so in love with her Bridegroom that she is consumed with being perfect for Him.

Christian television, conferences, books, and magazines have helped develop a healthy interchange between movements and denominations that is bringing about a de facto unity among believers. It is quickly becoming impossible for controlling denominational leaders to keep their people isolated from the rest of the church. This is helping bring about a realization of how much each part of the Body of Christ needs the other parts. However, until authentic apostolic ministry is restored a functioning unity will not be completely possible.

Each great sweeping movement has helped restore the power of heal-ing, miracles, great teaching ministries, and prophecy to the church. However, these all still tend to clash with each other, and will until there is a ministry restored with the respect and stature that the apostles and elders of the first-century church had. There are great unity movements arising that are helping to prepare for this, but the actual stature of unity and power that the church is called to in these times is far from having been obtained yet anywhere in the world.

But before we jump too far ahead, let's examine some of the failures of our moral character that have been taking place in the church. This is not to discourage but rather to shine the light on the "gates of hell" through which the enemy is still gaining access into the church.

THE TRAGIC SLIDE

Just thirty years ago, divorce among evangelical Christians was only a fraction of the percentage in the general population of America. In the 1990s, however, the rate of divorce among evangelical Christians became equal to that of non-Christians. And in the latest study, the rate of divorce among evangelical Christians has exceeded the rate of divorce of non-Christians! How could this possibly happen?

Divorces can happen for reasons that are beyond our control. I personally do not believe that divorce necessarily disqualifies one from leadership in the church, as this would even disqualify the Lord. Jeremiah 3:8 says that the Lord gave Israel a certificate of divorce. Was this because the Lord was not a good or faithful husband? Of course not. Even with a perfect husband, Israel committed adultery with other gods.

Divorces can take place that are the fault of one partner, not the other. I, therefore, believe that we must consider each case individually. However, in the overall scheme, the divorce rate is certainly a barometer of our integrity and morality, in both the world and the church. The barometer is dropping fast! In meteorology this is an indication of an approaching storm. The same is true spiritually.

This barometer clearly shows that the integrity and morality of evangelical Christians is falling to an incomprehensible low. This is happening on our watch! What are the shepherds doing? What are the prophets doing? Presently "the accuser of the brethren" has them fighting one another while his hordes pour in through the unprotected walls and gates of the church.

Marriage vows are solemn oaths to live together until death parts us. For such a wholesale disregard of this most crucial oath, we can conclude that there is a profound departure from the basic integrity and honor of our word being our bond. One of God's most basic characteristics is that His Word is true, and if we are to be like Him and represent Him, our words must also be true. The divorce rate among Christians who claim to be born again now exceeds 50 percent. This is a basic indication that most Christians are following their flesh rather than the Spirit. As the Word of God is clear, the ultimate result of that will be death.

Lust is counter to love and works to destroy it. The flesh wars against the Spirit, and if we follow the flesh, we will die spiritually. We can attend church, read our Bibles, and even witness to others but still be spiritually dying. If we are going to become the new creation we are called to be, to grow up into Christ, we must put the evil deeds of the body to death. The result of compromise in this will be our death. The apostle Paul warned the early Christians about this:

> I am speaking in human terms because of the weakness of your flesh. For just as you presented your members as slaves to impurity and to lawlessness, resulting in further lawlessness, so now present your members as slaves to righteousness, resulting in sanctification. For when you were slaves of sin, you were free in regard to righteousness. Therefore what benefit were you then deriving from the things of which you are now ashamed? For the outcome of those things is death. But now having been freed from sin and enslaved to God, you derive your benefit, resulting in sanctification, and the outcome, eternal life. For the wages of sin is death, but the free gift of God is eternal life in Christ Jesus our Lord. (Rom. 6:19–23)

Those who are led by the Spirit of God are the sons of God. We are called to be joint heirs with the King of kings, to reign with Him, and be seated on His throne with Him. This is the highest calling that has ever been offered in all of creation. To sacrifice this for the temporary, empty pleasures of sin is worse than what Esau did by selling his birthright for a bowl of stew!

The evangelical church in America is failing at some very basic issues. If we do not face them, humble ourselves, and repent, seeking the Lord's grace, the spiritual relevance of the church in America will soon cease to exist. That is the enemy's strategy, and presently he is winning this battle.

Let us not continue to allow sin to abase us, but rather set our faces like a flint to walk in the integrity and nobility of the high calling that has been so generously bestowed upon us by the Lord.

Could the church still become the bride of Christ? Of course. This could happen very fast, particularly if we repent and are open to

God's call to righteousness. We must always remember what we read in 2 Peter 3:8–9:

> But do not let this one fact escape your notice, beloved, that with the Lord one day is as a thousand years, and a thousand years as one day. The Lord is not slow about His promise, as some count slowness, but is patient toward you, not wishing for any to perish but for all to come to repentance.

We may think the church is decades, or even centuries, from attaining the glory that she is prophesied to have at the end, but as Peter explained, the Lord can do in one day what might take a thousand years for us. He can speed things up. If He does not speed them up, but seems to be delaying, He is being patient so more can be saved.

Scripture exhorts us to give honor to whom honor is due, and it is right that both the founding fathers, and most of the leaders of the United States, have navigated a course through human troubles that is extraordinary in history. There has never been an empire or great power to arise like her. When the United States was the lone possessor of nuclear weapons and could have easily dominated the world, she refused to do it. In fact, she expended her own resources to help rebuild friends and enemies alike. When she has projected her power, it usually has been to fight tyranny and promote liberty. As a Frenchman recently wrote, wherever there is a great tragedy anywhere in the world, whether it is from war or a natural disaster, Americans are almost always the first to respond with help. No great nation in history has ever shown the kind of benevolence America has demonstrated. But is this the beginning of the kingdom of God?

America is not the kingdom of God, but it could be a part of what will become the kingdom. Revelation 11:15 says, "And the seventh angel sounded; and there arose loud voices in heaven, saying, 'The kingdom of the world has become the kingdom of our Lord, and of His Christ; and He will reign forever and ever.'" The Greek word that is translated "become" in this verse is *ginomai* (ghin´-om-ahee), which Strong's defines as "to cause to be" (gen´-erate), "to become" (come into being), is used with great latitude (literal, figurative, intensive). This implies a process, not an instantaneous change.

The definition of this word is in harmony with the way the Lord has dealt with man from the beginning. He took generations, from Noah to Abraham to Moses, to establish His covenants with mankind and prepare us for the redemption He would provide through Jesus. The church has been going through a process for nearly two thousand years. It is apparent that in the millennium, the earth will be restored, but it is also likely to take an entire millennium to do it. Yes, the Lord could do what we think would take a thousand years in just a day. Why not give ourselves to Him in such a way that we might, as Peter encouraged, "hasten" the coming of the day of God?

Even so, we often misunderstand what the Lord is doing because we expect the conclusion to happen instantly, but that has never been the way He has done things. The coming of His kingdom will be like the sun rising, which does not happen instantly! First a faint light is seen in the direction from which it is coming. Then a few rays appear, gradually getting lighter until the sun finally appears. Even then it is hours before light is at its fullest.

In this process some instantaneous events, such as the Rapture and the coming of the Lord, will occur. Of course, as many have pointed out, the word *rapture* does not appear in the Bible, but there is a time when we are changed "in the twinkling of an eye" (1 Cor. 15:52) and caught up into the heavens with Him. However, it can be biblically supported that the establishing of His kingdom on earth will happen over time. Peter called this the "period of restoration of all things" in Acts 3:21 when he affirmed that this was what the prophets had spoken of from ancient times. The Greek word that Peter used for "period" is *chronos,* which Strong's defines as "of uncertain derivation; a space of time or interval; by extension, an individual opportunity; by implication, delay." It is a word that purposely emphasizes a time period that indicates a process.

What is my point? Some biblical prophecies indicate a quickening of events at the end, and others seem to indicate that we will need patience. We often apply the things that we care the most about to the things that will be quickened, but those are probably the very ones that we will need to have patience to see. We all still see in part. Until the whole Body of Christ comes together we will not have the complete picture. Let us hold faithfully to our part and seek increasing understanding of it, but also reject the presumption that we see it all.

Even though the end of the age may be very near, we can do things today to establish the Lord's domain in our own place of influence. We prepare the way for His coming kingdom by living in that kingdom now. We can also establish a foundation now that can be used in the millennium for the restoration of all things. It is obvious that people will be living on the earth during this entire period, and afterward. I was told that even new buildings should be built to last a thousand years. Though the Lord may return very soon, we should be writing school curriculum that can be used during the period of restoration. Certainly our buildings, curriculums, and procedures will be modified and improved upon, but we can lay the foundation to build upon.

Let us guard our hearts by humbling ourselves with the reality of just how far short of the biblical stature of the church we now are. We must rise above building our own little ministries if we are to be a part of building the true church. We must rise above preaching the church, and preach the kingdom, which is the glorious domain of the King. We must seek His glory, not our own, if we will again be apostolic. In all of my encounters with the Lord, He has said that we must have a long-term vision in everything that we are doing. In everything we do now, we should be thinking of the generations to come.

16

God Will Do It Again

As extraordinary as the Welsh and the Azusa Street Revivals were, they are just a foretaste of the harvest at the end of the age. Just as the Israelite spies brought back fruit from the promised land to testify of its abundance, these revivals are foretastes of the abundance of God, which is about to be realized as the church crosses its Jordan River to begin the conquest of its inheritance.

The Israelite spies brought back several kinds of fruit (grapes, pomegranates, and figs); likewise, the Welsh and Asuza Street Revivals are just one kind of fruit we will find in our promised land. There may not have been another move of God in history that accomplished more in such a short period of time as the Welsh and Azusa Street Revivals, but the Great Awakenings, ignited by the ministries of Jonathan Edwards, George Whitfield, and the Wesleys, were every bit as effective in turning multitudes to Christ. In some ways they had even more far-reaching and longer-lasting results because they laid the foundation for the future moves of God.

We must also understand that while all of these moves of God were different, they were all moves of God. The Reformations that originated in Germany and Switzerland were extraordinary moves of God in their time, as were the Anabaptist, Pietist, Puritan, and many other great movements.

There is much common ground between all these great movements and revivals, but they all seemed to include an aspect of God's ways that the others did not have. Likewise, they all seemed to include characteristics that were not God's ways or His truth, but He used them anyway. Every revival or renewal in history has been at least a little bit out of control. The area that was beyond man's control seemed to be the place where the Lord would move in the greatest way, and also where the devil or the flesh would gain some influence. In every field that the Lord sows, the enemy will come along and sow tares, but if we become so afraid of the tares that we will not go to that field, we will not get the wheat, either! This all seems by God's design to separate the cowards and unbelieving, both of which He has declared will not enter His kingdom (see Rev. 21:8).

The Lord has had a few Joshuas and Calebs who have been outstanding in their time, full of faith in doing great exploits. But now, at the end of the age, He is raising up a generation with the faith to cross over and possess their inheritance. Sam Jones, Evan Roberts, and William Seymour were great men of faith, but the Lord is about to release ten thousand like them, along with those like William Booth, Hudson Taylor, John Wesley, George Whitfield, Jonathan Edwards, Count Zinzendorf, John Knox, Luther, Peter, and even Paul—*all at the same time!* Together they will ignite a multitude of Nashville, Welsh, and Azusa Street Revivals, multitudes of Great Awakenings, and many Reformations—all together. A generation is arising that will see all of the things that every prophet and righteous man from the beginning longed to see. For those who love God, there has never been a greater day to be alive. The Lord has saved His best wine for last.

Afterword

THIS BOOK IS INTENDED TO BE THE BEGINNING
of an investigation into a most important subject. As you probably
noticed, some crucial events in church history, like the Reformation,
were hardly addressed. I know very well that these are necessary for
understanding the church in our own times, both Protestant and
Catholic. Even so, to address the Reformation as it deserves would
require at least an entire volume of its own, which will be forthcoming.

Please also understand that my purpose for writing this book as I did
was not to present the material in a form that would be completely con-
vincing to anyone. My goal was simply to challenge those who love the
truth to begin questioning some of these issues and search them out in
more depth for themselves. I am convinced that every sincere seeker of
truth who does so will find that I have not even told half the story, but
what I have told is accurate, even conservative.

Even the most superficial observer of the modern church must see
the multitude of contradictions and confusion that many popular doctrines and eschatologies project. Those with a love for the truth must

begin to examine and challenge these doctrines. When viewed in the light of history, the different pieces to the puzzle presented by biblical prophecies begin to fit together. Then a pattern that reveals the glory and wisdom of God can be seen, which must cause the knee of even the most stubborn to bow.

There is a treasure of wisdom and understanding to be found in studying history, which makes the times of tedium and drudgery well worth it. However, the greatest treasure of all is fellowship with God and union with His purposes. It is His purpose to heal all of the wounds of the past and establish the trust between His people in every different spiritual tribe or movement, so that they will all be one. But such true healing must be based upon the truth, for it is the truth that sets us free. If we are going to have the truth we must also have the courage to see things differently from the present, popular views.

I fully expect this to be a controversial book. However, I did not write it for that purpose. I am determined to never seek controversy—or to run from it. My goal is to speak the truth, in love, for God and for His people. I know that this book can be used to cause divisions. Whenever I have presented some of this material, some have accused me of being anti-Catholic, and others have accused me of being pro-Catholic. Some people will read or hear everything in extreme terms and will interpret them from their own biases.

I do not claim to be free from my own bias, so I do not expect most of those who read this book to be. Even so, I have striven very hard not to present what I have from being for or against anyone. I am only for the kingdom of God and for the truth. I also know that if I am faithful to that I will probably be shot at from both sides. I do not consider that to be my concern.

I could have been much more brutal in presenting the history of the dark times that the church, and the world, suffered. However, my goal was to be not brutal but honest enough to present the issues that must be addressed if there is ever to be true healing and unity in the Body of Christ. Just as the United States had to fight a Civil War in order to preserve, or have, a true Union, some issues in the Body of Christ must be addressed, and overcome, before true unity can ever come. I do not intend to compromise the truth for the sake of a superficial, and flawed, unity.

I have been warned a number of times by close friends that if I published certain things, it would ruin my ministry. I have not let this affect me yet, and as it has turned out my most controversial books have become the most popular, and effective, ones that I have written. However, I realize that one day these friends may be right. Yet my goal is not to build my ministry, but to be obedient. I do not care about the effect as long as I know that I have been obedient and have written the truth. My goal is to hear on that great day, "Well done, good and faithful servant." I realize that if I am to hear those great words from the King, I will hear much less pleasant comments from men. As the apostle Paul wrote, "If I were still trying to please men, I would not be a bond-servant of Christ" (Gal. 1:10).

So, am I saying this to deflect the obvious criticisms that I will be getting from this book? To some degree, yes. I appreciate and try always to remain open to genuine correction that is biblically based and done in the right spirit. However, many seem determined to influence me with threats about how my ministry will be hurt if I do not yield to them. If that is your point, I do not want you to waste your time, or mine. I am not concerned about the effect that the truth has, but I am very concerned that what I am speaking or writing is the truth. If you can help me to do better there, it will be greatly appreciated.

I always feel too clumsy and rough to handle the truth of God and will always agree that I need serious improvement there. I know that there are many who could do a much better job at this than I can. Maybe my poor attempt in some of these areas will provoke them to do it. But the pressure politics that are still dictating policy throughout much of the Body of Christ are, I believe, the reason for many of the most serious errors we are still plagued with. Therefore my goals are simple: to be obedient to my calling and to finish my course—and not yield for a moment to such devices of men.

Without question, the truth will prevail. The kingdom of God is going to come, and His will is going to be done on earth just as it is in heaven. All things are going to be summed up in Christ. I trust that you and I, and many who may now seem to be our personal enemies, will all be a part of that. I am continually convinced that His kingdom includes much more than even the greatest visionaries have ever been able to perceive. Even the greatest seer only sees in part. Even so, His kingdom will be much closer if we live in obedience to Him today. Those who are in His kingdom love Him above all things, and they love His people. They also love their enemies, and those who are still in error. They love them enough to speak the truth without compromise.

Notes

CHAPTER 3

1. Adapted from an article in the *Morning Star Journal*, "The Apostolic Ministry of John G. Lake," by Keith Davis.

CHAPTER 4

1. Adapted from an article in the *Morning Star Journal*, "An Odyssey of Reconciliation," by Gail Harris.

CHAPTER 8

1. *Fox's Book of Martyrs*, by John Foxe (1516–1587), is available on-line at www.ccel.org/f/foxe/martyrs/.

CHAPTER 9

1. The historian Eusebius, bishop of Caesarea in Palestine, records this conversion in his book, *Conversion of Constantine*.

CHAPTER 10

1. John Henry Cardinal Newman, *An Essay on the Development of Christian Doctrine* (Notre Dame: University of Notre Dame Press, reissued 1990).
2. Henry H. Halley, *Halley's Bible Handbook* (Grand Rapids, MI: Zondervan, rev. ed. 1979).
3. Alfred Baudrillart, *The Catholic Church, the Renaissance, and Protestantism,* 182–83.

CHAPTER 11

1. This story is taken from "The Hidden Calling" by Stephen Mansfield, an article published in the *Morning Star Journal.* Mansfield has also published one of the great books on the life and character of Winston Churchill, *Never Give In: The Extraordinary Character of Winston Churchill.*

CHAPTER 12

1. Adapted from an article, "The Forgotten Legacy of Sam Jones," written for the *Morning Star Journal* by Ray Hughes, a musician, songwriter, Christian historian, teacher, and humorist with an international ministry to whom God has given a special love for Nashville.

About the Author

RICK JOYNER IS THE FOUNDER AND EXECUTIVE director of MorningStar Publications and Ministries in Charlotte, North Carolina. He has written more than a dozen books, including the bestsellers *The Final Quest* and *The Call*, as well as *A Prophetic Vision for the Twenty-first Century*, *The Prophetic Ministry*, and *The Harvest*.

Rick is also the editor of the *Morning Star Journal* and the *Morning Star Prophetic Bulletin*, and is the director of the MorningStar Fellowship of Ministries and the MorningStar Fellowship of Churches.

Rick lives in North Carolina with his wife, Julie, and their five children. Rick can be contacted by writing MorningStar Publications, 4803 West U.S. Highway 421, Wilkesboro, NC 28697, or by fax at (336) 973-5191. MorningStar's Web site is www.morningstarministries.org.